Opport

Us Kids

By
Dennis Canning

What great fun we had as kids,
Wooden swords and dustbin lids.
Airfix kits and Corgi cars,
Catching fish to put in jars.
Built a tree house in the woods,
Acting tales of Robin Hood.
Flicks on Saturday, Batman's on.
Eating popcorn 'til it's gone.
McGowan's toffee, teeth stuck like glue,
Blackjacks, Penny Bubblies, Spangles too.
Playing hide and seek 'til dark,
Tomorrow one last visit to the park.
Back to school for all us kids,
No more swords and dustbin lids.

Opportunity

By

Frank Canning

Published April 2014

By

David Cox

ISBN 978-1-291-63498-3

Copyright © Frank Canning 2014

Printed by LULU

Dedication

This book is dedicated to my dear family, especially my beloved sister Margaret Burgess, who couldn't stop giggling after she read about herself!

(She's the one in the back of the lorry leading the singing!)

Contents

Part One

Part Two

Part Three

Foreword

Expecting the worst, I pulled up opposite Hanratty's scrapyard. Mr. Hanratty was standing at his gate as if waiting for me, smoking his pipe. He was a big tough looking man: he must have weighed about fifteen stone and he looked like the sort of man I wouldn't like to have an argument with.

"Morning, kidda" he said.

Surprisingly, he greeted me with a big friendly smile, which gave me a little confidence. I thought at least a man with such a pleasant smile might not do me much harm if he physically threw me out.

"Come on. Let's have a look at what you've got. 'Ope you're not going to break me bank!" He chuckled.

To be quite honest to myself, I must admit that I really thought that I had a van-load of old rubbish. Had I seen this stuff a couple of weeks earlier I wouldn't have given it a second look.

Here I was – presenting my "rubbish" to Mr. Hanratty, trying to look as if I knew what the business of trading in old rubbish was all about, trying to control my trembling nerves and trying to accept that in a short while I would get a kick up the arse from the big man as he frog-marched me off his premises for wasting his time.

I don't know if it was excitement or desperation that made my heart beat fast. I had a strange feeling that this was my big chance and I had to take this chance, as it might be the golden opportunity that I had been seeking all my life; but on the other hand, it might be just another humiliating disaster.

Perhaps it would be better if I started at the very beginning…

Acknowledgements

For all their help and advice, word checking, grammar checking, proof checking, reading and reading and reading again, writing their memoirs, typing, changing, altering, inserting dots and commas, listening, laughing, remembering, crying, shaking their heads, rolling their eyes and taking the odd paracetamol and brandy or two!!!.

To my lovely wife Jane for her three years of patiently pulling her hair out and inwardly screaming.

The following are listed alphabetically and not in order of importance, either to me or to the book.

Christine Canning. Daughter in law.
Christopher Canning. Son.
Clifford Canning. Dad. Deceased.
Dennis Canning. Cousin.
Douglas Canning. Uncle. Deceased.
Granddad Canning. Deceased.
Jade Canning. Granddaughter.
Wilfred Canning (Wig). Brother.
Josephine Chadwick.
David Cox.
Robert Ilett.
Christina Jones.
Angela Mead. (Bookworm)
David Michie.
Amanda Nelthorpe. Daughter.
David Robinson. Cousin.
Gordon Robinson. Uncle. Deceased.
Peter Satchell.
Bill Veitch.

Author's Notes

This book was created because for many years, friends, acquaintances, grandchildren and other recent members of my family, kept asking how all this began. I have often told the story about how I was so desperate, that I grabbed an "Opportunity" which happened to come my way. With a lot of drive and luck it changed my life, and the lives of my family, forever.

My Grandson asked me the same question and I repeated the story to him. He later commented on how it had inspired him. He said "Why don't you write it down as a book. It might inspire other people, who like you, are desperately looking for inspiration, and it might drive them on to take a chance. It might work, it might not."

I come from a family of writers and diary keepers and must have picked it up from them, as for many years, I have kept diaries of my own activities.

My grandson's comment inspired me to start re-writing my diaries and memoir's. It became an obsession, and for three years practically took over my life. I found that once I started to remember and write about a certain point in my life, it stirred up other memories of things that happened later – then, earlier memories were brought back to mind, and so it went on, and on.

I found I was also re-living and re-tracing my forgotten life through diaries and records, endlessly remembering all the silly, stupid and interesting episodes from the past. I am quite sure this would encourage anyone, once they found a good starting point, to write their own memoirs.

Part One
A Poor Beginning

Heading north, out of the small Yorkshire town of Thorne, was Marsh Lane – "marsh" being the obvious name for a lane that was probably created as the way to cross the bog between Thorne and Moorends. It was a single pathway with a grass verge and a ditch at either side. The only people who had any reason to use this path were people who needed to pass from one village to the other, as it was a road to nowhere. It was very lonely, dark and forbidding. There were no such things as electric lampposts, as electricity and gas were only just beginning to be piped into the surrounding villages.

About one and a half miles from the very last house in Thorne, standing on its own, was an old railway carriage. It had no wheels or axles as they had been removed for the war effort. It stood there, as it had stood for many years, perched on old railway sleepers, slightly tipped at one end as it sank slowly into the marsh. The wooden sides were showing distinct signs of rot and the roof had been patched up so many times that the original roof was no longer in existence. There was a row of windows either side, which displayed pretty gingham curtains. A metal chimney protruded from the roof with smoke coming from a neat little stove. Over the ditch, in front of the carriage, was a two-foot-wide wooden plank bridge, which was used to cross over to the lane.

Mam and Dad had lived here since their marriage in 1932. They had two children: Margaret, aged three, and Wilfred, aged one and a bit. Mam was about to have another child.

Dad was a keeper of diaries. His diary at this time said that the ditch was full of water from the heavy rains and water was covering the planks. Mam was screeching that the baby was coming out and wouldn't wait, and told him that he should fetch the midwife immediately. The diary recorded that "this one was going to be a lot of trouble." Dad pulled on his boots and, without lacing them, put on his pullover and a balaclava and dashed out of the door. As soon as his feet touched the soggy plank he went arse up and landed in the ditch. Swear words came out as he pulled himself out of the ditch, minus one boot. He rolled over back into the ditch but couldn't find his boot, but, because of the urgency and the terrible screeching coming from inside the carriage, he decided to proceed without it. He hobbled the one and a half miles at Olympic speed. Having a telephone at that time was only for the very rich and there were very few of them about on Marsh Lane. In fact, the only telephone near to him was at Moors' Farm and if he had gone to ask their aid at two in the morning he would have been eaten alive, because old Bill Moor's dogs were as black and savage as the Hound of the Baskervilles, as Dad's diary reads. Undeterred, he hobbled the last half mile down the lane to the home of Nurse Parr. There was no doorbell or doorknocker so he used her clothes prop to tap on her upstairs window. She wasn't very pleased about doing business at this early hour, particularly as a thick fog had set in. He rushed back home and stood by the door just in case she couldn't see the wooden plank because of the fog. It seemed ages before he spotted her bicycle lamp through the gloom and saw the stern look of urgency on Nurse Parr's face as she entered the carriage.

I was born at half past four in the morning of December 7, 1935.

A couple of years later, after a fair share of unemployment, Dad got a job at Thorne Colliery and moved into a "pit house" in the village of Moorends for which he paid an abominably high rent of seven shillings per week. My earliest recollections of this house were the damp smell, hoards of cockroaches, gas lights, and newspapers on the table for a tablecloth. I remember that I always seemed to wear only a shirt with no pants. I don't know if it was because I wet myself or because Mam couldn't afford any. I distinctly remember often following Margaret and Wilfred to school with no pants on, much to their annoyance. I also remember that the table was always full of food. It was plain and simple, usually bread, jam, a bottle of sauce and a pot of dripping. I probably remember that because those were my favourite foods and that was about all I ever wanted to eat for years. I also remember that with our meal we used to drink tea out of jamjars as we only had two cups and they were for Mam and Dad. I probably dwell more now on our living conditions in those days than I did then, because at that time, this was "our lot" and we didn't really have anything to compare it with, so we were happy to drink out of jamjars and have newspapers for tablecloths and the food we had was enough to fill our bellies. There were certainly no obese kids in those days!

Another brother, George, added to the fold shortly afterwards.

In 1939 war broke out. Dad still worked at the pit and so was not called up for service in the forces.

It seemed that this particular area of Yorkshire was in direct line of the war front and subject to possible bombardment. By now we had settled into the type of lifestyle that all the coal miners enjoyed on Barnsley Road. Most of the men in our street were engaged in digging holes in their back gardens, covering them with corrugated sheets and placing some soil back on top, leaving a small entrance for the family to enter. These were for possible use as air raid shelters. Most of these men worked down the pit, so the constructing of these shelters was a doddle to them. Depending on how fussy the particular owner of the shelter was, some were made into quite comfortable little dens with walls and floors lined with planks of wood; they had seats and a table and candle holders; some even had places to sleep.

I remember seeing the skies full of aeroplanes and hearing the continuous droning of the engines as they flew over to Germany on bombing missions. I particularly remember hearing explosions as the Germans bombed the nearby town of Hull. When this happened the sirens started howling and Mam ordered us to hide under the kitchen table, just in case we were bombed, as we didn't have an air raid shelter.

Were we frightened? No, of course we weren't. We were only kids. We were all too young to understand what was happening and it all became another exciting adventure.

The First Move

For some reason, which wasn't mentioned in his diary, Dad was transferred to a job at Askern colliery and we all, as a family, moved to the village of Askern to live in lodgings with our Granddad Canning. Soon after this, Dad became unemployed and was called up to have a medical to join the army. Due to his health and eyesight, he was passed as "Grade Two," which meant that, although he couldn't join a combat regiment, he was placed into the Royal Army Ordinance Corps, who were, as he wrote, "the suppliers, cooks and general dogsbody regiment."

He was to be based in Lincoln and was suddenly whisked away, leaving Mam to cope on her own. It must have been a struggle for her with her kids to cope with, and having to manage on army allowance. For us kids it was all good fun. Poor old Mam – Dad away, four rowdy kids to feed, clothe and get off to school, and food on ration! Poor old Granddad - having to put up with this rowdy lot day after day. What a hard life it must have been! I can now put myself in their shoes and can understand what strong characters Mam and Granddad must have been to cope and try to survive during such hard times. Child number five, Irene, was born at Askern; something must have happened whilst Dad was on leave!

We kids could only see, and were only interested in, what we were doing at the time and on any particular day. We were quite happy. We were fed and we went to school or to play – it was a great life! The war didn't mean anything to us as we were too young to understand what was going on anyway, and we certainly had more important things to do like playing and going to school, or rather, in my and my sister Margaret's case, playing truant! I hated school and, according to the diaries, we were always in trouble for not attending. I don't know what my sister's problem was, but I just didn't like learning. Reading, writing and arithmetic (commonly referred to as the three R's) were a pure waste of time. I found out much later that we were constantly in trouble with the school authorities and, in fact, Dad was once fined for our absenteeism, which, of course, Dad never paid as he was away "fighting for the country."

Flitting

Mam's life certainly wasn't sweet and easy. Dad was away in the army and, naturally, Mam wanted to be close to her family for help and companionship. Dad's large family lived in and around Askern, but most of Mam's family – consisting of Granddad and Grandma Robinson, her sister and her brother-in-law, Auntie Mary and Uncle Vic - lived in the mining village of Langold, in north Nottinghamshire. This, of course, and quite understandably so, led to our next exodus. I often think we were like gypsies moving from one place to another. We always seemed to be waving "Ta-ta" to our friends from the back of a removal lorry. I remember our friends running alongside our lorry as we pulled away, waving their arms about until they disappeared from sight, never to be seen again.

It was a little sad waving to them, watching their figures get smaller and smaller until they disappeared completely.

Just imagine: four kids wedged on the back of a lorry full of beds, chairs, table, pots and pans, all of us wrapped in rugs and blankets to keep warm, hanging on like grim death, trying to hide from the wind, and all laughing and shouting and singing. Margaret always led the singing. "We're off, we're off, we're off in a motor car, fifty bobbies are after us and they don't know where we are." We would chant this over and over until one or the other of us started the next line at the wrong time and it all became a screeching babble. What a terrific adventure, travelling off to a new land far away!

We were to live in lodgings with Auntie Mary and Uncle Vic. They must have had hearts of gold to accept us into their home.

A standard pit house in a standard mining village consisted of three bedrooms, a front living room, a kitchen, a bathroom, and a downstairs toilet, situated in the passage adjoining the kitchen.

The kitchen had a sink and wooden draining board, and what was called an "oven range," which was heated by an open fire, with

Flitting

movable rings which on which to place a kettle or pans for cooking. The front room also had an open fire which heated an oven with similar cooking rings. The ovens and fire-grates were always kept in pristine condition. They were "blackleaded." Blacklead is a sort of jet black polish, which was spread onto the oven door and the fire-bars and rings with a cloth, then rubbed with a clean cloth until it looked like shiny varnish. Some houses were lucky enough to have an electric cooker with a cooking range and an oven, but our house hadn't advanced that far. Our family lived in the kitchen and shared two bedrooms, although two of us occasionally slept on the floor of Mary and Vic's bedroom, when Dad came home on leave. Auntie Mary and Uncle Vic lived in the living room and had the large bedroom. We all shared the toilet, sink and bathroom.

Washing machines were only for the well off. It might sound funny but washdays were a bit of an adventure to us young kids. We didn't realise then that Mam usually reached a point of near exhaustion on those days. We just sat about trying to be patient, waiting until she had finished "dollying," and then we could use the tin bath and dolly stick for our chosen game.

It took two days for Mam to do the washing. A tin bath was full of dirty clothes. Firstly, she emptied the clothes onto the floor, and then half filled the bath with hot water and added soap. The first lot of clothes were put back into the bath, now full of water. Then she placed a "scrubbing board" into the bath amongst the clothes. A scrubbing board is more easily recognised as the instrument that Lonnie Donegan called a skiffle board. It had a metal corrugated surface on which Mam vigorously rubbed the dirtiest of the clothes up and down to get the dirt out. The next operation was to swap the rubbing board for the dolly stick. This was a three foot long wooden pole and attached to the bottom was what can more easily be described as a three legged stool. At the top was a bar, which was slotted through a hole which became the handle. Once again, with great vigour, Mam lifted the dolly stick up and down and swirled it around and around in a motion similar to today's electric washing machines. After the clothes had had a good bashing and swirling they were put into a sink of clear cold water for rinsing to get rid of the soapsuds. They were then ready for mangling. The mangle was a heavy steel frame that held a pair of wooden rollers that were rotated by a winding handle. The rinsed clothes were slotted between the rollers and the rolling motion threaded the clothes through the rollers and squeezed out the remaining water. The clothes were then hung out on the clothes-line to dry. This operation was repeated several times during the day and would normally take the whole day to finish, depending on the amount of dirty clothes there was to launder.

After the clothes were dry, Mam would iron them using a couple of heavy steel flat irons, which were heated up by placing them near to the fire. As one was being used, the other was being heated up. The ironing would probably take all of the next day to complete.

By the time Mam had finished her "dollying" my brothers and I were getting very impatient to play our game. The tin bath and the dolly stick became our ship. By placing the dolly stick into the bath it became a mast. We then sat in the bath and happily sailed around the world or became pirates or something similar, oblivious to the fact that our Mam was on the verge of exhaustion.

There is another operation which was sometimes used on washdays and which helped to pass Mam's time away. This was the boiling of the clothes. Most houses were fitted with a "copper" boiler which was a large steel urn mounted in a brick-built frame. Beneath the urn was a coal fire that boiled the water in which the clothes were put to be boiled. Our clothes must have certainly been clean and germ-free! Poor old Mam, and all the Mams of those days, who must have had muscles like Samson!

Dad was a very strict man and we all had to keep in order otherwise it was the belt! I know we were a rowdy lot with only our Mam to keep us in order whilst she was simultaneously cooking, washing, cleaning and shopping. She couldn't have had much time or energy to even try to keep us in order. We must have been a proper handful. The Wild Bunch, Dennis the Menace, Bart Simpson - just think of these characters put together into one free-for-all package and you might be somewhere near. How did she cope? When Dad came home on leave, we were terror struck.

"I hope you are going to sort your damn kids out," Mam said as he entered.

The belt was deliberately unbuckled in front of us as he entered the house and we suddenly became perfectly behaved children – but only because we had tasted the belt previously. During his short home leave, if ever we happened to become a little rowdy, Dad would stand up and, with a super stern look on his face, his hands would clench his belt. We would all go quiet.

There was another side to Dad's coming home – his kitbag! As I have explained, Dad's regiment was the RAOC.

They were the stores and the suppliers of kit and caboodle: clothes, boots, food, ammunition, uniforms – in fact, every item which could possibly be required by the soldiers both at home or abroad on the fighting front. Dad's kitbag – or, in most cases, kitbags – were full of goodies for us hungry devils. What did the soldier need when he was on active duty? Every soldier carried a survival box in case he was cut off by the enemy. In it were biscuits, a tin of beans, a tin of dried fruit, dried milk, chocolate, and all things to keep a soldier alive for a week. It was so exciting, sheer luxury: we pigged ourselves. He also pinched army jackets for us to wear, army blankets for our beds, army socks, army shorts, army boots, belts and braces. Simply everything! He was our lovely Father Christmas, until we had eaten our fill from the survival tins; then we would be asking him, with the belt in mind, how long was he stopping? Upon reflection, he must have loved us and tried to do the best for his family to take such risks by bringing his bags of "loot" home.

I could never understand why Mam was always expecting another baby after Dad's parcel of leave.

Mam
enjoyed
her
washing
and
mangling

While we
enjoyed
our pirate
game.

WASH DAY.

A vivid memory of Mam in those days was that she was always fat! Brother Gerald was born in May 1943, making a nice round number of six in all.

I remember Dad telling us once, many years later, about the time he was on the train coming home on leave and there was a search being carried out by the military police. He had two bags full of goodies for us. The search came down the carriage. The MPs were examining all the soldiers' papers and searching their bags. He thought this was it – jankers for the next two years! Just as they reached him, a fight broke out further along the coach and the MPs rushed along to control it and arrested the men who were fighting, frog-marched them to the guard's van and never came back. Dad said he wasn't religious but he thanked God that day.

We – that is, my brothers, sisters and I – went to Langold School. My sister Margaret and I once again hated school and got into the usual routine of one day present and two days off. We must have invented truancy, although we were not really playing truant, as we were too young to know what truancy meant. It was just "not going to school." Dad's diary said that Frank invented everything from mumps to scarlet fever, besides other complaints not yet defined in the medical journals. The "School Bobby" became a personal friend of Mam as he saw her so often. I remember setting off to school in the morning, but cannot remember arriving. I used to sort of lose my way or take the wrong direction and finished up playing all day with the other kids in the street as they too, funnily enough, must have been playing truant also. Then, at the end of the day, I used to sit looking through the window, full of excitement, waiting for my brothers and sisters to come home with my bottle of school milk.

End of the War

I don't know which came first, the end of the war or Dad's demobbing, but I will take the end of the war first.

Our village must have been generally classed as below the poverty line, the reason being that all the able-bodied men and quite a lot of women were in the armed forces, leaving only old people, people who were not in good health and poorly paid mine workers, who were exempt from call-up because they had to keep the pits running. Food was on ration and generally it was a case of survival for the village residents.

VE Day was the end of all suffering and, to celebrate, the whole village (like the rest of England) had street parties. I was nine years old. I had three brothers and two sisters. We were so preoccupied with our own lives and growing up that we didn't give much thought to simple things like food and, after all, we had a magic mother who always filled our bellies. The thing was, we had never seen anything different to compare our lives with, and so what we got and what we had was quite sufficient. If, for instance, we were suddenly to be presented with a table full of roast beef and three veg, covered with a lashing of gravy, followed by apple pie and custard, a cup of tea with sugar in it and sweet biscuits to dip in, we probably wouldn't even have known how to eat it and, if we had, we would probably have been sick or have had bellyache followed by the shits!

May 8, 1945 was the day we did have the shits! It was the end of the war. VE Day. Victory in Europe Day. The whole country had a damn good reason to celebrate. Every city, town and village celebrated in a way that had never been done before. Our village, like the rest of the country, held street parties and celebrations. No one had ever done or seen anything like this before.

Firstly I remember the parade of the Home Guard, sometimes called "Dad's Army." The Home Guard consisted of a battalion of all the old and unfit men who had not been called up by the forces.

They were all dressed in army khaki clothes with tin hats and all were carrying rifles. They marched along the streets following their Sergeant, who just happened to be old Mr. Baker, a giant of a man with half inch thick glasses, a fat belly and about six or seven feet tall. Mr. Baker was leading his regiment, calling the usual "left, right, left, right" in the way we had often seen during their practices on Sunday mornings. The only difference was that this time they marched from street to street, stopping at the individual parties to do a very well rehearsed drill. Mr. Baker barked his instructions and the soldiers snapped to attention and performed a perfectly remarkable and orderly routine with their rifles. They then saluted, right turned and forward marched on to the next street party. We kids were all goggle-eyed and full of admiration, knowing that had the Germans attacked us we would have survived.

Everyone clapped as the soldiers were marching away. Then, as if by magic, tables and chairs appeared and were lined end to end along the street. The tables were then covered with white tablecloths on which masses of food suddenly appeared. There were cakes, buns, jelly, custard, Spam, jam, fish paste and potted meat sandwiches, pies, blancmange, scones, and red, yellow and orange pop. Where did it all come from? We kids had never seen so much food in our lives. We ate, we scoffed, we were all drunk with pop, we were all singing *Roll Out The Barrel, It's A Long Way To Tipperary* and *One Green Bottle*, and our Mams were leading the singing. Some of them were drinking this brown stuff out of pint mugs, which smelled horrid. It was loud, happy and glorious. Then the sickness overcame us. One by one we suddenly went a pale colour and up it all came. But what a great party! I'll never forget it: one of the happiest days of our young lives.

Flitting Again

Dad seemed to have a lot more leave after the end of the war and things got a bit strained at Auntie Mary's house. Although I didn't feel or see it myself I know that our parents and our auntie and uncle were a bit squashed and, according to the diaries, we had to move again.

There is no record in Dad's writings or in my memory as to how we acquired the next place to live, but Dad wrote that when we arrived he felt ashamed and disgusted with the sight and the smell of our new home. We were old hands at flitting. We weren't gypsies but I often think we would have easily been absorbed into the gypsy fraternity because of our record of moving.

We moved to the nearby village of Oldcotes. Now, Oldcotes was an old fashioned type of village, straight from the pages of a Charles Dickens novel. There were two main through roads, north to south and east to west. Where they crossed was the village. There was another minor street, which curved round, joining the two main roads. It could really be described as a one-street village, and not much of a street. On thinking back, the only car that passed through in any one week must have been lost! There was no electricity, no tap water, and no gas. One shop, a two-classroom school and a large Roman Catholic Church. There was a Police House and about forty or so houses, and a few surrounding farmhouses, and there was a new pub called the King William IV.

Our house was the "Old King William IV." It was a condemned building. It hadn't been used as a pub for at least ten years and had stood empty and dilapidated since then. It was a rat-infested hole. There was a living room, which used to be the bar, which had an open fireplace, and a second smaller room, which used to be a "snug," also with an open fireplace. There was a kitchen with a sink but no taps, a fireplace with an oven and rings for cooking. Alongside the open fireplace was a steel compartment which, when filled with water, was heated by the fire, and became the main form of hot water. There was a large cold room called a pantry. A spiral flight of wooden stairs led to three first floor bedrooms with concrete floors. The stairs continued to a top floor with two large bedrooms with adjoining double doors. Out in the yard was an old-fashioned water pump, which was the only supply of water for the house.

Down below the house was a large cellar, which was previously used for storing the beer and now stored about a thousand empty beer bottles. Outside the back door was a small yard covered with cobblestones, which led to the toilets. The toilets (The "Shit House") was a sight and smell to be always remembered. When we first entered we had to burst open the lock. I don't know why on earth it was locked because anyone who entered did so at their peril and was liable to be overcome with fumes from pans full of mouldy shit, which was covered with a green, translucent fungus. There was a box seat, which stretched from one wall to the other with four holes to sit over. It must have been quite a sight, during its pub days, seeing four persons shitting at the same time. In front of the boxes were four doors which opened to pull out the shit pans. The pans had not been emptied since the pub closed, and the door and window were closed and locked, probably just in case someone broke in and died.

Although The Shit House was the most horrible place, it was the first place to be cleaned up, for obvious reasons. Dad and Mam fearlessly set about it and in no time it was spick and span except for the constant collection of cobwebs which seemed to appear again overnight after cleaning.

For us lads, The Shit House gradually became our group meeting place, especially during winter evenings. It was a bit frightening to go on your own having only a candle to light it, so we started going in pairs but the one left out soon realised; rather than going on his own, he felt safer to go three together. It soon became quite a fun place for Gud (George) and myself sitting there listening to Wig's (Wilfred's) jokes. We sometimes sat there for ages until the candle began to flicker, or until Mam called us in for bed.

Toilet Humour!

Although we, as a family, were just a little above the poverty level, our Mam and Dad were very clean and fussy people. Mam always kept a nice house. She was the original "washerwoman," always cleaning, scrubbing, dusting, washing and ironing, and Dad always had his apron on, also. I remember, wherever we lived, our home was always kept as pretty as possible, with curtains and cushions, and colourful rugs.

Everything smelled of disinfectant and polish. I can understand how they must have felt when they first entered the new house, but the only moan I ever encountered were the comments in Dad's diary. They didn't even comment, as far as I can remember, on the toilets. They set to, with the help of Margaret and Auntie Mary and Uncle Vic, and cleaned, scrubbed and painted the whole house from top to bottom, and in no time at all it looked like a pretty country cottage. There were gingham curtains at all the windows and a matching gingham tablecloth. There were freshly painted doors and windows, vases of flowers, and cushions on the chairs. I really think our Mam was more house-proud than she had ever been in her life, bless her. She had had a pretty rough time and, for her, it all looked like a fresh beginning. Here she was with her own house, with Dad about to be demobbed and get a good job. Here was a nice little country village and a nice new school for her children. I can only imagine what was going through her mind: security, happiness and contentment.

Miss Booth and the School

We lived about half a mile from the school. It was a two-classroom school with a small house attached in which lived the headmistress, Miss Booth – Miss Adeline Martha Booth, a giant of a woman with a face like thunder, hair cut short like a man's, muscles like Desperate Dan, massive bulbous tits, and fat legs on which she wore men's socks up to her knees; to finish off, she wore a pair of man's boots. Her clothes probably came from an Army Surplus Store. She suddenly had six new pupils named "The Cannings" and she didn't like it. We seemed to be instant misfits, but being kids it took a long time to sink in that we were not the chosen ones. We had entered into a closed territory, which was very settled, comfortable, neat and orderly, as it had been for the past hundred years. It could even be called a clique. I can see it more clearly now as a much older person, more worldly and wise, but at that time we thought the world was fair and equal, and in our naivety it all looked like a great new adventure. Let me explain.

Oldcotes was an old fashioned village with old established residents, some of whose families had lived there for generations. Their kids and grandkids and probably great-grandkids had all lived and been educated there. They were all pedigree "Old Cotians" through and through. Most of the families had occupied the houses they lived in for generations. Many of them were farm owners or were employed locally in the woodlands or farms or the surrounding estates. Over the years most of them had developed a reasonable standard of living and were well established. None of them were miners! There had probably not been any influx of new people into the community for the last hundred years. Suddenly, there arrived in their midst a large family of rough kids who wore army jackets, and whose father was away in the army. The whole lot must have seemed to be of a lower standing. They were not very well off and to top it all they came from the "Wild West" mining village of Langold. Wow! How were these village folk going to cope with us?

Five of us signed in at the school, which consisted of two classrooms: Infants and Juniors. Our sister Irene started her school life here in the infant class under a nice Miss Smith. The rest of us were in Miss Booth's class. I can honestly say it was not a pleasant school. We were constantly in bother with Miss Booth and our Dad was constantly having arguments with her because of her continuous bullying of our family. At one time, even the police were involved!

It was by Miss Booth's hand that I tasted my first caning. Although I know now that I thoroughly deserved my caning, I do think it was a bit harsh and my bum was quite black for a while afterwards. It was the night before Bonfire Night. Like all kids we were testing our fireworks. A bunch of us were in the toilets letting off a few bangers. I placed my Jumping Jack on the floor and we all stood back. Just as it was about to explode, Miss Booth strode in with a fierce look on her face. She stood there with her hands on her hips and demanded to know what the banging was about. My Jumping Jack suddenly exploded and jumped up her skirt and got lodged in her undergarments. As each bang went off she jumped and screamed and patted her clothes but the firework was lodged and didn't come down until all the bangs had exploded – or in this case imploded. We all were in hysterics, but she somehow didn't find it at all amusing.

"Who? What? Who?" she screamed.

Everyone went quiet when they saw her red face. They all pointed at me. She grabbed me by the ear and dragged me into the classroom and bent me over a table. I received four lashes. She was so angry and embarrassed with all the laughing that I probably got the hardest caning she had ever given. The next day Dad visited school to give her a proper telling off.

But it was not all bad, and we eventually established ourselves in the school and the village, and we made good friends with the local kids.

Dad was demobbed and started work at the Langold coalmine named Firbeck Main Colliery and we began to settle down and become part of the community.

I am not quite sure what rewards a soldier receives when demobbed but I was aware that Dad received a new suit of clothes and a sum of money. Even though when he finally came home he didn't have his usual kit bag full of goodies, I distinctly remember it was a happy time. Mam and Dad bought a few new things for the home and we kids had new shoes. But the most memorable thing was our holiday. A week at Cleethorpes, a holiday I will always remember.

None of us kids had ever been to the seaside before. Dad gave us an allowance of a shilling per day to spend on anything we wished. It normally took less than ten minutes to lose it in the penny slot machines. Then we had to find some other entertainment to occupy ourselves with such as paddling in the sea or digging in the sand, but these soon became a bore and we finished up hanging around the beach facilities and the donkeys were our first challenge. The ladies who owned the donkeys were only too pleased to let us hold a donkey's head and walk up and down the beach with the riders, as they sat under their umbrella, reading the paper and gossiping. It was all good fun and we felt so important being the donkey lads. At the end of the day the ladies gave us an ice cream as our reward, even though we must have walked at least fifty miles a day. The next day one of the ladies, who also owned the swing-boats, asked us to look after them while she sat in her box taking the money. It involved taking the punter to their particular swing and holding it steady while they climbed in and then helping them out at the end of their time. The swing-boats were not as tiring as the donkeys. At the end of the day we were all given our ice cream reward. The next day we were introduced to the roundabout. This involved helping the kids on to their seats and helping them off at the end. The best bit about this particular job was that we could also have as many rides as we wished, free of charge! For the rest of the week we were darting between donkeys, swings and roundabouts. It was so exciting and we all felt so proud and grown up.

The ladies must have loved us. They kept calling us "sweetheart" and gave us our ice cream every day and then, on the last day of our holiday, they gave each of us a shilling, which went straight into their slot machine. One of the ladies said that we were such good workers that there would always be a job for us whenever we visited Cleethorpes again.

What a great holiday! What a golden memory!

Dad and Mam must have had a nice holiday as well, sitting in their deckchairs with their mugs of tea. We only saw them at mealtimes and bedtime.

Good Memories

The most treasured memories of Oldcotes were our days on the farm. My brothers George ("Gud") and Wilfred ("Wig") and I were forever wandering down to Clarkson's farm near our home. We became very friendly with the workers and used to spend most of our time there after school and at weekends, and especially during school holidays. Although we were only young – ten, eleven and twelve years old – we were accepted by them and became helpers. We became part of the operations and they gave us jobs to do which were easy enough for kids like us to do and which we thought were fun to do. As we were only kids we couldn't do manly things like hoeing or loading or the heavy lifting of bails of straw, but we were very handy with the horses and carts.

They didn't have the sort of heavy machinery like tractors and mechanical equipment that farms have today. Most of the work was done by horsepower.

The horses were "human" and we got to know them personally and they got to know us and trusted us. Although they were massive bay horses we were able to treat them like pets. Bay horses are the largest horses on earth. We stood about as high as the top of their legs and they were so heavy that the ground shook when they walked. But they were the gentlest of animals. They all had names and they all knew their own names. If you gave an instruction to a certain name then that horse pricked up its ears and obeyed. We knew all their names: Daisy, Mary, Blackie, Tom and Sam were the main workhorses. A few others never seemed to do anything but eat and follow the other horses around. One of our jobs was fetching the horses from the meadow, back to the farmyard, to be hitched up into their harnesses and hooked into whatever cart was needed for that day's work.

First thing in the morning the men got their instructions from the "gaffer." They were given specific jobs to do depending on the time of the year, the weather and what particular crop they were handling at the time. Depending upon the job, they had to take certain tools; for instance, rakes, hoes, scythes, pitchforks; and for these particular jobs they needed certain wagons and certain horses. For instance, in late autumn they were "muck-spreading," so they hitched up to a two-wheeled muck-cart with high sides to carry as much cow manure as possible. A dray was for carrying corn, wheat or barley, and was a long, flat, four-wheeled base with a front and a back rake to hold the bails or sheaves. The same dray was used for carrying turnips, carrots or potatoes, but then it had to have side-boards fitted so that none of the vegetables would spill overboard. When the men had been given their instructions, Gud, Wig and I were told which horses were needed. A certain horse was best for a certain cart. We strolled down to the meadow called the Manor Yard, which had a wide gate that we didn't open until we were ready. We clapped our hands and the horses cantered towards us. The ground actually shook as they came towards us. We had to pick out the particular horses and lead them to the gate and let them out, closing the gate immediately to keep the others in. Off they cantered, up to the farm. They knew exactly where to go and didn't need leading. By the time we got back to the farm the horses were already being harnessed up. We were lifted on to the cart and handed the reins and we set off to the field with the men sitting on the back of the cart having a good old chat and a fag.

We were heading for a particular field, which could be half an hour or even several hours away. All the fields had names that must have been passed on by generations of farmers: Champion Herons, Manor Yard, Long Acre, Long Orchard, River Bed, White Water. We knew exactly where the fields were and we were in charge of the journey, and there was no way we could speed up the journey as the horse plodded along at its own speed – clip-clop, clip-clop. They were happy days, peaceful days. I even used to put a stick of straw in the corner of my mouth like most farmers do. It was pure contentment.

Our school summer holidays were spent in heaven. It was harvest time. The corn had been cut and bailed into sheaves, and the sheaves were stacked upright against each other into "stooks" so that the rain would run off in case they were stood for a while. The stooks were about a hundred yards apart. Our job was to drive the dray from one stook to another. One man picked up each sheaf with his pitchfork and threw it on to the top of the dray. The man on top placed the sheaves, interlocking them so that they held each other in place during their journey home. They were stacked about ten feet high on top of the dray. We then had to take the dray back to the farm.

There were men waiting at the farm for the drays to arrive. One man stood on top and, using a pitchfork, he threw the bales into a barn where another man stacked them under cover of the barn until all the harvest was in. After all the harvest had been collected, a threshing machine was brought in. This machine separated the corn and put it into bags and at the same time bundled up the hay into bales. The bales were then stacked to form a haystack ready for use in winter as animal feed. It was quite a long drawn out, labour intensive system, which had been used for hundreds of years. Nowadays a massive machine called a combine harvester, driven by one man, cuts and separates the corn, and rolls the hay up into large rolls, all in one quick operation.

We learned how to speak horse language from the farmers. "Whoa – cum back – gee up – gee over – goo on – steady – whup whup." Just repeat the words "over, over, over, cum back, gee up" at the end of the field and the horse would turn right around, find its position to return and set off back down the field again. Just say "Whoa" and it would immediately stop. You didn't have to pull on the reins. They knew exactly what they had to do.

One hot summer's day I fell asleep on my journey back to the stackyard, which was about a couple of miles, and woke up to find myself back in the farmyard and the dray being unloaded. Imagine the ribbing I got from the men!

They were all laughing their heads off and saying things like, "You must have been at it all night," which they thought was very funny, but I didn't know what they meant.

It was all good, healthy fun. I wonder what the kids of today would think of it if ever they had the privilege of doing something similar during their school holidays. I doubt whether anyone, adult or child, would ever have the opportunity or privilege to enjoy such an exquisite experience. If only they could – I am sure it would change the way of the world as it is today. We all think of the past, the good old days – if only!

A good thing about our days on the farm was that it also helped with our family food supplies. There was an abundant supply of rabbits. During the corn-cutting season the corn reaper-binder worked around the field in an ever-decreasing circle and the rabbits were gradually squeezed into the middle, too frightened to make a break until the very last cut. The farmers, my brothers and I encircled the last remaining cut with our arms and coats opened up, ready to throw them on to the rabbits as they made a break for it. They were very fast and we had to be alert and ready for their mass life or death dash to freedom. They were like a bolt of lightning, but we were used to it and ready. If we were lucky and our timing was right and we were standing at the right spot then the poor suckers jumped straight into our coats. It was relatively easy to catch our prey but sometimes they dodged us; then there was a mad panic to try to catch them, but they were always too fast for us. Once they had dodged our coats there wasn't much chance of catching them. Even so, it was a very exhilarating – but fruitless.

When we were successful we wrapped the rabbit up in our coats and gave it to the farmer who killed it by gripping its back legs, hanging it upside down, and giving it a quick, sharp chop at the back of its neck. I could never have done this: I was too squeamish. Mam was so pleased when we brought a rabbit home. She was an expert skinner. She cut off the bottom of the legs and the head, then cut the skin from the bottom, underneath the body, to the neck. She then ripped open the piece of skin at the bottom end. Then, gripping the back legs, she whipped off the remainder of the skin in a quick, jagging movement. The skins were hung outside to dry and were eventually collected by a rag and bone man, who paid for them.

Rabbit was then and will always be my favourite meat. The way Mam used to do it was to make rabbit stew or rabbit pie. The first day we had it fresh with potatoes and greens, and with a good helping of bread. We had the same the second day made into a pie, or stew, served with more veg and more bread. The third day she put in more potatoes and peas and reheated it; the fourth day it made nice gravy with chips or something else and bread. We ate well and were never hungry when there was a rabbit on the go. The bones and even the heads were sucked dry. Gud was a devil for sucking the head dry – brains and everything. My mouth is watering now whilst I am writing. You haven't lived until you have tried Mam's rabbit pie!

In those days there were certain foods that were taken for granted that we never see today. They were foods of substance. They filled up your bellies and were affordable. The mums and dads of those days created dishes from nothing. When Mam bought a piece of meat, which could not have been very often, she would also ask the butcher for a piece of fat for rendering. I think it was a freebie because the better off people probably only wanted the best pieces of meat. Mam used to cut off the rind and cut it into small cubes, which were put on to a flat dish in the oven and cooked until the pieces were crispy. They were called "scratchings" and they were delicious. They had a crunchy, meaty taste. The other piece of fat was melted down for cooking and eventually the much-used fat was put into the "dripping pot." Dripping was so tasty and nourishing when spread on bread. Every bowl of dripping put on the table was firstly drilled with the knife in order to get to the bottom where the brown juice had settled. It was first come, first served, and Wig, because he was the eldest, had the privilege of being the first to dig in and spread his bread with the lovely brown juice.

Dad spent some of his time in the army in the cookhouse and he used to cook a very tasty pudding called jammy fritters. He cut one-inch-thick slices of bread and spread one with thick jam and placed another slice on top. Then he cut it into quarters and dipped each quarter into a batter and fried it in deep fat: delicious when drowned in custard.

Faggots and haslet were scrumptious belly fillers, and Mam and Dad were great bread makers. They made a great ball of dough, which was placed in a large earthenware bowl with a tea towel on top, near to the fire, to rise. Then they cut the dough into pieces and flattened them with a rolling pin. They then cut the pieces into circles about twelve inches diameter and baked them in the oven. They were called "flat breads." At the table they were cut into triangles like modern-day pizzas and were slit and spread with dripping or jam or treacle or Nestlé's condensed milk – lovely!

No food or scraps were ever wasted. Potato peelings, pea pods, vegetable cuttings, stale food, and waste of any description was put into a special container and collected by Mr. Sutcliffe who lived a few doors away, and owned a pig. He probably couldn't afford proper pig food, whatever that was, and collected these scraps of food from us and the surrounding neighbours. His pig was the biggest thing I had ever seen and, to think what it was fed on, it seemed to thrive. He lived for his pig and called it Porky. (An unusual name for a pig!) We used to make jokes about him and we thought it quite funny to say that Mr. Sutcliffe used to take Porky to bed with him, but our sister Margaret innocently stood up for him and contradicted us by saying that he was such a nice kind man and it was a kind thing to do to sleep with his pig. One day he had Porky slaughtered and he came to our house and told us the news. He explained that Porky was bred only for food and that he had lived a good life and was ready for slaughtering. Whilst he was telling us he took out his hankie and cried, and we all cried with him. Mam was inconsolable. A few days later Mr. Sutcliffe brought us a joint of pork and a giant pork pie. It was the most delicious pie I had ever tasted and to this day pork pies are still my favourite food.

Shortly after we had settled into our "pub" we explored the cellars and found, in the very back cellar, thousands of empty beer bottles. This was probably the dumping ground for them in earlier days. Just for sheer devilment my brother picked up a bottle and threw it at the opposite wall: it made a popping sound. He picked up another one and it also popped.

The popping sound was probably due to us being in an underground cellar with little or no fresh air and being completely enclosed like a cell. Of course, we all had a go and then another go; this at first, made quite an interesting, puzzling sound. Then someone went a little further and threw a little harder. After which, it was the force of the throw that was the challenge and not the popping sound. After a few hundred bottles had been thrown, someone noticed that there was a prominent stone on the wall and said he could hit it. However, missing it encouraged the next person to show that he was the more accurate thrower. The challenge was then to hit the stone, which created another very serious competition. After a few hundred more bottles were thrown, another competition had to be created to relieve the boredom.

Someone had the brilliant idea to throw a bottle at the ceiling and bounce it off onto the wall to smash. Some smashed on the ceiling, which was not in the bottle-smashing rulebook – it had to bounce off the ceiling and smash against the wall. A clever alternative was to hit one wall and then for the bottle to smash against the adjacent wall. Arms were beginning to ache and another boredom patch was beginning to set in. We were tiring. All sportsmen reach the point of exhaustion where they either have to struggle on or stop.
"What the hell are you little buggers doing?"
I froze to the spot. Wig and Gud backed towards the wall. The belt was off and I got the first swipe and the second and the third. My arse was on fire – thank God, when the others were getting their share, I had space to escape. I scuttled up the stairs, out of the back door, across the yard, across the field, non-stop, clutching my burning bum. Nowadays I draw cartoons and have used my experience of scampering away, clutching my bum, in several of my cartoons. Remember Dennis the Menace of the Beano? I stayed out until I was hungry. Dad had calmed down by then and we listened to the reason he was so angry. He had intended to take the bottles back to the pub who gave a refund of a penny a bottle on returns. Poor old Dad. But we got carried away – and we did have such a smashing time!

Living in our condemned house had so many very pleasant memories and some very scary ones. Margaret sometimes sang to us before bedtime. She had such a wonderful, soothing voice. One of our favourites was the Irish melody *If You Ever Go Across The Sea To Ireland*. I still remember the words to that song even after all these years.

There were no such things as electric lights so we used candles for lighting. We took a candle to bed and usually left it lit until it burned out. There were four of us sleeping in one room, three of us lads sleeping in one bed, two at the top and one at the bottom, head to toe. Margaret had a smaller, separate bed. Quite often Margaret was allowed to stay up later than us because she was older. One night the three of us boys were tucked up in bed but were awake for a long time until Margaret came up. We heard her creep upstairs as quietly as she could but, unfortunately, all the stairs creaked and we could hear every step. We waited for her to enter the room but she didn't. Someone had walked up the stairs but no one entered the room. We all lay there perfectly still and quiet for ages, wondering what had happened to her, occasionally looking over the blankets to see if she was there. We did not dare speak and we were all feeling a little scared and huddled closer to each other. Then we heard Margaret say "Goodnight" to Mam and Dad and come up the stairs. All the stairs creaked once again and she came to bed. Complete silence that night. What were the creaks we had all heard? We were never the same again. We had heard stories about the house being haunted and every strange sound we heard from then on scared the pants off us.

One winter's night Mam and Dad had gone out to the pub and they left Margaret in charge. They needed a break. Irene, our younger sister, had been very poorly for a long while. She had a temporary bed downstairs at the back of the room in order to keep her warm, and Mam or Dad took it in turns to sleep downstairs in the chair to watch over her and keep the fire burning all night. Margaret had told them to go out for a drink to have a break. Later that night, Margaret told my two brothers to go to bed and said that I could stay up with her for a little longer to keep her company. She put a few more logs on the fire and we sat there talking for quite a while. She sat in the armchair until she dropped off to sleep. I moved closer to the fire to keep warm. It seemed like ages and suddenly the candle burnt out. It was dark except for the light flickering from the fire. I was beginning to feel a little scared and moved closer to the fire. I sat there for what seemed ages thinking about horrible things like ghosts and evil spirits, and then I heard a rustling behind me. I dared not turn around. It was quiet for a while, and then I heard a cackle of a voice. I was frozen to my seat, praying for Margaret to wake up. It went quiet again for a while. I could only hear the sound of the fire and then I heard this witch-like cackle behind me. It sounded like a deep throat cackle as if someone was laughing. I was imagining a witch standing behind me with her long nails poised ready to stick them into the back of my neck. She was cackling and gasping. I tried to move away, closer to the fire, which was by now fiercely blazing. I was petrified. I couldn't speak or move in case the witch struck me. I sat paralysed for what seemed like an eternity. Suddenly the door opened and Mam and Dad came in.

"What, what, what's happened Frank? What's happened to Irene? Why is she lying on the floor behind you? Why – why – why?"

They picked Irene up and put her back into her bed. Margaret woke up and yawned, rubbed her eyes and strolled up to her bed, still half asleep. Mam scolded me for sitting too near to the fire and treated me for burns on my legs.

Television was not yet in the public domain and we didn't have a wireless (radio), so we had to entertain ourselves. Most evenings were spent playing games, doing jigsaws and hobbies. We didn't ever get bored. Boredom was a word we never used. We had lots of things to do and created our own entertainment. One thing we all liked to do, under our Mam's supervision, was to make our own rugs! Rug making was quite an interesting pastime. We all sat around a table on which was spread a piece of hessian cloth cut to the size of the rug we were about to make. This operation made use of any old rags or materials from worn-out clothes, which were cut up into "clippings" one inch by four inches (2.5cm by 10.5cm).

These could be of any colour or of any type of material. The clippings were placed in the middle of the cloth in piles of various colours. Each person had a "pricker." This was a homemade tool that Dad made out of a clothes peg. One leg was broken off and the other leg was sharpened and smoothed off by burning it with a match.

This is the simple method of how to make a rug. First you prick a hole with the pricker and push one end of a clipping through the hole; that is then pulled halfway through with the other hand. A second hole is made and the other end of the clipping is pushed through. This procedure is repeated in rows until the whole of the cloth is covered. When it is turned over the fluffy ends of the clippings form a soft comfortable rug.

We became very skilful in rug making and were able to do fancy patterns and shapes with various colours of materials. It might sound boring but this wasn't only a time-filling operation – while we were clipping, we were in conversation and having games and quizzes, laughing and joking. Dad was always inventing some sort of word game or a "guess what" game. Nowadays I think they call it quality time. Time flew by and we were all happy and the end result was a gorgeous, warm, cosy rug that we all took pride in because we had manufactured it ourselves.

Back to School

It took a while for any of us to settle in at the school. For one thing, we were not as well off as most of the other village pupils and we wore army combat clothing, which Dad had conveniently "borrowed" from the army stores. I personally felt very conscious about it as the other kids wore normal coats and trousers and it made me feel different from them. The fact that we were new to the school, as I have previously stated, didn't help as the people who lived there were old-established families who had probably lived there for many years. We were new kids on the block and they were not used to it.

The first thing every morning, about a dozen of us older kids were marched into the playground for our daily PT. We had to "reel off"; that means to stand to attention in two rows with an arm's length between each person. Miss Booth stood in front and told us what exercise we were to do.

"These exercises are to wake you up and get your blood circulating," she told us.

We were instructed to jump with legs apart, then again with legs closed, ten times; whilst jumping, clap hands over heads, then clap hands down by sides, ten times; and, whilst still jumping, circulate arms ten times. These exercises were not for the weaklings! Legs apart, touch toes ten times; arms outstretched, swivel left, then right, ten times! By now we were waking up and our blood was circulating! I remember one such session vividly. I wasn't jumping properly. Miss Booth thought she would set an example of me.

"Frank, come out here and stand in front of me," she hollered.

I sauntered over and stood to attention, facing her.

"Now, hands by your side – jump, jump, jump, jump. One two three four, up, up, up, up."

She still wasn't happy with my jumping so she pulled me to her, placed her hands under my armpits and began to jump with me.

"What's the matter, boy? Can't you jump properly?" she shouted.

She then pulled me right up to her and put her arms around me, pulling me so close that my face was in between her massive tits.

"Now jump, jump, and jump!"

We both jumped up and down and her tits buried my face. It certainly made my blood circulate. I never stopped thinking about it.

I probably shouldn't have been thinking about things like that at such an early age, but I had a pretty good imagination for one so young!

My very first moneymaking venture started at about this time. I must have been about eleven years old. The creative activity at school for the boys was fretwork. A fretsaw is a very fine saw blade that is stretched tight by a steel sprung frame. A pattern or picture is stuck on to a piece of plywood and the fine fretsaw cuts out the outline shapes of the picture. I made several animals such as giraffes, lions, tigers and zebras, by cutting out the four legs and fastening them to the body with a cotter-pin and painting them in glorious colours. They were freestanding and the legs moved. I was thrilled with them and thought they were a wonderful invention. I approached the local shopkeeper and asked if she would put them in the window for sale at three pence each and, lo and behold, they sold. I replaced the ones that sold and was proud to have made a few shillings.

I also spent time after school at the local wood yard helping them during their log-cutting process. Branches of trees were cut into logs, which were thrown into the back of a lorry; then each Saturday the lorry was driven to Sheffield to sell the logs door to door for firewood. My job was holding the bags whilst the men filled them with logs. We didn't come home until everything was sold. They gave me two shillings and sixpence for my efforts, which I gave to my Mam. I felt so proud when I gave it to her!

Dad was a chain-smoker. He was rarely seen without a fag in his mouth. As soon as his fag was just about to burn his lips he lit another from the same ember. We all took it for granted that this was the norm and couldn't wait for the day when we could walk about with fag in mouth. One day we were playing in an old shed when one of the lads brought out a cigarette and a box of matches and quite calmly lit up. We all thought this was quite a spectacular, manly thing to do.

"Giz a drag," we said.

He passed the cigarette round and, just as I was about to have my turn, Dad appeared in the doorway. Everything suddenly went quiet.

"If you are going to smoke you had better learn how to do it properly," he said.

He took the cigarette out of my friend's mouth and handed it to me.

I was quite taken aback as I fully expected a good telling off, but Dad handed me the fag with a sincere smile on his face.

"None of you know how to smoke properly," he said.

He then turned to me and said, "Now put the cigarette between your lips and hold it gently with your teeth. Now, think of it as if you are drinking milk though a straw and suck in the smoke."

I felt as if I was on fire. My throat, my chest, my lungs were burning. I nearly coughed my heart up.

"Now," he said. "Perhaps that will teach you a lesson about smoking. It's not good for you. Do you think I enjoy it?"

He put his fag into his mouth again and walked away; I think I detected a slight grin on his face. I never touched another cigarette until I was thirty.

I will always remember with much glee what we call the "scrumping incident."

My brothers Gud, Wig, and myself were probably the world's best scrumpers. A scrumper is a person who steals apples and pears from other people's trees.

The Roman Catholic Church had a large, long orchard, which happened to be just across the road from our house. It was surrounded by a high wall with an entrance gate from the church at one end and a gate at the far end of the orchard. All the apple and pear trees were in prime condition, having being looked after by the Church gardener.

We were often in there filling up with gorgeous fruit. What we did was to climb over the wall, with one of us stood at the church end as the lookout. He was placed there to keep an eye out for the gardener. If ever the gardener was seen he hooted like an owl by putting his thumbs together and blowing downwards to produce the owl sound and that was the signal to disappear. We collected fruit by putting it down our shirts, which were held tightly round the waist with a belt. When our shirts were full all around our bodies and bursting open, we scampered off.

One day we all went a bit mad. We arrived home with shirts full and took the stolen fruit up to the top bedrooms and placed them on the floor very carefully in neat rows. Then we went back for a second lot and did the same. Then a third lot and then again and again while the going was good. We thought we would stock up for winter and the cold concrete floor was ideal to keep the fruit fresh. Mam and Dad never went up into the top floors as far as we knew. After about four or five visits the floor was full with what looked to be about ten thousand apples and pears – or so we believed!

That evening we were all relaxing, playing our games, and there was a knock on the front door. We always dashed to the front window when anyone came to the front door, to peep behind the closed curtains to see who it was. To our shock it was the priest – God! We'd been seen! Our hair stood on end! We expected the worst – the belt, at least. Mam quite calmly went to the door. I hid behind the chair. Gud scampered upstairs and Wig dashed into the front room.

"Good evening, Mrs. Canning," he said in a charming voice. "Would your boys like to pay a visit to my orchard to pick a few apples and pears?"

Poor old Mam! If only she knew!

"What a kind priest," she said to us later. "Now, we don't really need any fruit as I have just bought a few apples from the greengrocer this morning. However, we can't throw kindness into his face, so just take a small bag and pick only a few, now, don't be greedy, and don't forget to say thank you," said Mam, with that silly, kind, smiley look on her face.

There are many stories I can clearly remember about Oldcotes, some nice, some horrible, some frightening. There were now six kids. Mam always seemed to have a fat belly. After about a year we had settled down and had made friends with the village kids. We were eventually accepted by Miss Booth. Although we still didn't have tap water, electricity or a flush toilet we were all quite happy in our home. Dad worked at the nearby coalmine as a surface worker and all seemed fine. Then the inevitable happened just as we were settled – once again we flitted.

We were quite dab hands at it by now. Pack everything up into boxes, pile everything on to a lorry, lodge ourselves in amongst the rugs, beds and blankets, and away we go.

This time we went back to Langold. Because Dad was working at the local colliery, Firbeck Main, he became eligible for a pit house at Langold. The big difference was, it was a proper house with electricity, hot and cold running water, even a flush toilet and a front and back garden. It was for us only. We were no longer lodgers and it wasn't a condemned old pub – it was sheer luxury. A new life was about to begin.

When we arrived at Langold, in 1946, it was a well established mining village. There was a row of shops on the main street which included a hardware shop, a newspaper shop, confectioners, shoe shop, chemist, dress shop, fruit and vegetable shop, toys and bikes, a hairdresser's, a milliner's, curtain materials and a hardware shop.

There was a Co-operative Society grocery store where most families were members and used their "Divi" number for every purchase. They were able to collect their "Divi" twice a year to spend on essential luxuries. "Divi" was the word used for a Dividend, which was similar to stamps or bonus point cards used by many stores today. For every pound spent, your card was stamped and each stamp was worth a penny or two, which mounted up annually and helped to pay the bills.

There was the Hill Top Workingmen's Club, the Smokey's Workingmen's Club, and the British Legion Club, a picture house, a billiards hall, a Church of England Church, a Wesleyan Chapel and a Salvation Army Hall. There was also a "Turf Accountant" (although off-course gambling was illegal at the time), who employed a "runner" who went round the pubs and clubs taking cash bets and who was probably paid commission on winnings.

The school consisted of Infants with three hundred pupils, Juniors with four hundred pupils and Seniors with five hundred pupils. There was a district nurse/ midwife who lived in the village and there was a doctor's surgery with three resident doctors. There was a fire station, which was manned by village volunteers. They were paid a small retainer and were paid per fire. It once got around that one particular fireman was setting fires during a nice hot summer so that they were called out and paid per call and he didn't have to go down the pit!

Langold Lake

Close to the village was Langold Lake, a well known and popular resort that was visited by flocks of people, some of whom had travelled hundreds of miles to spend their summer weekends there. The lake was about half a mile long and a quarter of a mile wide at its widest, and had a children's swimming/paddling pool with changing rooms. It was a haven for fishermen and swimmers. It had rowing boats, a café and a bandstand from which different colliery brass bands played on Sundays (at that time every colliery had its own brass band). One of the main attractions was its ten metre high diving board.

The local residents thought of it as their own lake, because it was the focus of everything for the children and youth of Langold. The lake was, and still is, completely surrounded by a footpath, which passed through woodlands and fields and has, over the years, become a nature sanctuary and is now called Langold Country Park. Adjacent to the lake was a recreation park with swings, roundabouts, slides and a sandpit. Young children enjoyed the roundabouts such as the King's Crown, Spider, Ocean Wave, and the Mechanical Hobbyhorse. Older ones liked the Flying Boat, the Bumper and the Swinging Plank. It was quite the Disney Land of its day.

The following excerpt is taken from a booklet published by the Nottinghamshire County Council Leisure Services:

A Look Back At Langold
"When the bathing pool and recreation park were opened, the Co-operative Guild marched the children round the village in fancy dress. It was a hot sunny day and each child was given a bag of sweets, buns and sandwiches. The first Langold gala was held in 1929. It was held on August bank holiday weekend and soon became the highlight of the year with ten thousand people flocking through the park gates in its heyday. Firbeck Colliery Band provided a selection of music from the bandstand. Numerous swimming events and competitions were organised. There were

relay and novelty races, high diving competitions and underwater races with aqua-lungs. The British Long Distance Swimming Association Championships were traditionally held at Langold Lake.

There were children's events in the swimming pool and demonstrations by the country's top swimmers, also synchronised life-saving displays and comedy items by swimming club members. Spectacular stunts included explosions, with first aid exercises carried out by the S.J.A.B.Corps. One year mock submarine explosions took place in the lake with frogmen. There were also trapeze artists. The Great Alganso, a world class act from Blackpool Circus, walked a tightrope over the lake. As a finale, Mr. Jack Revill – Mr. Langold Lake – did his daredevil dive from the 35 foot high diving board into a patch of burning petrol.

Life saving awards were presented to successful members of the Gala. A Royal Life Saving Trophy – The William Henry Memorial Trophy – was awarded to the Firbeck Life Saving Club, the first Inland club of its type in the country. Mr. Jack Revill founded the club and helped to form the Royal Lifeguard Corps and pioneered a method of deep-water resuscitation that was adopted worldwide. In 1956 he gave a lifesaving demonstration to Princess Margaret and Lady Mountbatten the Queen Mother, and the Earl of Scarborough. Jack was dedicated to instructing young people who gained thousands of awards over the years, besides saving a number of lives. He was eventually bestowed an honorary life membership of the R.L.S.

Village Life

I was about twelve years old when we moved to Langold. Once again, it was a case of getting to know who was who in our area. We already knew quite a few people from when we last lived there, but this time we lived in another part of the village. It didn't take long to make friends, as the surrounding kids were even more curious to meet us than we were to meet them. It seems that every neighbouring house had kids. We were surrounded by them. The place was alive. There were lots of people and lots of kids – a far cry from Oldcotes. I remember thinking that we were going to like this place!

We were signed in at the school and compared to our last school this one was like a city. I was in the Juniors, Class Two. All my brothers and sisters were in different classes, with different teachers. It seemed strange at first as we were used to being all together, but this was quite normal in any secondary school – the unusual situation was in our previous school.

We soon made friends and the ones who lived near to us soon became our best mates. We walked there and back to school with them, played with them at playtime and ate our dinners with them. Then, after school, we were running wild with them. Our parents must have enjoyed the new situation much better as we were not hanging around the house and they no longer had to entertain us and make rugs and suchlike.

It must have had something to do with the contentment of living at Langold, but the family became even more enlarged. Alan, Janet, Richard and Linda added to the fold. The village seemed to be split into several areas and groups depending on where one lived and, obviously, because we lived on Markham Road, we were called the Markham Road gang. When I say gangs, they were not as gangs are today, armed with knives and even guns. Our village gangs were only formed due to whatever street you lived on, and even then you were not all that separated as we all knew one another and often mixed. However, gangs we were and, at that time, we were building up our own individual identities. For instance, the Knott End gang were quite a tough lot, only because they consisted mainly of one family who were renowned fighters. It was difficult to bump into their eldest without him wanting to bash you. He always walked around with his fists clenched and arms bent upwards as if he was about to have a fight. His brothers seemed to follow his example and they walked about all looking quite threatening. It was wise to keep clear of them at all times. The School Road gang were a mixed up bunch of funny-sized kids. A couple of them were rather small and some were quite lanky. In fact, one was nicknamed "Lank" - but only to be used by his friends. I once called him "Lank" and got a right earful and was cautioned by the schoolteacher who told me to learn my manners. There were also the Sankers, the Boldries, and the Bashers. Some took on the names of their streets and some were just called after a certain person. It was all innocent fun but it became an identity and it became an easy way of identifying who you were talking to or about at any particular time.

Naturally, there were a few fights but nothing too serious. Whenever there was a fight it was well broadcast. For instance, we were once having a game of football between two gangs, and one of our men knocked over one of the opposition. It became a free for all shouting match, and then someone suggested that the fairest way to sort it out was to fight it out. Both sides agreed and a match was announced at the lakeside bandstand at ten o'clock the following Sunday morning. The whole village was alerted and this fight was the most important topic of conversation for the next few days. Sunday came and we made our way to the Lake. On the way, there seemed to be quite a lot of people about and, as we got closer, we realised that practically all the village were attending. It was like Wembley Way before a World Cup match. We couldn't get anywhere near the bandstand and we waited for the opposing contenders. We waited – we waited – and we waited. After about an hour people started to chant "Why are we waiting?" but no one turned up.

Later that day, I called at "our man's" house to find out what had happened and his Dad told me that he had been to see the other guy's Dad and between them they had banned the fight.

There was a famous incident when our gang crossed swords with another lot. We were going to school and some silly person shouted something to one of the other gang members. He picked up a stone and threw it at him and obviously the correct thing to do was to throw one back. This was the key to a mad stone fight. We were on opposite sides of the road and as all of the houses had a wall along the front of their houses it was naturally safer to jump over the walls and bob behind for safety. There were probably about ten of each regiment and we picked up a stone from the garden and lobbed it over to the enemy's position, and then bobbed down again. We quickly found out that the safest and most tactical way to fire a missile was to suddenly stand up and throw, then bob down. If someone from the other side just happened to be standing up at the same time then – if you could think quickly enough – you could direct your fire to them; but usually you were too afraid of being hit, so you just stood and threw your missile blindly.

Everything was being thrown: stones, pebbles, and wood, even the odd brick. Any missiles that landed nearby were returned. The battle went on for some time and was encouraged by the onlookers, who stood at a safe distance shouting encouragement to their particular side or player. No one seemed to be hit and we were all thinking just how long did we have to carry on throwing at each other, and how could we stop without the other side thinking we were cowards? The householders were knocking on their windows and shouting for us to stop. People from neighbouring houses were also screaming for us to pack it in. How could we?

I picked up my next stone and stood up. The next thing I knew I woke up and I was lying on the ground surrounded by people. I didn't know where I was and I couldn't see very well because blood was pouring into my eyes. Someone had put a cushion under my head and a lady was wiping me with a wet cloth. The fight had stopped as I was hit. It must have been a relief to everyone, for probably the battle might have lasted longer than World War II if I had not received a direct hit on my forehead.

Back to School Again

Once again, I must confess – I hated it! I was in the second class of the Juniors. Miss Wheaton was the teacher – Miss Wet Neck, we called her! There is nothing much to say about her except she was typically the three R's, and the three R's, I wasn't! I couldn't read, my Maths was hopeless and, although I found writing OK, I couldn't spell. My time spent with her was, pretty well, nothing.

Nearly everyone had nicknames in those days. I don't think Miss Wet Neck ever knew what she was called, otherwise I think she would have gone mad, but some of the teachers knew their nicknames and seemed to like them as long as you addressed them by their proper title when speaking to them. There was Tusky Garner – big teeth, of course; Mr. Wood the headmaster was called Woody; Miss Jelly Legs had long, skinny legs. Ricky was Mr. Ricket; Buck Brien inherited Buck simply because it sounded pretty clever; Tash Avery had a massive R.A.F. moustache, and Mac was short for McCarthy. It was a mark of popularity for a student to have a nickname: Wig, Gud, Dick, Ally, Spike, Wogger; Bummer Brown's name was pretty rude but it didn't seem to bother him. We had Geg, Nog, Smiggy, Piggy, Coll, Bazz and Nobby. We also had a Blackie, a China and a Nigger, and names like this never seemed to bother anyone in those days. But the best nicknames were Mavis Cross who was naturally called Jumper and Betty Green who was called Theresa. I have often wondered why all Clarks are called Nobby! All the Cannings inherited the name Canno.

The Art teacher was Mr. Avery (Tash). Now he was my sort of teacher because he was the Art teacher. He was a very tall man and his big bushy moustache gave him an air of kind authority. I liked Art and the way he spelled it out. The best times were when he gave us a piece of white paper and told us to express ourselves. When he first said this, I couldn't understand what he meant and asked the person next to me what it meant. He told me that you had to do whatever came into your mind and put it on to the paper! My imagination went wild and the first thing that came into my mind was something like a house in the distance with a lorry full of boxes travelling towards the house on a winding road. Well, that's what it looked like to me. The boy next to me said it looked stupid and Mr. Avery wouldn't like it as he always liked a simple drawing. At the end of the lesson he collected the work in and it was home time.

The following week I couldn't wait for the Art class. We entered the classroom and sat at our desks. Mr. Avery placed a bundle of papers on the table. Immediately he called me out to the front of the class and I froze. I was a very shy person and to have my name called out was quite alarming. He asked me to explain what the picture meant and explain what was meant by the lorry and the winding road. I was frozen, thinking that I had drawn something really stupid, as my friend had told me last week. I was a little frightened to speak and Mr. Avery must have sensed my dilemma and spoke for me.
"I seem to think, Frank, that you are trying to portray what happened to you recently when you and your family moved from Oldcotes to Langold on a removal lorry."

I nodded my head.

"And the winding road is to signify that because you were all sitting on the back of the lorry you were unable to observe the road you took and you didn't quite know where you were heading."

I nodded my head again.

" Now Class Two, when I ask you to express yourselves and draw whatever comes into your mind I would like you to think about what Frank has done and try to portray your own exciting experiences."

I felt so proud. I had always liked drawing and Mr. Avery made me feel that even if I couldn't read or add up, I could at least draw.

As far as I was concerned school was OK except for Maths, English and reading out loud – mainly the three R's. I was often absent from school. Many times I just didn't turn up if any of these lessons were on the timetable. It wasn't that I didn't like school, it was just that I couldn't get my head around the main subjects. I couldn't seem to concentrate on the books and, when I looked at them, the words seemed to move about. The teacher often said to me that I wasn't concentrating! Yet, if it was a creative subject or something that required thought and imagination, I was great. I couldn't understand why. If we were doing sums I did them differently to how the teacher had presented them. For example, she wrote a few long division sums on the blackboard, which we had to copy into our books and calculate the answer. I mainly did them wrong but sometimes got the right answer using my own method. I used to draw a picture of the sum using lines and squares. I couldn't explain how I did it; the teacher must have thought I was on another planet. I usually finished up being told off for doing it differently to the method they were using, but I quite often got the right answer.

The lesson I dreaded most was reading out loud. We each had our own book. The teacher read a few lines out loud, then pointed to a certain child who had to stand up and carry on reading. The teacher carried on a little more, then called out to someone else to carry on. I was dreading my turn as this was my worst subject. She then called my name. I had followed the story so far by putting a ruler under the lines and following each word with my finger so that I could concentrate. I stood up and left my ruler on the desk as it might have looked silly whilst I was reading out to the class. I looked at my book, precisely at the line where the teacher had left off, but the line moved upwards. I tried to follow it and it moved sideward. I found the word again and the word moved upwards again. The teacher snapped at me to concentrate. I was concentrating so hard that I was sweating, but still the words moved. I managed to say the word but the next word disappeared and I read out the word next to it. At this the class started to laugh and I was so embarrassed and red faced. I didn't know why this happened but it always happened unless I put my ruler under the lines. I knew I could read as well as anyone else but I couldn't read the proper way and, because of this, the teacher thought that I couldn't read at all. I had my own way of doing things and I got by, but I would always finish up with egg on my face trying to do it the normal way.

Playtimes, home-times and four o'clock on Friday were my favourite times – I thought it was a waste of time trying to learn.

In those days there were certain games children used to play. These games must have been passed down for generations and were played in the playground or in the streets. There were games which used to involve a lot of people and games that only two could play.

One such game was Hits and Donks, as we called it, more commonly known as Hits and Spans. It was played with marbles – mibs. It was an on-the-pavement game. One person flicked his mib as far as he could with his thumb; the other person then flipped his mib and tried to hit his opponent's mib. If he hit it, then it was his or, if he landed near enough to span it with his little finger and thumb, then it was also his win. If neither happened, then the other person could flick his mib for a second chance, which usually was successful. The winner then shot off again for the second bout. This game could be played as the children journeyed to or from school.

Picture cards was another two-person game. Picture cards were collected from cigarette packets. These cards were collectable, with pictures of sportsmen, trains, flowers or ships. One person skimmed a card as far as he could; the other person skimmed his card to try to land on top of his opponent's card and, if he landed on top, he won the card.

Hide and seek was another favourite. For this game a lot of people can play. Someone has to be "on." He or she hides their face and counts to one hundred whilst all the others go away and hide. The "on" person shouts, "Coming, ready or not" and goes off to find them. When someone is found they have to be "tigged." Tigging means that they have to touch the other person; then they go to base or jail and he has to stay there until everyone is found. Then another "on" person is chosen and the game is repeated.

The way people are chosen is by "hand switching." Two people face each other with their hand behind their backs, and then both together bring their hands to the front, showing one of three hand signs. The signs are: clenched fist, which is a "stone," a flat hand, which is "paper," or two fingers apart, which represents "scissors." A stone will blunt scissors, so stone wins. Paper will wrap a stone so paper wins. Scissors will cut paper so scissors win. The one who is first to win three is the winner. If both bring out the same sign at the same time then it doesn't count.

Leapfrog is a very energetic game. The kids form a line, and the first one bends down with his hands on his knees to form an arch with his body. The second one leaps over and then bends down. The third one leaps over the two people in turn; then he also bends down. Then the fourth one and so on until all are bent down. Then the last in line, who was the first to bend down, will leap over all and then bend down and then the next will leap over all and bend down and so on, forming a continuous chain which is forever moving forward. This can be played on the way to or from school or in the playground with as many people who want to join in.

Tin Can Alley or Rallico is a very rough game and was my favourite. A lamppost is "home." There are two teams: one team is "on" and they have the home and have to hide their faces while the other team run off and hide. After a count of so many seconds, the home team chant "Rallico, Rallico, Rallico, co, co" and chase after the others to find them. When one is found he has to be "head and tailed." This is done by putting one hand on his head and one on his backside. He then has to go to jail at the home lamppost and he has to stay there with two people from the home team guarding him. The home team have to search out all the others and head and tail them, sometimes with a struggle, until they are all captured. They can all be released at any time by one of the opposing team dashing out of his hiding place and running up to the "home" and spitting into the lamppost area. If the "spit" lands in the home circle then all are free and run away, but if they are stopped by the guards, who head and tail them, then they also have to go to jail. Many a fight has broken out during this rough game and it is not a game for girls.

The girls used to do skipping games, chanting skipping rhymes, hopscotch, and cat's cradle.

Truth and Dare was a favourite game for both boys and girls. The person who is "on" can ask anyone if they want a "truth" or a "dare." Usually, if it's a boy, they ask for a dare and sometimes they are dared to kiss a girl or do something similar. If it's a girl's turn they usually choose a "truth" and they are usually asked if they have kissed a certain person or if they love a certain person or something "girly." There were usually lots of red faces and embarrassed giggles but it was always a favourite and sometimes sexually motivated. This game was probably the first introduction to boy-girl relationships.

The streets were much safer than today as there was not much traffic in those days, and the street could become a football pitch with coats placed at either end for goalposts or a cricket pitch using the gateposts for stumps or something similar.

I don't want to sound condescending, as these sorts of games are still played by the kids of today, but there is no comparison to how we always played such energetic, fast-moving and sporty games, rather than the computer games of today. There weren't many overweight people in those days, most probably because we didn't have the exotic and fattening foods. Chocolate, crisps and similar things were a rare treat. Well, I suppose we would have eaten beef burgers if they had been available; after all, we were only human – but we ate rations and we did more physical things.

Every other week we had to do a long-distance run. We started from school, through the woods towards Langold Lake, round the lake and back again. It must have been about five miles. Not many people did the distance. I didn't ever complete the course. People were very crafty and knew all the short cuts. Usually the gym teacher, Mr. McCarthy (Mac), took us on this run. He was a keen sportsman and was in many local teams and even played rugby for the nearby town of Worksop. He had his special "fit mob" that always ran with him, but the majority of us only kept up with him for about a mile and then started to slow up. We couldn't ever have kept up his pace and he knew this and so didn't try to encourage us to keep up.

'STONE - PAPER - SCISSORS'

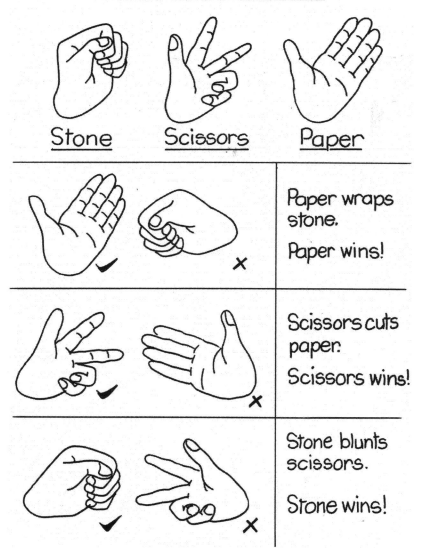

Stone	**Scissors**	**Paper**

Paper wraps stone.

Paper wins!

Scissors cuts paper.

Scissors wins!

Stone blunts scissors.

Stone wins!

He had his favourite people following him and they disappeared in front of us. My gang always did the same trick. We ran with him for about a mile, trailed off until the runners were out of sight and then we walked as far as the recreation ground just before the lake where there was a large open-fronted wooden shed with seats.

This was as far as we went, and we lay down and had a good old time telling jokes and acting about for the next half hour until the runners came back into view. We peeped through the holes in the shed and kept quiet until they had run past us and disappeared from view, and then we all set off and trotted back to school. When we got back to school the fast runners were usually flat out on the grass, exhausted, puffing and panting. Poor sods! We trotted in, pretending to be exhausted, and flopped on to the ground to be congratulated by Mr. McCarthy.

"Yes, well done, well done!" the elite lot were saying to us with a silly, knowing look on their faces.

Others in the running class had other ways of dodging the miles, like hiding in the woods. In fact, as I remember, our lot only ever ran about a mile during any long-distance run.

A funny thing happened to one of our lot one day on a cross country rendezvous. We had arrived at the shed and drank our water and one lad, who will remain nameless, had a small school milk bottle. As we were acting about and getting more and more ridiculous, he decided to wee in his bottle, and next thing he had put his penis into the bottle and got an erection. It got stuck in the bottle. We all thought it was hilarious. He was walking about proudly holding up the bottle with his erect penis. We just couldn't stop laughing. Then, when we had settled down, he couldn't get it off – it was wedged in and it seemed to get tighter the more he struggled. He then began to panic as elite runners came into sight. The more he pulled and tugged, the tighter it got. Most of our mob had left to finish the course and just a couple of us stayed behind to help him out of his dilemma. We told him to sit down and calm down and try to "cool off" and then someone had a bright idea. He took an empty bottle and filled it with cold water from a pond and poured it into the bottle with the trapped member to help cool it off. After another session of cold water his red and sore penis was finally released. We arrived back very late and told the teacher a pack of lies about him tripping over and that we had to help him to stagger back. My mate and I were congratulated by the headmaster at the end of the week assembly for the kind gesture of stopping behind and helping our comrade back to base.

At the end of the street where we lived there was a path that led into the wood. This wood became one of our main playgrounds. We climbed trees, we made swings and swung about like Tarzan; we chopped down trees; we had fires, played games like tracking and we became wild woodmen.

We disappeared into the wood on Saturday morning and didn't come out until we were hungry. My brother Gud was a true "wild woodman." He was palling about with a girl from our street and they often played in the woods together. One day we followed them. We had become excellent trackers and we thought we were like Davy Crockett! They took the back wood path to the big trees. It was quite a long way into the wood and they stopped at a certain tree that had good climbing branches. About halfway up the tree was a platform carefully fastened by ropes to the branches. We watched them skilfully climb up and swing themselves onto the platform until they were out of our sight. God knows what they were doing up there! They were up there for ages, as quiet as mice. We hung about for quite a while and then took off to do our own thing in our better known part of the wood.

We kids were all interested in comics. Dad allowed us to have *The Dandy* and *The Beano* every week, delivered through the letterbox. It was always a mad scramble to get to read it first. Simple things like comics were very popular in those days. Every Saturday evening at about six o clock the "Comic Man" parked his van in a certain position on the main road near to the shops. He was a very popular man and all the kids in the village kids gathered around his van as soon as it arrived. He opened his back doors wide and spread out two side tables on which he displayed his comics and books.

Superman, Captain Marvel, Spider-man, Action comics, Marvel comics – I was completely hooked on them. I liked them not only because of the exciting comic stories, but also because of the drawings. I used to study them and copy them. I found it so fascinating and skilful how they had been drawn: the shapes of the faces and hands and the way they drew the muscles on the characters' arms and legs. I was always sketching them and I took advantage of every scrap of white paper in the house to practice my drawings. As far as I was concerned, if ever I came across a piece of white paper, it was there for me to draw on and it gave me another reason to draw.

Swapping comics was a great and cheap pastime. What it meant was that if you could only afford one comic you didn't miss out because by swapping you could read all the comics, and everyone in the village was involved in swapping. The girls did the same with their comics. The Comic Man must have done a roaring trade. He was such a character himself. He was so fat he could hardly move but, like most fat men, he was jolly, always telling jokes and pulling our legs. Everyone liked him.

"Do you want anything for the weekend?" he kept saying.

Then he laughed away as if he had said something really funny, especially if you didn't know what he meant. It was funny to him because he knew that we were so naive. Even so, I did notice that the older lads used to buy these little boxes of something very discreetly so no one could see them buying them. I thought it might be tobacco and they didn't want anyone to know they were smoking. The older lads also used to buy the Hank Jansen books, but I didn't realise just how interesting they were until I was a few years older!

These books became the new thing. It was no longer Superman or Spider-man comics for the older boys; it started with Hank Jansen and suddenly the Comic Man's van was full of *Tit-Bits* and *Razzle* and a host of "girly" magazines.

Suddenly they didn't want to swap me a Dandy or Superman comic: they were only interested in Hank Jansen. It was an education.

My school report was a disgrace. I remember reading it before giving it to my Mam. Maths – must try harder! Reading and English – must concentrate! Writing -"composition" - Frank has a vivid imagination but must concentrate on his spelling and grammar. The reports always finished off by saying something about my "poor effort" and "must try harder," "disruptive in the class," now in a "C" class and "must try to improve himself." The only good thing any teacher said was, "Frank excels at Art."

We were asked to express ourselves once again in the Art class. This time I drew Superman – muscles and everything, including his bright blue costume with the "S" sign on his chest – on a large piece of white cartridge paper about two feet high and eighteen inches wide. Whilst I was drawing it the kids kept coming over to look at it and admire it. Even Mr. Avery himself came over to see what all the fuss was about.

The picture was pinned to the wall and it stayed there for as long as I can remember. It gave me a lot of pride and self-esteem and was even mentioned in my school report. From that day on I decided that I wanted to be an artist and draw comic strips.

The village cinema, the Picture House, was a main attraction to everyone in the village. It showed three different films per week. Most films were black and white with just a few Technicolor ones. Films like *The Black Swan* with Errol Flynn, and *Tarzan's Secret Treasure, The Maltese Falcon, The Third Man, The Mark of Zorro*, and *Lassie Come Home* filled the cinema. Everyone liked cowboy and indian films and Tarzan films. A new Tarzan film with Johnny Weissmuller was always the talk of Langold, as were the heroes like

John Wayne, James Cagney, Kirk Douglas, James Mason and Humphrey Bogart. I seem to be only mentioning the boys' films, but films with Lana Turner, Bette Davis, Katharine Hepburn, Barbara Stanwyck and Lauren Bacall were also popular.

If children under fifteen wanted to go to the pictures then they would have to stand outside and ask an adult to take them in. "Take a nine-penny in, please, mister?"

There were sometimes twenty or more kids standing bothering all the adults to "take them in." We sometimes stood there for ages until the last person had gone in and then we went home as miserable as sin. I remember once, it was a Tarzan film; we had asked everyone to take us in and there were about six of us unlucky ones left. I was nearly in tears as it was the last time it would be shown and Tarzan was my favourite. We were just about to go home when the manager, Mr. Johnny Walker, stepped outside and said that we could go in by ourselves as long as we didn't make a nuisance of ourselves or make a noise. Forget the heroes of the films: he was our hero that day!

It was quite a challenge to get into the cinema without paying and there were several ways to do it. My friend, Colin, was great at devising ways and means of getting in without paying. The cheekiest and probably the most dangerous way was to simply filter into a group of people and boldly walk in with them. It was risky but occasionally it worked. One day we found out just by accident, by rummaging through boxes of rubbish, that all the torn-up tickets were put into a cardboard box and dumped at the back of the cinema to be collected by the bin-men. Sometimes when they were showing a popular family film the usherette was rushed off her feet having to handle her torch and trying to tear a large bundle of tickets up, so quite often a few of them were not torn in half. We filtered through the box to find tickets that were nearly whole and used them on the Saturday matinee shows, when kids were allowed in without an adult. We didn't often pay to see a matinee and used our cinema money to buy ice creams and sweets.

Another way to get in free was a more daring ploy and was only used when we were really desperate. This only worked after the lights had gone out. The toilets were located near the exit doors, which were at the rear of the cinema near the stage. One of the boys who was in the cinema having paid his fee waited for the lights to go out and the first item was being shown on the screen. The chances were that at that particular point no one would visit the toilet. He then quietly went towards the toilets, but instead opened the emergency door and let the rest of the gang in, closing the door quietly behind them. One by one they entered the cinema looking as if they had visited the toilet. Only one went in but three or four came out. No one ever noticed: their eyes were on the screen.

During this time at Langold we acquired another two sisters and a brother - Janet, Richard, and Linda, making a nice round figure of ten. Our eldest sister, Margaret, had left home and was married to a soldier, Tony, and they were stationed at Catterick in North Yorkshire. Wilfred was fifteen and had started work at the family business – the pit – Firbeck Colliery. It was called a family business because it was expected that when you left school you went to the pit where your dads and uncles and brothers worked. It was a tradition – unless you were clever at school and passed your Eleven Plus exam.

At the age of eleven every child sat this examination. I personally cannot remember what the exam entailed but, of course, like the majority of the pupils at our school, I failed. There were a few, like our friend and neighbour Ivan, who passed and were then transferred to Retford Grammar School.

Large families were common in those days and were not looked on as unusual, but it became quite a joke with the teachers, who said at the beginning of a new term, "Welcome to class so and so, and what Canning do I have this year?"

I remember that every reference book I was given at school had the name of a Canning scribbled in it somewhere.

Life-Savers

I have mentioned Langold Lake, the nucleus of everything for Langold folk. Wig was already a member of the Life-Saving / Swimming Club. I joined soon afterwards and other members of our family joined over the next few years. It took over our lives. We often used to say we lived at the lake. We were there every day, summer and winter. We were members of the Life-Saving Club and *Bay Watch* had nothing on us. It was a time in our lives when we were turning into young men and women. We were approaching puberty and beginning to think about our physical appearance. We were bashing weights about in the swimming hut and swimming long and fast distances as if our lives depended on it. We had so much energy and it had to be released. We thought we were God's gift to women – supermen, in fact – and the girls were super sexy wonder women! We lads all joined NABBA, the National Body Building Association, and wore white vests with the logo NABBA and an image of a muscular man printed on the front. Can you imagine a group of fresh-faced, cropped- haired, bronzed, muscular he-men swaggering along the lakeside on a crowded day, pushing out our chests, sticking out our bottoms trying to walk like John Wayne, flexing our muscles. Charles Atlas in the flesh! How could the girls possibly resist us?

The best years of our lives! We did save lives and we also pulled out a few drowned persons, but mainly we had fun. The swimming club was an all-year club. We swam all year round, winter or summer.

During winter the stove was loaded with logs so that the club hut was hot and we did our weight training until we were wet through with sweat, then ran down the pier and dived into the lake. If it was iced over, we broke the ice and dived in. We must have been slightly mad but we were convinced that it made us healthy and super fit.

During the summer school holidays we practically lived at the lake. We left home early morning and walked through the woods with our pals to the club. My particular best swimming club pals were Sim Cockayne and Ivan Cavell. We called ourselves The "Cav-Can-Cock Club." It didn't matter whether it was raining or sunny, this was our daily trek. In those days, it always seemed to be sunny. The mornings were spent swimming and diving and when we were hungry we went home for food. Then, in the afternoon, off to the lake again. Home for tea and then in the evening back to the lake again for the evening swimming club. Jack Revill, the club coach, was home from work and it was then that we did our life-saving practices, exams, exercises and weight lifting.

There are three ways of handling a drowning person in the water. The three methods were practised every session until you were proficient enough to do them automatically, without thinking, during a life-saving incident. Method one is to be used if the person is not panicking and just wants help – grab the person at the back of his neck with your left hand, then reach round and place your right hand under his chin and swim backwards, pulling him along. Method two is to be used if the person is big or fat and difficult to handle, and then you have to turn him around facing away from you, place your hands beneath his elbows and drag him along. Method three is to be used if the person is struggling and then you turn him round facing away from you, slip your arms under his arms and around his chest, pull him to you to stop him struggling and then pull him along to safety. I say "him" but it applies to both sexes. We had an equal number of girls in the club as boys and we all did the practising together, most times boy with girl. I think you will have already guessed what happened when we practised the seemingly very popular method three, but if we didn't practise it properly we were ticked off by our instructor because, after all, it was to save lives.

At weekends, when most of the club members were there, we did silly things like mud fights, swimming costume football, high-dive showing off, underwater aqualung practice and generally had fun in between our duty stints as lifeguards.

LIFE SAVING HOLDS

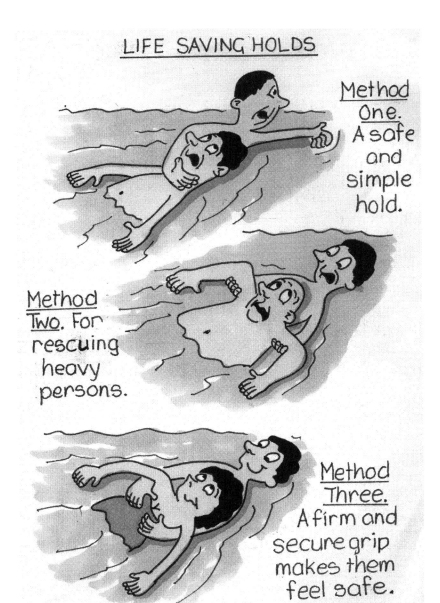

Method One. A safe and simple hold.

Method Two. For rescuing heavy persons.

Method Three. A firm and secure grip makes them feel safe.

The lifeguards had a special stand built for them, which was located on the end of the main pier and had a high seat for the duty person to sit on and observe the swimmers. There were two other seats for a couple of other lifesavers, who sat either side of a "reeler." The reeler was a winding device, like a mangle, which wound up a long rope, and fixed to the end of the rope was a harness which, in case of an emergency, the lifeguard fastened around his chest. The reeling manoeuvre was practised every day, as it was a very important piece of life-saving equipment. It was simple but enabled the lifeguard to rescue someone in a very speedy and safe manner. Imagine a person in difficulty about 200 yards away from base, shouting for help. The duty lifeguard quickly puts on the harness with the rope attached to it, dives in and swims to the person who is in trouble. He then turns him onto his back, grabs him around his chest, under his arms, and then, at a given signal, the team reel them in. It is a quick way of recovering a person in difficulty. We all practised regularly, and felt confident and proud that we were performing an essential duty.

During my few years as a life-saver there were quite a few people saved but unfortunately two people drowned. I will always remember an experience when a boy disappeared under the water. We were called to help by his sister who was screaming from one of the floating rafts that her brother had not "come up" after a long time. We all dived in and quickly swam to the raft and then started diving under the water searching for him. It was ages before we found him. He had drifted underneath the raft and had got tangled up in a rope. We pulled him out and lifted him into a boat to take him ashore. It was quite an ordeal for me and I was exhausted after many deep dives under water looking for him.

We tried to console his sister, who was hysterical. I never again want to handle a person who has drowned. It is a horrible experience having to tightly grip a dead body when there is no reaction or feeling in them. Their skin and muscles move like jelly. It feels as if the skin is coming off the bones into your hands. The normal reaction of a living person is for them to tighten their muscles to compensate the pull.

Life Saving Club

I will always remember a more pleasant incident. One day when I was on duty, a girl of about my age asked if one of the lifeguards could swim alongside her to the high diving board to give her support as she was a little unsure. Everyone volunteered but I said that I was the duty officer that day and pulled rank! She was a beauty and looked quite sexy in her swimming costume. We got into the water and started swimming. She was quite happily chatting away and confidently swimming when, suddenly, she decided she wanted to go back and turned around. When she saw that it was further to go back than forward she started to panic. I swam up to her to calm her down. I told her to turn around and float whilst I held her head and helped her along. We continued quite calmly back to the pier. When she climbed out she threw her arms around me.

"I thought I was going to drown and you saved my life, and, because you saved my life, I now belong to you," she said.

She was ever so grateful to me and we built up a nice friendship and saw each other regularly for a few months afterwards. She came to the lake most Sundays and sought me out. I got quite a lot of ribbing from the club crowd.

"Here she is again, looking for her hero, ha ha."

We often walked round the lake and found a nice spot to sit in the long grass, and, eventually, a bit of snuggling and cuddling took place. One day we were lying down and I put my arm around her shoulder and my other hand strayed on to her breast. She sat up and angrily said something like, "I am yours in soul only – not in body." She got up and marched quickly away, with me trailing along behind saying that I was sorry. That was the last I ever saw of her.

Making Money

We were a large family of twelve and, being not too financially well off, it must have been quite an arduous task for my parents to feed and clothe us all. Even so, we didn't seem to want for anything. We were happy and we didn't know any different. We didn't have anything to compare our lives with as everyone around us was of a similar status. However, it was quite natural for the older ones of the family to try to help with the finances. One of the most popular and simplest ways to earn a little extra was pea picking and potato picking, when all the family could take part. In fact, at times, it seemed as though the entire village used to take part. We were picked up by a local farmer in a lorry or a large trailer and were transported to a field where we spread out across the full width of the field, practically shoulder to shoulder. The line of people moved slowly forward, picking up each and every pea plant by the root, plucking off the peas and placing them into sacks. As each sack was filled it was carried to the scales where the farmer weighed it and paid in cash. It all depended upon the farmer and the demand for peas at the time as to what you were paid but it wasn't very much. The value was accounted for in "pecks"; there were about five pecks per sack and the payment was between 3d (just over 1p) and 9d (about 4p) per peck. Nevertheless, if the whole family worked hard for a full day, then Dad used to go home a happy man, with a pocket full of money and, of course, we always had peas for dinner that evening.

Pea picking was a summer job. Potato picking was done in the autumn. This was work for only the oldest and strongest of children. The school had what was called the "potato-picking holiday" or, as it was called locally, "spud-lugging." Only children with written permission from their parents were allowed to do this. It was just one week in the autumn when the children were allowed to participate in this activity and it was only the children from the top two classes. We arrived at school as normal in the morning to be picked up by the farmer in a lorry. For some of us this was a great adventure. Although it was hard, backbreaking work, it was much better than schoolwork. The clothes we wore were our oldest and dirtiest as this was the dirtiest of jobs, grovelling in soil for up to six hours a day. The field was measured out on to "stints" of about ten yards, one stint for one person. A tractor rode along the furrows pulling a machine, which spun out the crop of potatoes, scattering them out onto the floor ready to be picked. Each person wore an apron made from sacking that was tied around the waist and which hung down to the floor. The bottom of the apron was gathered up with one hand to form a pocket; the person stooped over and walked along the stint, picking up the potatoes with the other hand and putting them into the pocket. When the pocket was full they were then tipped into large baskets that were placed along the length of the field. It was not work for the weak, but boys and girls did it. It was hard work but good fun and good pay and, of course, we always had fresh potatoes for our evening meal.

I always grabbed every opportunity to earn money and was always looking for ways to earn a bit of extra cash. I don't really know why – perhaps it was the desire to buy something more or perhaps it was just a desire to earn. I will never know but it has always been inside me and for as long as I can remember.

During our playing in the woods days I thought it would be a good idea if I made bundles of sticks for firewood and tried to sell them. Every house in the village was heated by an open fire and all miners have an allotment of free coal so there were coal fires in every house. In the morning the fire had to be lit. Firstly you cleaned out the old cinders from the day before, then you placed a bundle of screwed-up paper in the grate. On top of the paper some sticks of dry wood were placed and then a few pieces of coal on the top. Once a match was put to it you had a fire. Paper and coal were always available, but you had to find sticks of dry wood. This was where my bundles of sticks came in handy. They were made from dead wood and chopped into pieces about six inches long and tied up into bundles, which I sold for a few pence a bundle. Nearly everyone wanted them and it turned into quite an industry. After a few weeks some of my friends were helping me and we shared the money. I gave most of it to Mam and she let me save some of it to go to the pictures and buy sweets and things.

My next enterprise was the holly business. A few weeks before Christmas, I watched Mam decorating the front room with Christmas trimmings. She said that she wanted some holly with berries and asked us if we could find some for her in the woods. It just happened that I knew of a magnificent holly tree in a wood near Oldcotes. I collected a few sprigs, and Mam was delighted with them and said that holly made Christmas, but was difficult to come by just when you wanted some. I wondered if other people thought the same way. I wondered if people might buy some. It was worth a try. I told a friend about it and we both decided to give it a try. We collected a few sprigs each and showed them to our close neighbours who "snatched our hands off." They said the same thing as Mam – "Christmas just isn't the same without holly!"

This was it – we were energised. So off we went back to the tree and collected a slightly larger amount. We knew that holly was prickly but didn't realise just how much. Our hands and arms were scratched to bits. We knocked on a few of our neighbours' doors and asked if they would like to buy some and we sold the lot after a few knocks. Next time we were better prepared: I wore three shirts, a thick coat, two pairs of gloves and a balaclava. Complete with a sharp knife and a ball of string, we now meant business.

This time we cut off a pile of sprigs and tied them up into several bundles, fastened some around our waist and some we put over our shoulders. You can now see why the thick clothing was essential. Good thinking, eh? We also carried another bunch of sprigs in our hands. We must have looked like walking holly trees. We got a lot of funny looks. When home, we separated it into a few nice looking sprigs and knocked on a few doors.

"Do you want to buy any Christmas holly with berries, Mrs? Only threepence a sprig."

The lot went in no time.

Walking holly trees.

Everyone said the same thing: "What a good idea! We can't get holly anywhere nowadays."

"Yes, please. Three sprigs, please."

The reaction was unbelievable. We sold everything and went back time and time again.

That Christmas I was given a bike for my present. It was second-hand but it was the most wonderful present I had ever had. I still get an excited feeling every time I think about that bike. It was standing on the landing at the top of the stairs for two weeks before Christmas and was covered over with a blanket, but I couldn't help taking the odd peep at it whenever Mam and Dad were out. God only knows how they could have afforded such a thing as there were nine other kids to buy for. I often think back to how they must have struggled at a time like Christmas. We all had presents. We all had a Christmas stocking full of goodies and we all had such an exciting time, but my bike has always been the greatest present – ever!

My bike gave me a chance to apply for a paper round, which was only available to people who owned a bike. There must have been about ten paperboys employed by this shop to deliver papers to various areas in and around the village. I took over a round from a lad who had just left school and was about to start work. He gave me five days' training to get to know what newspapers and magazines were to be pushed into which doors and how to mark them up with the house numbers or names. It was quite mind boggling to start with as there was so much to remember. In a matter of five days, he had pumped into my brain the many different papers etc. He also explained full details of who lived in the various houses, their names, what sort of people they were, who gave him Christmas tips, how many kids they had and also a few other interesting and sordid details about some of them. In particular number 103.

I distinctly remember number 103. We left our bikes at the gates and as we walked up the drive he started whistling very loudly the tune from "Popeye the Sailor Man." He slowly pushed the paper into the door, waited a few seconds and then we walked slowly back to the bikes. He then explained why. Apparently the lady at number 103 sometimes opened the door with very little clothes on and one time she was naked, he said. He usually whistled to let her know that he was delivering her paper, hoping that he might have another show, but this particular week we weren't so lucky.

Weeks went by and I thought he had been pulling my leg. I had gotten into the habit of whistling the "Popeye" tune on the way to 103 but my whistling wasn't very loud. One morning I was trying my best to whistle louder, with cheeks nearly bursting. The door opened and the lady, clad in her housecoat, took her paper from me, wished me good morning and asked my name. She said it was a cold morning and I answered that I had a balaclava and gloves so I was warm enough. A few days later she opened the door and her housecoat was slightly opened.

"Good morning, Frank, it's a cold morning."

I answered that I had my balaclava and gloves, and didn't know what else to say.

A week later she opened the door standing in her bra and knickers. I think I turned bright red and stuttered the usual answer that I had my balaclava and gloves. I remember looking her in the face, not daring to look anywhere else. I slowly retired back to my bike thinking no wonder she was cold standing there with so little on.

The next time I had a showing, a week later, she was in her underwear again.

"Good morning, Frank, not so cold today," she said.

I couldn't say my usual balaclava and gloves speech and said something more intelligent like "I like this warmer weather."

Realising that I was conversing, she said something like "Do you like delivering my papers, Frank?"

By now I had lost my stage-fright and said the first thing that came into my mind.

"Yes, I even told them at the shop that I like delivering to number 103."

She quickly slammed the door and I never saw her again after that day. I wonder why? Even now after many, many, years I still glance at number 103 when I drive past.

The money I earned on my paper round was given to Mam and she gave me some pocket money. The first time I had been given regular pocket money and, wow, I felt like a man – rich!

We were growing up. I was about fourteen years old and life was sweet. We were all flirting and girls were always on our minds. All my pals were girl mad, and if we didn't have a sweetheart at the swimming club then we had one whom we fancied at school. The subject was always the same – girls, girls, girls! I had a fancy for a girl called Phyllis. Phyllis was quite a clever girl. She was in an "A" class and although I was only in a "C" class it didn't make any difference. She seemed to like me and we always seemed to be passing each other in the corridors and waving to each other and smiling and blushing.

We used to stand in the schoolyard at playtimes talking to each other, laughing and joking. I wish I could remember what we talked about but we were never short of something to discuss. We didn't have a romance, or anything like that: it was one of those magical associations where we always seemed to meet up together, even though we hadn't arranged to meet. It seemed that wherever I went she was there, and wherever she went I just happened to be there. It was as if we could read each other's minds. For instance, on a particular Sunday morning I went to the lake as usual but for some reason I sidestepped into a rain shelter within the recreation ground and there she was! We spent all day happily walking, chasing and generally acting about like lovesick idiots. We never kissed or cuddled but it was sheer joy to be with her. The only time we touched each other was the day when we arranged to meet at the lake on a swimming club day and we walked around the lake holding hands. I will never forget it. My hand was sweating and aching but I wouldn't let go in case she ran away. She was a good friend and our friendship continued for many years even after she got married. Many years later, when I was much older, I happened to be working alongside her brother at the pit and he told me that she always talked a lot about me and she wished that we had become closer. Shucks! Missed out again!

The last year at school was my best year. Everything the teachers had strived to put into my brain was now suddenly sinking in. I was promoted into a "B" class. I conquered Maths by doing it by my own secret method. I became quite good at "composition," now called English Language, and although I still couldn't spell any word that had more than three letters in it, the teachers now accepted me for what I could do and didn't pester me to try to do what was impossible. I felt as though I was achieving at last. I felt as though I had suddenly become aware of education and I wanted to know about everything and anything and, funnily enough, I realised the only way I could learn was if I really wanted and needed to learn and then, and only then, I could take it in to my brain. I was what is called a late starter!

School suddenly became acceptable and agreeable. I wanted to catch up with all that I had missed. I suddenly became part of the class, not just a part of my own gang and friends. I was no longer just the troublesome dumb kid who was known for disturbing the class. I became a team member and part of the whole class and it was my pride and joy when I was voted captain of the Roman team. My eureka moment came too late – I was about to leave school.

We had a visitor called a Careers Advisor who interviewed everyone to talk about their ambitions and career prospects. It was such a laugh. We were all hysterical with laughter afterwards, probably to cover up our embarrassment over our inadequacies.

"What sorts of careers have you in mind?" was the question.

Our answers were: space ship drivers, ships' captains, prime ministers, bank managers. The girls' answers were: models, film stars, air hostesses and celebrities. It was so ridiculous and we all fell about in stitches for the rest of the day with our outrageous quips. We boys were sons of miners and we were educated in a secondary school in a mining village and any thoughts of anything other than following our fathers' footsteps into the pits were simply out of the question. Of course, we all wanted and wished for better things, but, for most of us, it was pretty well "What's good enough for your Dad will be good enough for you."

Still, it clicked our minds into a thinking mode. There are other careers for boys with a secondary school education, such as carpenters, builders, electricians, farmers, plumbers and lorry drivers, but we were left in limbo. The Careers Advisor saw so many kids in such a short time she hadn't told us how to go about getting one of these wonderful job opportunities and we were still as mixed up as we were before her visit. Still, our minds were wandering and wondering! Perhaps that was what this visit was all about?

A couple of my school friends, Harry and Sim, and I had decided that we would like to work as carpenters when we left school, as we enjoyed the woodwork class so much and the Careers Advisor had put careers into our minds. We had heard about a woodyard business located about five miles from Langold. Well, we were interested in wood and so it sounded just right. We biked along to the woodyard one day and saw an office lady who gave us a form to fill in. A few weeks later we all had a reply and were offered jobs to start as soon as we had left school.

We left school on Friday and started work on the following Monday. I cannot remember if I gave much thought to the fact that I had left school and whether I was happy or sad or whether I would miss school. All I could think about was how nervous and pretty scared I was at the thought of starting work on the following Monday. I distinctly remember telling Mam that I couldn't stop thinking about it and I couldn't get to sleep with it on my mind. I remember her pulling me to her and cuddling me and having a cry. I think she felt sorry for me and it made me cry also. She tried to console me and encourage me, but even though I enjoyed the cuddle very much I was still scared to death.

Work

During the weekend, which seemed to pass very quickly, we made arrangements to meet at an unearthly time of seven o' clock in the morning to get to the woodyard for eight. We all had bikes and we all had been to the woodyard previously, so we knew roughly how long it would take us to get there. Our parents were advising us to be conscientious and get there a bit earlier, just in case. "Just in case" was good advice, especially when we were only halfway there and Harry's bike had a puncture. We were all in a bit of a dilemma. None of us had a puncture kit and even if we had we wouldn't have known how to mend a puncture and we wouldn't have had time to mend it. What a predicament we were in! There was only one thing to do and that was to walk, pushing our bikes. We couldn't leave Harry behind, so we all set off at a trot, or rather a hobble. Have you ever tried running whilst pushing a bike?

We arrived half an hour late, sweaty and flustered and thoroughly pissed-off, expecting the sack. The boss wasn't very happy but accepted our reason and sat us down for our first introduction. We were all given different jobs and introduced to our "skilful person" for supervision and training. I was introduced to "old Harry." He looked about a hundred years old, a little wizened chap with blue overalls and a flat cap. He was to look after me and train me to be a "crosscut leg sawyer and bundler."

Harry surprised me. Although he was old and looked old (probably because I hadn't seen many old people before), he was the nicest, happiest and funniest man I have ever met. I am not really a very good judge of people, as I learned to my detriment later in life, but there are certain people who, as soon as you set eyes on them, you know that that they are OK and you like them and you trust them and you feel good about them. Harry was one of them. The manager was straight to the point. He told Harry that I was his lad and he had to teach me all about the job. He then spun round and strolled off back to his office.

The very first thing he said to me was, "You look like a randy little bugger. Have you been on the nest all night?"

I knew I would be OK with old Harry.

Harry's job was cutting long pieces of pre-prepared timbers, two-inch by two-inch square, into certain lengths to be made into chair legs. A length of timber was placed next to a template on a saw-bench. He held the timber with his left hand and pulled a crosscut circular saw across it with his right hand, cutting off the chair leg piece. He threw the pieces into a basket. Then, pulling the piece of timber forward, he repeated the process again and again for hours and hours, all day and every day.

My job was to place the long timbers onto the bench for Harry to cut and then to dash round to the other side, pick up the smaller, cut pieces from the basket, stack them into a bundle of twelve, and strap them together. This was my destiny. After a few weeks it became so monotonous and boring. My only consolation was Harry. His continuous jokes and chatter kept me from going mad. After about a month I found that I was counting everything to twelve: twelve steps, twelve pedals of my bike, twelve mouthfuls of food, twelve steps when walking, twelve, twelve, twelve. I was going twelve crackers! How I longed for school! Oh, how I longed for playing in the woods, for the swimming club, the weekends, the pictures! How on earth had Harry survived this torture for all the years he had been working there? It's no wonder he looked old.

Poor old Harry. Probably he was quite happy with his job. Perhaps he was so relaxed, calm and contented with himself that this was the perfect job for him, for life. He didn't have to think, he didn't have any responsibility, and he didn't have to make any decisions, just plodded along day after day, laughing and joking and telling his mucky jokes. Then, one day, he was well into a pretty vulgar joke about his mother-in-law when he cut his thumb off!

Blood splattered all over the place. I nearly fainted. I screamed. People came running. People were panicking. It was frantic. As someone was wrapping a cloth around his hand old Harry just turned to me and said, "It's OK, Frank. Don't worry, lad, I can't feel bloody thing." He winked at me and started to laugh as he was taken away.

Pit Work

That night I told the story of Harry to my Dad and told him that I didn't want to go back there again. He told me I might be better off working at the pit and he said that he might be able to get me a job there as a surface worker. I told him anything was better than the woodyard. It would have been OK if Harry was going to be there, but I didn't think Harry would be going back to work after losing his thumb. Also the work I was doing wasn't really anything to do with carpentry. Dad got me a job at the pit as a surface worker. After resigning and collecting my pay I saw Harry at his home and he wished me all the best for the future, told me another joke and we said our goodbyes. I saw him a few times afterwards but he seemed to grow older every time I saw him.

A surface worker covers a multitude of jobs. My job was working in the stockyard where all the materials and equipment were stocked ready to be called off when required. They were then loaded on to special wagons to be sent underground. The materials, such as steel rings for the tunnels, planks of timber to face the tunnels, wooden "chocks" for supporting the roof, electric cables, steel rails for the tubs to run on, girders for roof supports, wooden props, steel props, hydraulic props and wire ropes – dozens of parts and types of equipment – were all stacked neatly in rows awaiting loading. Every day orders were received by the pit top manager who distributed them to the workers, who loaded the specified items into the specially made wagons and containers; then, with the order requisition attached to the wagon, they were transported to the top of the pit shaft for delivery underground. Every day was different. It was quite interesting and was so different it made such a change from the woodyard.

I worked there for a couple of years. It was steady work but the pay wasn't very good and I started to hear about the sort of wages the underground workers were earning. My brother Wig was working underground on the coalface and earning over three times as much as me.

Mining, especially for underground workers, is hard graft and I would have no hesitation in stating that coalface work is not only one of the most dangerous jobs in the world but must be also one of the most gruelling, and miners well and truly deserve every penny they are paid. Gud joined the pit and went straight underground and I followed him underground shortly afterwards.

My first job underground was as a haulage worker. Once again there were many types of jobs connected with haulage. The tubs of coal were transported from the coalface to the pit shaft, a distance of about one and a half miles, by fastening them onto a series of endless wire ropes that were moving continuously throughout the journey. On their journey they were directed and redirected along certain routes. At the junction of each route the tubs had to be unclipped from one rope and clipped onto another. A clip could be described as very heavy steel paper clip, which is firstly fastened onto the front of the tubs; then, by pressing a long handle, it closes its jaws to grip the endless moving wire rope, which pulls the line of tubs forward. My job was the "clipper." I had to await the arrival of the tubs and fasten them together until I had a full amount of twenty, then clip them onto the rope for their journey onwards. I also had to mark each tub with chalk with a special number. In between the tubs leaving me, and the arrival of the next consignment of tubs, I had a certain amount of waiting time. To fill in the time I started drawing on the side of the tubs with my chalk. After a while this became an obsession and after a few months nearly every tub in the pit was decorated with one of my drawings. The drawings were mainly cartoons and caricatures of some of the miners.

This was my Art training course. The reason it became such an obsession was that quite often people asked me to do certain drawings for them of certain people doing certain things. It soon became something like a political cartoon in a newspaper.

'TUB CARTOONS.'

If anyone who worked at the pit had done something special or had said something silly or controversial or had had a new baby or had won at bingo or scored a goal for the local football match – anything – then they became the subject of a cartoon on the side of a tub, which would travel throughout the length and breadth of the underground system and would be seen by hundreds of workers. My tub cartoons became quite well known within the walls of the pit and, even now, after nearly sixty years, people still remark and remind me of my tub cartoons.

It was a grand training for my drawing ambition. Since my schooldays I had dreamed about becoming a cartoonist and I thought that this was as near as I might ever come to being one. I made friends with a pit official called Arthur, who had a locker next to me in the pit baths, and we used to shower and get changed together while discussing world affairs. He often remarked on my tub cartoons and said to me one day, "Why don't you try to get your cartoons published in the newspapers?"

He told me of a magazine which was published specifically for the coal-mining industry called Coal. I had seen this magazine as it was sold in the pit canteen shop. I wrote a letter to them and told them what I had been doing and how my cartoons were talked about in our colliery, and they asked me to send some samples to them. I didn't have a reply for about a month and had forgotten all about it. Then, to my great surprise and shock, I opened up the next magazine to see my cartoon published. I couldn't wait to see Arthur the following day and approached him with a beaming face, and before I could get it out he showed me his copy. How proud I was! I felt like hugging him with excitement. Had it not been for him I wouldn't have even thought of doing it. He became my friend for life.

I received my fee of £1.10s, and they asked me to send more. Eventually I had a series of cartoons published called *Trainee Trouble* about a young trainee like myself getting up to all sorts of troubles and quirks. It gave me so much pride and my Dad never stopped telling everyone about it.

Once again we moved house. This time we didn't go very far, just into another street. The family were growing up and needed more room. It was not uncommon for people to swap houses in this village and we swapped a three-bedroom for a four-bedroom house. Wig, Gud and I were working at the pit. Irene, Janet, Alan, Gerald, Richard and Linda were all still at school. Alan and Janet had followed the mob and had joined the swimming club.

By now the family seemed to be in a much better financial position. Dad was still working at the pit. Margaret was happily married and was living with her soldier husband, Tony, in the army barracks in Edinburgh. We three older boys were employed and were handing over our wages in exchange for pocket money. Mam and Dad had found themselves a nice little weekend job looking after the changing rooms at the lakeside swimming pool. The pay for this must have been only a couple of pounds or so but they both seemed so much happier and contented, and Mam always looked so beautiful after all the struggles and hard times she had been through. It might have been a combination of earning a few pounds, the fresh air and mixing with all the happy people enjoying their weekends swimming and picnicking. All in all, I think for the first time in their life they were reasonably happy and contented.

Girlfriends

Wig, Gud and I were now all earning good wages as underground workers. We worked hard and played hard. We were enjoying our new life as all young men of our age did. A bit of money in our pockets, a new suit, a wash and scrub up, and off to town at the weekend for a night on the town! Don't get me wrong: a night on the town wasn't at the nightclub or disco, getting drunk and disorderly. No, no, a good night out for most of the lads was to catch a bus to town, pick up the girlfriend and go to the pictures, preferably with seats on the back "snogging" row, or to the Palais de Dance. We would have a drink, if we could afford it, and then walk the girls home. Snog until midnight, miss the last bus and walk home, about seven miles, usually with a bunch of other revellers who had all done the same thing.

We all had our share of girlfriends. Some were seeing girls from our home village who caught the bus out and walked back home with us, or some met girls from Worksop. Wig was seeing Monica, and he was pretty hooked on her, and I was seeing Betty, her next-door neighbour. They lived in Worksop and their houses were in a block of eight terrace houses with "gennels" or passageways dividing them. The gennel became our Saturday night snogging place. It was dark and dry. Wig and Mon had one end and Betty and I had the other end, all of us having a good old snog at the end of every Saturday evening.

With me, it didn't go any further than a snog as I was still a bit too shy to try anything serious, but one evening Betty's Mam and Dad had gone out for the evening and she invited me inside. I thought this was my chance: it's now or never! After a while, she asked me if I would like to see the rest of the house and we eventually finished up in her bedroom. My heart was pounding. I hadn't yet "done it" – nearly there – but not quite the finished job. I was nervous. We sat on the bed and I was quite sure that she was thinking about the same thing. We started to snog and my hand went up her dress and hooked into the top of her knickers and I started to pull them down as I thought this is what you did. She sat up looking so startled.

"What do you think you're doing?"

She was really angry and pushed me away, patted her dress down and marched out of the room with me limping along behind. She opened the back door and pointed her finger outwards.

"Good night."

I had got it wrong again!

I had got a lot to learn about women. I tried many times to see her again by sending messages, but no reply.

"Take your time. It will happen, but the girls usually take the lead," Wig advised.

How much time did I have left? I was getting older and cracking up with frustration.

Mary was much easier – so I thought. We went to the pictures and snogged so much on the back row that I can't even remember what the picture was about. Afterwards we went for a beer and she seemed quite merry and laughed a lot and I thought my time had come at last. We walked towards her home and I suggested that we go into the local scrapyard, which was on the way to where she lived. This was one of the favourite stamping grounds my mates had told me about. The gate was slightly open so I thought there must be some of them inside and already at it.

It was a bright moonlit night and we could see quite clearly. There was a pile of old tyres that were stacked in a certain way so that they made a sort of a circular wall, with a gap to get into the middle with a nice space to lie down. Wow, this was perfect!

No one could see us and I said to myself once again, "This is it." We lay down and she started to take off some of her clothes. My trousers were off and we were about to kick into gear and then she said, "Ow!" and slapped her thigh. Then another "Ow!" Then I said, "Ow!" We started scratching and patting and saying, "Ow, ow!" I could see these things crawling all over her body and I was covered in them. We both jumped up and ran and then I realised that we had left our clothes behind so I went back and grabbed them. Can you see us running down the road, half naked, shaking our clothes, scratching and screeching, "Ow?"

I was at the local pub with a friend having a quiet drink and watching these two girls playing darts and they kept giving us the eye. They were very friendly and they seemed to enjoy our banter about "double top" and who got it in the "bull's-eye." We got chatting to them, bought them a drink, had a good laugh and walked them home. We made arrangements to meet Vera and her sister the following weekend. Vera was quite attractive. I fancied her. We got along famously and it wasn't long before we were going out together. She met my parents and I met hers. She lived quite close to me and from that day we became very close; in fact – as it was called in those days – we were "courting."

There was no more Worksop and long frustrating walks home after missing the last bus home. From now on I was made: it was pub, pictures, bike rides, walks in the country, anywhere where we could get it together. I didn't have to make up any more fantasy stories to keep up with my mates. In fact, I hardly ever saw my mates: I was busy getting it together with Vera. Even the swimming club was neglected. My life was work, beer, and Vera. What else could any red blooded male want?

We weren't courting very long before the inevitable happened. In those days couples were stigmatised if they became pregnant out of marriage - more so in a small village like ours where everyone knew everyone. It was looked down on. Dad wasn't very happy: he kept saying words like "disgrace" and "scandal" and "ashamed." There was no such thing as contraceptive pills like today's privileged people take for granted, but, even so, we should have taken precautions. The Comic Man was always offering "Something for the weekend, sir," but I never really took much notice of what he was on about. How could we take care? We were both as bad as each other. We were both passionate and we didn't think about the consequences. We had to get married. It was what was called in those days "a shot-gun wedding."

Even though we were both very young and immature, we managed to acquire rooms in the house of a good friend and, with the help of friends and family, we furnished the rooms and settled down.

Our daughter was born on February 8, 1955. We called her Amanda Jean after the film *Mandy*. Princess Mandy, I called her. She was a true Canning – a wanderer. Fifty-odd years later I still call her a gypsy as she, dragging along with her, her devoted husband Cliff, has travelled the world and seen nearly every notable sight in the world. I'm sure there is some sort of wanderlust in her genes. They have spent half their lives in aeroplanes. All her life she has been dashing here and dashing there, surrounded by loyal friends. When she was a toddler we lost count of the times she wandered off exploring and finished up in some neighbour's house. She had only just learned how to walk. Her favourite toy was a pull-along ding-a-ling roller. While she was out on one of her "visits" all we had to do was to open a window and we could hear the ding-a-ling in the distance and we knew where she was – visiting someone and chatting away to them. Everyone said she was a lovely little chatterbox. We thought she was a little devil but such a sweet little devil.

"Where the devil is she now?" we used to say.

Thank goodness it was in those days when things were relatively safe. Today you cannot leave children out of your sight for one minute, in case they are kidnapped – but if ever she had been kidnapped we would have had no fear that they would soon have handed her back as she would have chattered their heads off!

88

Coalmining

I was now a married man with a family and responsibilities. I needed to earn a decent wage and decided to apply for training as a coalface worker. I was really chasing the big money as coalface workers were the better paid miners; but the job was arduous and dangerous and not healthy. In fact, to put it mildly, it was the worst type of work in the world. I have often said that I would have been better off in jail as a convict, for at least a prisoner learns a trade even if it is stitching mailbags.

After I had finished my six months' training period I became a fully-fledged, qualified collier. At first I had to work a week in rotation of all three shifts until a regular position became available to me. This was called "working the market." At the beginning of the shift I signed in and was given whatever job was available. I didn't know what I was going to do or who I was going to work with until I had arrived. I hated every minute of it. After a few months I was having nightmares about it. This wasn't what I was put on this earth for. I found it strange that some people actually enjoyed working in this environment, working all sorts of ungodly hours in the most hellish places, eating black dust, coughing up black phlegm, being so tired at home that you were unable to function properly. I dreaded going to work and had to force myself to do it. I began to envy other people's jobs. I envied the milk-man early in the morning delivering his milk, and wished I was him; I envied the man who drove the pit bus and I often wished I was him – even a dustbin man. Anything was surely better than my lot. However did I get into this situation?

I didn't seem to mind working as a haulage worker as I could fill my time with drawing on the pit tubs, but coalface work was a dread. I felt like a prisoner doing hard labour with no way of expressing myself. There was a black seam of coal in front of you which had to be removed and whichever job I did at the coal face there was only one way it could be done – no thought – no planning – no creativity – just face up to it, with bent back, naked except for a helmet which carried a lamp, a belt which held a lamp battery, knee pads, and boots. After ten minutes you were wet through with sweat and totally black with coal dust.

The only way you could tell who was who was if you had started your shift with them. To come into contact with anyone else after the first ten minutes, all you saw was a moving lump of blackness, as black as the coal they were working on.

The dread started in my mind as soon as I had changed into my jet black working clothes which were stiff from sweat from the previous day. The first thing was to fill my bottle with water, then pick up my lamp, thread the battery on to my belt and make my way to the pit shaft. There were two shafts. One was the inward fresh air shaft into which air was sucked through the system down into the mine by means of a gigantic fan. The air circulated through the complete coalmine through many miles of tunnels, circulating through the coalfaces and eventually back along other tunnels, up through the outward shaft and finally expelling into the atmosphere.

At the beginning of the shift the workers could enter the pit by any of the shafts they chose. The only difference was that the air in the inward shaft was cold and damp, and the air in the outward shaft was bad air – hot, putrid and smelling of Shot powder. I always opted for the fresh air shaft because at least for the first half hour breathing was easier.

The shafts at Firbeck Colliery were nearly half a mile deep. The lift, which was commonly called a "cage" as it was made from open steel mesh, had two decks and carried twenty-four men on each deck. A cage operator at either end would open or close the gates, which were waist-high and made of open mesh. The operator opened the gates and counted the men in, two abreast. They had to stand front to back, squashed tightly against each other in order to fill the cage with the full number of men. As they entered, the men from the previous shift exited from the back door. The mesh doors would then be closed behind them. At the bottom of the shaft a similar operation was being done, with the new shift men exiting the cage from the back gate as the men who had finished their shift entered through the front gate. The top and bottom cage operators then pressed their signal buttons to inform the winding gear operator that all was ready. For the first ten seconds the cage slowly gathered speed; then the breaks were taken off and it dropped freely under its own weight, then started to slow up for the last ten seconds. With a whoosh, the two cages passed each other halfway at a phenomenal speed.

For a new starter at the pit, this was a most frightening experience. On descending, the stomach lifted up into the chest area, then gradually settled; then for the last few seconds it dropped down to the bottom of your body. The ascending men got the experience in reverse. It usually took about three or four weeks to get used to this daily unnerving experience.

I remember one day I was waiting to descend when a man jumped down the shaft. His friends said that he had been very depressed for a long time and continually talked about his hatred for pit work and how he could not stand the thought of another day down the pit. His body was never recovered. Apparently when anything is dropped down the shaft the speed of the fall and the velocity of wind causes it to bounce from side to side all the way down, and all that was found of the body upon examination of the shaft was gruesome bloody marks every so often where the body hit the sides.

I felt what I call the "dread" at the beginning of every shift but, thank goodness, I never got the urge to jump down the shaft.

Strangely enough, not everyone thought the same as I did about coalmining. My opinion was heavily biased, probably because my mind was set firmly and I always knew that one day I would leave the pit to do other things.

A mining community was a unique, close-knit group of people. Although there was another world outside, most people within the community were quite happy and satisfied with their lot and had no great desire to change. When born and brought up in a mining village and a mining environment one naturally tended to become swallowed up by the mining ways and thoughts, and even speak mining language. Everyone knew each other and everyone fitted into the community system. The village, the school, the shops, the pubs and clubs were all geared up to cater for the community. No one was financially better off than anyone else. The work was regular and constant and everyone felt safe and secure.

There were many such mining communities scattered throughout the UK, and although they were all conjoined by the National Coal Board they were all unique in their characters and all had their own specific, identifiable accents. The basic broad accent was what could be called Pit Slang, but mixed with the dialect of the particular county where they were situated. For instance, the words "thee" and "thar" were said slightly differently in different areas but meant the same thing.

A typical morning – it is five o'clock – a dozen or so men are waiting for the pit bus. No one talks as they are all missing their sleep and are in a dreamlike state. Some of them are half asleep, eyes closed whilst leaning on the bus shelter wall. The bus arrives. As the men get on the driver tries to communicate with them as they hand over their fare.

"Orrate then?"
"Arr orrate," is the reply.

"Ars thar gooin'?"
"Orrate, mate," is the answer.

"Arr thee orrate as well?" the driver asks.
" Knackered," is the reply.
"Thar orrluss knackered."

The next man hands over his fare. "Fuckin' 'ate earlies," he utters.
The next man says, "Earlies is bett'r'un fuckin neets."

This is pit slang. It is a tough, manly way of communicating, which is fully understood by mining folk with, of course, lots of swear words introduced between every two or three others.

A few typical simple phrases:

Arr thee orrate? – Are you alright?

Is thar on neets? – Are you on nights?

Arrs t'owd lass? – How is your wife?

Were an orrate do wern't it? – It was a good show, wasn't it?

When's thar gooing oowm? – When are you going home?

Is thar gooin' ta flicks t'neet? – Are you going to the cinema tonight?

Giz a swag a thee watter. – Would you please let me have a drink of your water?

"Ayoop, arr thee dooin', orrate?" is quite simply asking someone how they feel.

Wot yer on abaht? – What do you mean?

Even now, after being away from the pits for fifty-odd years, I still drift back into a slightly moderated version of pit slang whenever I meet an old pit comrade. One of my old pit pals often telephones me, and my wife always tells me that she knows whom I am talking to by the way my speech drifts back to pit slang.

Coalmining is really a very sophisticated industry and the production of coal can only work by a series of very intricate and elaborate systems. The coalface I worked on was two hundred feet long by four feet high and each day a four-foot-wide strip of coal the whole length of the face was taken out. The face was divided into approximately eight-feet-long "stints" and a collier or hewer, the man who digs the coal, had to remove all the coal from his stint, and while doing that he also had to put in place a series of roof supports to stop the roof caving in. At the end of his day he had to leave his area clear and tidy by shovelling all the coal on to a conveyor belt, which ran behind him the for full length of the coalface. This shift, the day shift – "days" - started at 6am and ended at 1pm.

The next shift, in the afternoon – "afters" - started at 2pm and finished at 9pm. This shift concentrated on "cutting." A large coal-cutting machine was used, which looked similar to a hedge trimmer but much, much bigger and weighing about two tons. It was driven by compressed air. The cutting blade, on which diamond-tipped cutting teeth were fitted, was located at the very bottom of the cutter. It slithered on the floor and protruded underneath the coal seam, cutting a groove about four inches thick by four feet deep so that the coal pressure was released. The cutter travelled the full length of the coalface, and was followed by the "borer." His job was to drill holes into to the coalface every few yards into which the "shot firer" filled explosive shot powder. A series of these "shots" was connected to a detonator that the shot firer exploded to smash the coal into smallish pieces.

The night shift – "neets" - started at 10pm and ended at 5am. This was the "drawing- off and packing" shift. The people on this shift had to remove the conveyors and belts, bring them forward and then reassemble them into the next space, which was a movement of four feet, and make them ready for the following shift. The packers then had to build "packs" or "pillars" by filling wire bags with waste material and stacking them to form pillars or supports which were permanently left to hold up the roof. Then the old pit-props were taken down and brought forward to be used again by the colliers on the next shift.

The Solution

I knew that there must be something else in life just waiting for me to find it, and I was brimming with ideas. The pit was like a dark shadow overpowering all imagination and ambition, and I didn't want to become locked in that sort of life forever.

If I said that I wanted to become richer or better off or even have a better life, I think it would sound facetious. I think the best way I can describe how I felt is to say that I wanted to "broaden my horizons." There must be a better, more interesting and more useful life, and I felt sure it must be there for anyone who wanted to have a go. I think these thoughts were embedded in my mind when I was very young and living at Oldcotes and wearing my army combat jacket.

What was the way forward? It was always on my mind – I was a married man, I had a lovely daughter who was the light of my life, but I felt like a misfit. I was bound to the pit as I lived in a pit house. I was a round peg in a square hole. And I somehow had to get out of that hole. Every day that passed made me more determined to try to change my life. I had made a decision to try to find other part-time work in order to ease off the pit work and perhaps even find another, more interesting job. It was a feeble plan and I didn't really know how to do it or if it would ever work, but it helped to drive me along.

My long-time interest in Art enabled me to be able to adapt to any type of artwork. I was already writing the deaths' entries in the register at the church, which involved precision writing in an Olde English script. I wondered if I could try to get more of this type of work. We were living opposite a row of shops that displayed posters and show cards. I visited all the shops and offered my services as a poster writer. It wasn't long before bits of work started coming in. I was asked to write chalked messages on blackboards and make small coloured posters advertising things for sale and bargain offers and price lists. The manager of the Picture House commissioned me to paint brightly coloured posters advertising the films that were showing on any particular week.

I was asked to paint a shop facia board – "G. Riggs. Butchers" – and after that successful contract, more shop sign work seemed to come along. I remember painting a high facia board in the middle of winter. My fingers were nearly dropping off. The board was very high and I was doing a balancing act on the top of a ladder. After completing each word I had to come down to warm myself up. The job took all day and I was so intent on concentrating on painting the letters accurately and trying to keep warm, that I didn't realise that I had spelled a word wrong. Of course, I couldn't spell at the best of times, but this time I was shivering and rushing to get the job done to get out of the cold and I wasn't thinking properly. The words were "Fruit and Veg" but I had written "Fruit and Vag." Lots of people looked up at me whilst I was signing but no one made any comment and some even said how nice it looked. I finished the job and was paid £1.10s. About two months later the shopkeeper came knocking on my door and told me about the mistake, but he couldn't stop laughing. He said that he had looked at it many times, and it was only when a lady came in that day and jokingly asked for some fruit and vag that he realised the error.

Funnily enough he said that he would leave it like that as it might create a good talking point in the shop. It stayed like that for many years and every time I went into his shop we had a laugh. He certainly had a good sense of humour.

My sign writing jobs led me on to painting and decorating work. One shopkeeper asked me to paint his shop front along with the sign writing and from then on people thought I was a painter and decorator – well, probably not, but I was cheap.

There was a new major road being built quite near to us. The road contractor had agreed with the NCB to purchase slag from the pit tip for use as a base foundation for this new road. It meant hundreds of lorries filling up at the tip and weighing off at the colliery weighbridge before delivering their loads to the roadworks. It was a great opportunity for many people who were able to drive heavy goods vehicles to buy old lorries and try to get a contract to do this work. Although it was only a short-term contract, it seemed that there was a rule that the lorries had to display the name, address and telephone number of the contractor. One new lorry contractor was a local man who asked me to sign his details on his lorry doors. Just a small job: it only took me a couple of hours.

I noticed that many of the lorries were displaying old names that didn't belong to them, and some didn't have names on at all. I decided to stand at the weighbridge and confront the drivers as they were weighing. I told them about the job I had just done and that I could sign their lorry whilst they were having their dinner break. It was only a simple requirement: it didn't have to be a masterpiece, just enough to make them legal and at £1.10s. it was a bargain. I did about fifty jobs before the demand dried up. It was a nice little earner and I gained a lot of experience from it.

I still carried on working at the pit but I became more and more resentful of it. Painting jobs were not regular and I couldn't earn a living doing it, and, unfortunately, working at the pit was still my main income. However, I must admit, I had more time off than going to work.

On November 3, 1959, our second child appeared on the scene. He was born at home. The midwife arrived and I was expected to leave the room and go and boil some water. After a very short time I heard her saying, "Come on. Push, push, push," and after a lot of screaming she said, "Good girl, well done."

I breathed a sigh of relief and thought she would call me in for the boiled water, but, after a minute or two, it started again.

"Come on, push, push, push." More screaming. Then, "Good girl, well done. Frank will be very proud of you."

Gosh, I thought, we didn't know we were having twins. I waited with bated breath for the call.

"Now, come on, Mrs. Canning. Try once more. Push. That's a girl. Push, good girl."

By this time I was panicking. Three babies, my God, what have I done?

"Mr. Canning, you can come in now. Bring the hot water in with you. We have a lovely surprise for you."

I didn't think I could take this. Why weren't we informed earlier? Why weren't we told during the examinations? Someone's going to pay for this. Three babies and I only have one pack of nappies! I plucked up all my courage and went in with the kettle in hand. The nurse handed me my baby.

"Where's the rest?" I said.

"The rest? What do you think this is, Mr. Canning? Some people are never satisfied! My word, some people, tut, tut."

She turned to my wife shaking her head and mumbled something about men.

We called him Andrew after a singer on the TV called Andy Cole. He turned out to be such a nice boy. Everyone liked him and he was always ready to do anything for anyone. Even as a very young person he was very caring and loving. He always thought about other people before himself.

It was during these early days that I began to have serious thoughts about fate and luck. Here I was. Every time I went down the pit I thought how unlucky I was and felt so sorry for myself. Then I looked at my two lovely children and felt so lucky to have such bright and sparkling kids. Then another stroke of luck came my way from my friend Arthur, the person who had the next locker to me in the pit baths' changing rooms.

The miners' changing rooms and showers were quite a well organised system. There must have been about two thousand lockers. Every man working at the pit, whatever job they did, was allotted two lockers, one at the "clean" side and one at the "dirty" side, which were separated by rows and rows of showers. This is how it worked. When you arrived for work in your clean day clothes you stripped off and put all your clothes into your clean locker. You then walked to the other side of the building, past the rows of showers, to the dirty side and your locker containing your dirty working clothes. You put on your dirty clothes and off you went to work. At the end of the shift you left your dirty clothes in the dirty locker, then walked into a shower area and had your shower, and then carried on over to your clean locker to put your clean clothes back on to return home.

The changing rooms became a centre for conversation, and for some unknown reason at the dirty side the conversation was about work and at the clean side you talked about home and nice things.

Arthur knew very well of my dislike for pit work as I was only there half the time, and I had told him that I would leave the pit if ever I could get out of my obligatory pit house. One day he told me that he and his wife had been talking about me and had said that they would fancy living where I lived. His wife wasn't very good on her feet, and they thought that my pit house was in a prime position for them, being so near to the shops. Would I be interested in exchanging houses? He also suggested that as his house was a council house, I would be able to leave the pit if I wanted to.

I was stunned and overjoyed. This was a point in my life when I knew my guardian angel was looking after me. I knew instantly that this was my chance to change my way of life and the life of my family. I had no hesitation and shook his hand and said, "Yes, please!"

We swapped houses and I never went to the pit again.

I wasn't aware at that time that, very shortly after this, I would be presented with an opportunity that would change my life forever.

Part Two
Odd-Jobbing

I had just left the pit and my pit house and was now living in a council house. It wasn't a very nice house: cold and damp. These houses were nicknamed "Airy houses" simply because they were cheaply built from blocks of pre-cast concrete; they were extremely cold in winter and hot in summer. The window-frames were made out of pressed steel that never fitted properly because of contractions and expansions with the changing weather. There was a continuous draught whining through the gaps, thus the name "Airy."

At this time I needed to earn a living, as I was married with two children and another one on the way.

Our next child we called Jay, after Jay North, the film star who played the part of Dennis the Menace. He was born on June 21, 1961. It has always intrigued me as to why we gave him that name, as he really turned out to be true to his namesake's character. Even from a baby he was a wild boy, always up to mischief, very spontaneous and hyperactive, and, in later life, always reaching for the stars. If there was a mountain to climb, then Jay had to climb it. If there was a hole, Jay had to jump into it. I think he is a little like me!

At this stage of our married life, my wife must have found things pretty hectic, with me frantically chasing spasmodic jobs and with no regular income. It was a pretty wild sort of life and it rubbed off on our marriage. We were constantly biting each other's heads off, mainly about money or the lack of it. I should have got myself a proper job. We were not what you could call sweetly and romantically inclined. We had had a shotgun wedding and we had a shotgun attitude to our marriage.

At that time my way of earning an income was by painting, decorating, and sign writing. I charged £2 or £3 for a shop fascia signing. For painting and decorating a house exterior I charged £2 or £3 per day. As a monetary example, when I worked down the pit on the coalface I could earn £18 for a full week's work (the top wages for an underground coalface worker), but I hated every minute of it. As I have explained, I took lots of time off, so I didn't very often bring home the top wage. I still tried to earn enough to live on with a wife and family, and my past experiences with painting, decorating and sign writing came in very handy. Now the pressure was on to keep my head above water, but my debts kept rising and I was desperate to earn more money.

Most Saturdays, I was helping out on a market stall, selling pots. The owner of the business was told by the market manager that a new law stated that he had to display a sign with his name and details. He asked me to paint a sign for him and gave me a couple of pounds. Wow! I thought this was a way to become rich. It only took me a couple of hours to make and paint a sign like this. It was now a legal requirement to have a sign and all the stallholders who didn't already have them had been warned. My super moneymaking brain clicked in. I made two signs using different lettering and different colours and traipsed round the market asking for orders, which I promised to deliver the following week. I reminded them very courteously of the law, and told them about the pot man's sign and showed them my two samples. That first day I picked up eleven orders.

My front room was converted into a "painting factory." The frames were made out of a piece of hardboard, which was nailed on to a one-and-a-half inch thick frame. All were given an undercoat of quick-drying emulsion followed by a quick-drying gloss top coat. This part of the operation took two days. I learned how to sign them very quickly; then I fixed a couple of brass hooks to the top of each frame to hang them with and, hey presto, they were ready for delivery the following Saturday. It was a local market, so I was able to carry the boards on the local bus to deliver them. All the stallholders were pleased with them and I actually got another batch of orders from neighbouring stallholders.

It is easy to imagine what was going through my mind: hundreds of markets all over the country – twenty, thirty, a hundred signs per week – mass production! I had some order/invoice books printed with my new business name, F.C. Stallholder Signs, and I was away – flying high. Richard Branson, watch out!

Getting to the various markets was a problem. The idea was to visit a market and take orders with a ten-shilling deposit. The following week I delivered them with an invoice, collected the balance, then travelled to the next town market and picked up another batch of orders.

I was taking driving lessons at the time but didn't have a vehicle, and a friend who had a motorbike and sidecar offered to help me out. We loaded the signs into his sidecar and I rode on the pillion. We covered most markets within a day's driving distance. My friend was good to me, and all he wanted was his petrol money and a few quid and some grub on the journey. Unfortunately it didn't last long - probably about six months. We did most of the markets and did some of them a second time, but the demand started to run out. For a short time I advertised in the *Market Trader* magazine but only got a few enquiries.

As the market sign business gradually slowed down, I became more occupied with other jobs like writing price tickets and doing posters and odd jobs for a man who sold slippers on the markets. His business was one of these opportunist types. He would buy all the "seconds" from a slipper-making factory in Manchester, bring them to his workshop at the back of his house, where a few part-time lady-workers sorted them out into pairs which matched in colours/size and which were not in too bad a condition. They were put into plastic bags and he sold them on the market at 2 shillings and 6 pence ($12^1/2$ p) per pair.

One of my jobs was to drive to Manchester and load up the van with slippers by actually shovelling them into the back of the van. I remember one day, in the wildest winter, I was returning from Manchester driving over the Pennines on the Snake Pass when I got stuck in the snow. The van had conked out and the snow was slowly getting deeper, covering the van. I didn't have a big coat and was only wearing my normal day clothes. I was frozen and frightened. I had heard of people dying in this sort of situation. Out of sheer desperation, I crawled over the back of the seat and burrowed myself into the middle of the slippers. It was so cosy that I soon dropped off into a deep sleep.

Next morning I felt the van moving. The rescue people had found the van, and, thinking it was abandoned, they were proceeding to tow it to safety. I called out and the rescue people couldn't believe that I had survived in amongst the slippers, as the van was covered in snow and ice. They wanted to have some publicity about it but I refused, as I wasn't really keen on taking the chance of anyone ever finding out that I didn't yet possess a driving licence.

The next two years had me surviving on a crazy mixture of odd jobs. If a sign writing job came along, or a house needed painting, or someone's kitchen needed decorating, I was always ready and full of enthusiasm and energy to take them on, but it wasn't steady and my earnings were up and down like a yo-yo. A more substantial project was window-cleaning. I touted a whole street and got a book full of orders which could earn me about fifteen pounds a week. I borrowed some ladders and started my new business. It was hard work but more regular.

One day I received an order to repaint and sign write all the fascia boards in my area for a group of butcher shops called Dewhurst. I had already taken a few driving lessons and knew how to drive, so I bought an old Commer van, booked some more driving lessons and passed my driving test. It was quite a hectic time travelling all over the place sign writing different shops but, for the time it lasted, it was what I wanted to do, and if you enjoy what you are doing, then you are halfway to happiness.

One day a shop owner saw me doing some poster work and offered me a four day a week job working for his chain of four shops called The Shopping Basket. He paid me £3 per day. My job was to write labels, price tickets and posters. This was a dream job for me. It was the first job I had ever had where I went to work in clean clothes. It was another sort of life, which I had never encountered before. Shop business hours were 9am till 5pm. I caught the 8.15am bus along with all the office and shop workers who were all dressed smartly in their suits and raincoats. All had shiny shoes and some had briefcases. All the ladies were wearing smart dresses and coats and carrying shoulder bags. It gave me an overwhelming feeling of importance and made me realise how other people lived a nicer, cleaner sort of life that existed parallel to the sort of life I had always been used to.

I bought a three-quarter-length gabardine raincoat so that I could look and feel like one of them. I will never forget how proud I felt sitting amongst those "city slickers" talking intelligently about the weather and things, feeling fresh, clean and smart, with shiny shoes.

I spent one day at each shop. It was a continuous task to keep up with the ever-changing prices. At each shop I was allotted one of the girls who advised me on the different prices and told me what items needed special display posters. In each shop there were about ten girls. Can you imagine my predicament? I was in a dream situation. I was the only male surrounded by all these beautifully made-up girls with miniskirts and bouffant hairstyles. It was my education on life. I didn't realise what girls were like! You see, normally, when a boy meets a girl, they talk about nice things. They speak to each other in a nice way, they are good-mannered, they certainly do not use harsh words, and are kind to each other. I thought all girls were like that. I was in for a harsh education. The first few days things seemed quite as I expected them to be, good manners and all that. Then, when they were used to me being amongst them, they seemed to change and think I was one of them. I heard the odd swearword and overheard the odd conversation about their sex lives, and, after a few weeks, they conversed with each other totally ignoring the fact that I was there.

Express Delivery Service

Girls are worse than men! I got to know how many times they had sex, how they performed, how big their boyfriend's "thing" was, how they thought their boyfriends were sex-mad imbeciles and how good they were at it. They suddenly took on a more masculine attitude and some of them deliberately said things to embarrass me. They thought it was really funny when I couldn't return their patter with some equally vulgar remark. To be quite honest, I learned more about life whilst working at the shops than I did working at the pit. The only way I could keep my end up (to coin a phrase) was to join them halfway. I gave a few of them nicknames like Sheila Feeler, Sally Shake 'Em, Sexy Sandra, Barbara Big Uns. Some of the names I cannot repeat but the more vulgar their names were, the more they liked it, and the more I was accepted into their fold. There were times when the odd one or two tried to molest me but I was a strong lad and fought well. Sometimes I didn't fight too hard, though. I don't think these things happen today, what with health and safety and all that.

My earnings were between £12 and £18 a week with my four days at the shop and my other jobs. I worked day and night and weekends. I slept when I could and where I could, sometimes in my van. Life was great - hectic but great! If ever I felt under pressure or worried whether I was doing the right thing I would compare this life to my pit life - days, afternoons and nights.

OK, life was hectic, but I was my own man. Sleep wasn't important and tiredness didn't matter. I was doing what I wanted to do and was getting paid for it. The money still wasn't regular or steady. Some weeks it was good and some weeks it was bad. If I had a bad week, pay-wise, then I had only myself to blame and I had to use my initiative and contacts to try to create more jobs. I could always work extra time at the shops, do a bit of window-cleaning, the odd painting and decorating jobs, even fetching and carrying in my van for a few pounds.

Whilst I was working at the shops I befriended a man who was a "rep" for Heinz Foods, who told me about his "other" job. He sold Hot Dog machines to pubs and market traders. These machines were a stainless steel box with a tray which held a small amount of water into which sausages and burgers were placed. They had a thermostatically controlled electric heating element which heated the water and kept the food hot. Once cooked, the sausages and burgers were placed into bread rolls. They were very popular at the time and, because I had market experience and a van, the man thought I might be able to sell them. I sold quite a few and the commissions were quite handy but, like every good idea, it didn't take long before they were being sold by everyone and better machines were being marketed.

The Opportunity

Unemployment benefit, or "the dole," was not my thing. I was once tempted to sign on and went to the dole office and joined the queue. The queue was a mile long. In the queue were quite a few people whom I knew from working at the pit – hands in pockets, fags in their mouths, all looking downtrodden and miserable. It was not a happy situation to be in. Many of these people were probably unable to get work and maybe some didn't want work. It was probably hard to manage on the money they received, and I suppose it all depended on what sort of a life they wanted. I stood in the queue for about an hour, then made my excuses about going to the toilet and disappeared. The dole queue wasn't for me!

The lessons I had learned over the past couple of years were embedded in my mind: hard work – keep an open mind – take on anything. Could this be the key that opened the door to opportunity?

I was certainly ready to take on anything. I was desperate to get out of this unsettled existence. I have always felt in my heart that there was something waiting for me; I couldn't go through life living from day to day trying to keep my head above water. It was only the thought of going back to the pit that drove me on, but surely the way I was living just wasn't the way forward? This must have been the time in my life when fate took me by the hand. There is a time in everyone's life when fate or circumstances or luck coordinates and takes over your life and your life alters; you just happen to be in the right place at the right time, or someone bumps into you at a certain time or your circumstances are such that something dramatic happens. I was ready and waiting.

I received a telephone call from a man who asked me if I would transport his goods to Bishop Auckland in my van, as his van had broken down. He offered me £6 to do the job: he said it would be there and back in a day. I grabbed it. £6 for a day's work driving was not bad! The man didn't know me; I didn't know him. He had made his own enquiries and heard from someone that I had a van and was always willing and able to do anything for a few pounds.

The next day I arrived at his house at six in the morning and helped him load six rolls of conveyor belting into my van. The journey took about four hours. On the journey he told me that this was how he earned his living. Apparently he dealt in rubber conveyor belting and rubber hydraulic hoses. I wasn't really interested in what I was carrying in the van; it was just another job, just another paying job. My man told me that he was a retired mechanical engineer and did this as a spare-time job to keep him occupied. The destination was a scrapyard called Hanratty's after its owner and was based in Bishop Auckland. When we arrived, my man asked me to stay in the van whilst he did his business. They took out the rolls of belting one by one and rolled them out on the pathway alongside my van, and Mr. Hanratty examined them by walking along them, occasionally feeling the edges, stamping on them and pricking them occasionally with a penknife.

Then he measured them with a long tape measure. After each roll had been carefully scrutinised, they walked to the end of the rolls, out of my hearing range, and discussed the price.

Hanratty then pulled a fat wad of notes out of his back pocket, peeled off a bundle and gave them to my man. They shook hands and away we went.

My mind was working double all the way home. I was tempted to ask questions, but thought he might not like it as he had told me to stay in the van whilst he did the deal. Obviously he didn't want me to hear what was said. So I kept my questions to myself and talked about sweet nothing.

Next morning I travelled on my own to see Mr. Hanratty and asked him if he would buy any of this stuff from me.

"Why, hi, kidda," he said. "I'll have as much as you can get hold of, but don't bring any rubbish."

He started rabbiting on about types and makes and specifications, which I tried to remember without letting him know that I didn't know what the heck he was talking about. I thought it better if he thought I knew a bit about it. I didn't ask what price he paid as I was too confused at this point. We shook hands and I escaped without him asking any embarrassing questions.

I was an ex-coalminer and, having previously worked in the pit yard, I had seen lots of conveyor belting as it was used in the coalmines. The pit yards are the most dirty and untidy places on earth. It is quite normal to see piles of disused and old rolls of conveyor belting scattered about waiting to be disposed of. People who work there don't give a hoot about it and don't ask questions about the disarray, dirt and untidiness, as long as they can get their work done and it doesn't interfere with them getting their work done. Every now and then there is a massive clean-up and the piles of rubbish, scrap, and broken and damaged timber, steel girders, pit props, rollers, and conveyor belts are loaded on to railway trucks and taken away for disposal. It wasn't unusual for someone who worked in the pit yards to take home bits and pieces of these scrap items if they could make use of them. Having lived in a mining village, I knew where there were a few bits of old conveyor belts lying about.

One chap, who was a pigeon fancier, had a piece of old belting from which he used to cut off pieces to patch up the roof of his pigeon coot. I offered him £2 for it and he said I must have won the pools. Another chap had a piece of belting lying on the floor used as a path. He gave it to me *free of charge*. He asked me to roll it up and take it away, as he said it looked untidy and was slippery when it rained. The third roll had been lying in someone's garden for a year or two. The man said he was going to use it as a barrier around his garden to keep the rabbits out, but he had later decided to use wire netting instead. I gave him £3 as it looked to be quite a long piece and seemed, to my inexperienced eyes, to be in decent condition.

I had spent £5; it was quite a gamble and I still needed more money for petrol – still, Richard Branson must have speculated to start his business and someone once said something about "speculating to accumulate."

I didn't sleep much that night. All sorts of things went through my mind. Would he throw me out? Would he laugh at me? Would he think I was an idiot travelling all that way with a vanload of rubbish?

I will never forget this day as long as I live!

I arrived at Hanratty's yard. He wasn't there – he was going to be out all day and wouldn't get back till late that night. The lady asked me to come back the following day. My first hard lesson: phone up and make an appointment!

I couldn't afford to go back home and travel back again in the morning, so I decided to stay the night in my van. I had a long, fretful day walking around Bishop Auckland. I went to the cinema, had a bag of fish and chips, and then tried to bed down in the van. It was only then that I found out that the seat back was fixed and would neither push back nor drop down. The passenger seat was packed with all the rubbish from the back of the van, and so I spent the night trying to sleep in all sorts of impossible positions.

No sleep, aching back, unwashed, and smelling, certainly not a pretty sight to do business. It was daybreak, about 5am. I must have looked like something the cat had brought in. I remember thinking this was not a good idea, as I didn't really know what I was supposed to do or say and I looked like a tramp. I was so nervous with lack of sleep that I had lost all my confidence. I told myself to forget it and just go home; after all, the man would probably kick me out for wasting his time with these rubbish rolls of conveyor belting. I remember driving away like a miserable wreck. On the outskirts of the town I passed a transport café and decided to stop for a coffee. It's funny what a cup of coffee, a bacon sarnie, a toilet and a wash can do for a man. I suddenly felt refreshed, and, with my confidence slightly lifted, I jumped into the van and went back to Hanratty's.

He was standing at his gate as if waiting for me, smoking his pipe.

"Morning, kidda."

I remember his big smile which filled me with confidence as he greeted me. I thought at least he didn't look like the sort of man who would physically throw me out.

"Come on. Let's see what you've got. Let's get it rolled out. 'Ope you're not going to break me bank!"

I had a feeling that he was secretly laughing at me - or was he giving me a bit of sympathy?

We unloaded the van, one roll at a time, and rolled them out along the pavement. He walked along each roll, occasionally stamping on them, feeling at the edges and pricking them with his penknife. He then stood for a moment, held his chin with his left hand and thought. My heart was pounding.

"How much do you want for it?" he said.

Stunned silence! This was probably the most important decision of my life, but I hadn't a clue. I held my chin as he was doing, pretending to think as people do holding their chin when thinking, but I wasn't thinking about how much to charge him. I was thinking about what to say next! My brain was stuttering, trying to think fast. £5 was what I had paid for it, plus petrol seven pounds, eight pounds. What if I guessed too much and he said no? What if I said too little and he laughed at me? I couldn't believe he had asked me how much. At least I knew he was interested and had not thrown me out.

"Er – um – er – leave it to you," I said.

A shiver went down my back. I shouldn't have said that. I should have said let me think about it, or I should have said I'll work it out, or something to give me time to think.

"Ninety-two pounds."

My ears popped. I think my heart missed a beat. I tried to keep what is called a poker face. Did he say ninety-two or was it nine pounds two? I couldn't let him know I was in shock. I couldn't ask him if he said nine pounds two, in case it was ninety-two. My brain went into overdrive. I pretended that I didn't hear.

"W-what was that?"

"Ninety two pounds. Is that OK?"

I clearly remember trying get my breath: I had never heard the words ninety-two pounds before, and I had never ever seen ninety-two pounds before, but, before I could answer, he pulled out a wad; he gripped it in his right hand and with his left thumb he peeled off ninety-two pound notes into his left hand as quick as lightning. He then creased them into a roll and gave them to me. With a false, cheesy smile I stuffed them into my pocket.

"Aren't you going to count it?" he said.

"No, I trust you," I replied.

I turned round to start rolling the belts up.

"Don't bother to roll them up," he said. "They need washing down and cleaning. Now then, kidda, it's obvious you've never done this before, so next time make sure you wash them down. I don't want your dirt in my yard . . ."

Ninety two pounds!

." . .make sure the belts are not rotten by pricking them with . . ."

Ninety two pounds!

." . . a penknife like I've shown you, and make sure they are . . ."

I wasn't listening to him. My brain kept repeating, "Ninety-two pounds."

." . . blah, blah, blah . . ." He went on but I wasn't hearing him. I was in a daze.

I often wish I had heard what he was advising me to do. I couldn't wait to get in my van and drive away in case he changed his mind. We shook hands, I said, "Thank you very much," and away I went.

To say how nervous and exhausted I was before the deal, I was now flying through space. My fixed smile spread from ear to ear and I couldn't stop the tears coming to my eyes. After about twenty miles I stopped in a lay-by and counted the money, slowly placing each note on to my lap. There were exactly ninety-two pound notes. I had never in my life seen so much money. I travelled another twenty miles to another lay-by and stopped again to count it, just in case I had made a mistake. This time I put a box on my lap and spread the money out into piles of five pounds each, plus two. There was exactly ninety-two pounds. I had been earning between eight pounds and twelve pounds a week for the last few months. One job had given me twenty pounds but it took ages to complete it. Twenty pounds had seemed like a lot of money, but ninety-two pounds – I won't say it again.

On my way home I called in to see my poor old Mam. I had to tell someone, and she was always so full of praise if ever we did anything praiseworthy. I gave her £10. Of course she wouldn't take it. She said it should be used as the start of my business. I insisted and she finally took it. I felt so good after it. After all she had done for me! I paid off a few debts, gave my wife £20 to buy some nice things for the kids and kept the rest to buy some more belts. I thought that this was a good formula to use if ever it happened again. If it didn't happen again, at least I had enjoyed an experience that I would never forget.

Was this the opportunity I had been waiting for? The man had told me to bring as much belting as I could get hold of. I knew basically what a conveyor belt was, but I didn't know much about the qualities and specifications of belts. I was also aware that if ever I needed to know anything I was a fast learner, but only if I needed to know, and this was one of those things I might need to learn about, and learn quickly. The main thing at the moment was to find more second-hand belts.

I soon let it be known around my village and other mining villages that I wanted old, used conveyor belts and that I paid good cash. I worked out approximately what I was paid by Hanratty for the belts. Although I didn't measure them, I estimated that there had been three lengths of belting totalling about three hundred and sixty eight feet and he paid me ninety-two pounds. Therefore he paid five shillings per foot. I could use this as a guide for the time being. If I could buy belts for a maximum of two shillings per foot, (depending on the condition of it), add my expenses (say one shilling per foot), then there should be a reasonable profit. The price would vary depending on the width of the belting, as well as the thickness, width, and condition of it. There was such a lot to learn. There was no such thing as a Business Education course devoted to buying and selling second-hand conveyor belting. The only way to learn was to fearlessly dive in and learn by trial and error, and try to gain knowledge by experience in the process; but to be honest I didn't really have time to think. All I wanted to do was to take advantage of this wonderful opportunity.

Since leaving the pit I had accumulated quite a few debts. Everyone for miles around Worksop town must have owed money to Wigfalls. This shop sold everything: televisions, washing machines, furniture, and electrical appliances. They allowed you to have the goods on hire purchase. I bought most of my things from them and the payments were collected weekly by the H.P. man. He knew all the excuses. I think he could write a book about the excuses that people made for not paying, but he was so understanding (a bit soft really) that as long as he got his cup of tea he allowed people to get further and further behind with their repayments. I was typical. In fact, I was so far behind with my payments that I kept receiving letters from Wigfalls threatening to take me to court if I didn't pay more. As you know, my income was spasmodic. Sometimes I paid a bit more to keep them happy, but mostly I missed payments all together.

The week I received my ninety-two pounds must have been the greatest week in both the HP man's and our life. We were actually waiting for him to arrive, and greeted him with smiles and my wife asked him if he wanted a cup of tea. We talked about the weather, the neighbour's dog, and the woman up the road who was expecting again, and about all the usual scandal on which he was an expert. We kept him waiting as long as we possibly could, just to enjoy the flavour of the situation. I think he was beginning to suspect the worst, but when we finally, casually, said we wanted to bring our account up to date he gulped and spluttered and nearly choked himself to death on his tea. My wife patted him on his back and we paid him off. He left saying that he liked calling at our house. I think he must have been a bit overwhelmed.

This was the turning point of my life. This was the point I had been waiting for. Throughout my pit days and my odd-jobbing days I knew at the back of my mind that someday something would happen which I could work at and which would fulfil all my ambitions. I knew that I could not take such a deal like this for granted, but I also had a gut feeling that this was something I could get my teeth into and put all my efforts into. It had a good, exciting feel and I wanted to give it all I had.

With my new enterprise the first and most important thing to start with was to find supplies of belts. At first it seemed easy, as friends or friends of friends who lived in the neighbouring mining villages informed me about the odd bits of belts, and they were soon snapped up and scrubbed clean and delivered to Hanratty's. The very first sale of £92 was a very lucky one. Over the next few months I delivered a few vanloads but never anything like the same value as the first lot. It was a good and hard learning experience, especially when he rejected the odd rolls for various reasons, like holes, wear,

118

rot, too short, bent, the rubber peeling off, the wrong type, too thick, or too thin. It was a case of learn or lose, but the pressures of covering my living expenses and maintaining a reasonable fund to buy belts and run my van were all driving me along at a hectic pace.

At first, each load I delivered was like a gamble. It was win or lose. A win was if I had bought a few good belts and was able to turn them into cash quickly. A loss was if I bought a belt which I thought was in good condition but it was rejected, and then I had to bring it back and store it in my garden, which was gradually becoming buried under pieces of bad belts and was beginning to look unsightly. It still cost me the same amount of money to take it and bring it back for no reward as it did for a good sale. It seemed simple and obvious, but I had to pay for my mistakes and, if there were too many and I didn't learn how to avoid making them again, it would be the end. In order to try to understand what I was doing financially, I kept a record of my dealings in a Simplex account book, which recorded my ins and outs of money and the names of those I paid and received money from.

It was time to think. I was getting nowhere fast. The source of belts was drying up. I had a reasonable knowledge of what good and bad belts were. I had been buying bits and bobs, some rubbish, some good, some bad. I needed to find larger amounts of good belts. I had already approached the NCB coalmine where I used to work, and they told me that all their scrap belting went to a central depot where they made hanging straps, knee-pads, hanging curtains and many other products which were used in the coalmining industry. I did remember when I worked down the pit seeing and actually using some of these things, little knowing where they came from or what they were made from. There was room for thought for my pile of rejected belts, but first things first.

Who besides the NCB used conveyor belting? First and most obvious came to mind: a quarry. Without a second thought (probably because I was desperate) I jumped into my van and drove to the nearest quarry: Tarmac Roadstone Co. at Matlock. I fearlessly went to the weighbridge, feeling and looking so confident (through desperation), and asked if they had any scrap belting for sale.

"Go to the main office," the man said.

My confidence took a nosedive as I looked at the big, posh office. Through the main door was a window that said "Enquiries," where a lovely young lady was sitting, giving me a big smile, which boosted my confidence again. In a rather "showing off" sort of way, I said, "I'm here to buy your scrap belting." She had a wry smile on her face and said, "I can see you are here! And which scrap belting is it you are here to buy?"

Confidence dropped again. Trying my best to backtrack, I answered, "N-n-no, I mean I wonder if you have any scrap belting to sell?"

She smiled again. Obviously she could see that I was a novice by my lack of experience and immature approach, and turned it into a light-hearted answer.

"OK, don't worry, I know what you mean. I'll ask Mr. Jones to see you. Would you like to take a seat? He won't be long. What's your name and what company are you?"

We chatted a while and she asked me what I wanted the belting for and how long I had I been in business. She told me that she had only been there a short while, and the casual, easy conversation went on for about half an hour and completely relaxed me. Mr. Jones came through, shook my hand, introduced himself and asked my name.

"Yes, it just happens we do have some used belting for sale, because the bloke who usually buys it isn't allowed here anymore."

He told me that the previous buyer had bought all their scrap belts for the past year and they had trusted him to load the belts up unsupervised, but they had found out that he had been helping himself to the odd roll of their new stock. Only when they did a stock check did they realise some belts were missing; so the next time he came, they spied on him and caught him red handed. No one had been to clear out the old belts since. He took me out into the works to look at the belts and I nearly fainted.

There was a massive pile of belts. Most of them were neatly rolled up into large rolls about as high as a man, and beside them was a pile of scrap off-cuts and pieces of broken and damaged belting. I had never seen so many belts as this before. It was hard to believe that he was classing this as scrap belting. I have since learned that it was more economical for them to change belts before they broke down, as they could not allow the plant to stand idle. He asked me what I would pay for the belts and I did a bit of smart thinking and said that I would give him the same as the other bloke, and that he would be able to trust me as I wouldn't take anything that didn't belong to me. He said, "OK" and held out his hand to shake mine. Although I was shaking with excitement, I didn't let him see it. He said he would like the belts taken away as soon as possible. As we started to make our way back to the offices, I suddenly realised that he hadn't told me how much the other guy paid. He probably thought I knew. Probably there was a regular standard price for this type of stuff. It was a drama – Agatha Christie stuff!

I had to find out, but how would I find out without asking him? If I asked him, he would know that I was new to the game and he would try to increase the price. I had to think quickly as we were getting close to the offices.

"What would you charge me if I took the belts – scrap belts included – all at one price?" I said.

"Well, that's the deal the other guy had. Everything at one price," he said.

Stalemate – think again!

"OK," I said, "I don't really want the scrap belts. What price would it be for the better belts only?"

Thinking that he might lose out here and finish up with the scrap belts on his hands, he snapped an answer very quickly: "Look, it's £10 a ton for everything. Take it or leave it."

Bingo!

We went into his office and agreed the terms. The deal was that I had to pick up the belts at my expense, using my transport. I had to completely clear the site every time. I must weigh it on their weighbridge. Payment had to be made in full within thirty days, and I was to confirm my quotation in writing on my letterhead by return of post. His instructions to me were very businesslike, and I suddenly felt very businesslike. The nagging things that were hovering at the back of my mind were that I didn't have any transport, I didn't have a letterhead and, most importantly, I didn't have enough money to pay for this lot.

On the way out the lovely girl on the reception gave me another of her big smiles.

"How did you get on? Did you do any business?"

I told her what had happened and she seemed so pleased. We had another little chat about things. I said my goodbyes, and she wished me the best of luck and told me to make sure that I called to see her next time I visited. I thought she fancied me! Or was it that she felt sorry for me? Anyway, I was glowing. On the way back I wondered what I had got myself into. My head was buzzing – was it excitement or sheer terror?

Now, imagine my predicament. I was living in a council house. I had a big garden that was on the corner of two streets where the front and back gardens were both exposed to the road. Everything that I did in my garden could be seen by passers-by. I already had quite a pile of what I called scrap belting, which was unsuitable for resale as conveyor belting.

I was about to import another ten or twenty tons. Neighbours were starting to talk about me. My next-door neighbour, who was a garden fanatic, was starting to give me dirty looks. Passers-by stopped to look and ask questions and query what it was all about. All this was affecting my marriage. Everything was covered in dirt, the kids were climbing all over everything and getting dirty, and my wife and I were continually at loggerheads. Still, I felt that I had to keep going. I was being driven along by it all, and I didn't have time to think about "trivial" things like neighbours and questions and the wife and the kids. Whatever happened would happen, and I would take it all in my stride.

The deal I had done was big-time in comparison to the small controllable "ins" and "outs" of the past months. This job would entail a lorry and a crane and, of course, the small subject of money.

It had been several months before that I had opened a bank account with the Midland Bank. I had made an appointment to see the bank manager, Mr. Cruikshank, and made an instant friend. There was a saying about your "friendly" bank manager: well, Mr. Cruikshank was such. He was totally bowled over by my business and called me an "entrepreneur." I had never heard this word before, but I later thought that "he" was an entrepreneur in spirit but stuck in a bank manager's position. He became one of my most special advisors without whom I could never have survived. Being only a simple mining lad with a poor education, I learned a lot from him. I didn't need a Harvard education with a friend like him.

My bank balance, although up and down, never went into the "red." Mr. Cruikshank had talked to me before about an overdraft facility but I never thought that I would ever need one. The thought of going into debt again after clearing my old debts was, as I thought, senseless. However, was now the time to take the plunge?
I made an appointment to see him, and explained about my deal with Tarmac. He was very impressed, saying that his bank had dealings with Tarmac. He went through the ins and outs of my account and commented on how pleased he was.

He said that although I did only a small amount of trading, it was done in a proper and careful manner and, perhaps now, with his advice and extreme caution, we could step onto the second rung of the ladder. He was so interested in what I was doing that I even thought he envied me a little. He seemed to take a personal interest. He gave me an overdraft facility, a bunch of papers to sign, a lecture about the money belonging to the bank, and that it was for the betterment of the business and not for spending on high living and foreign holidays. We had a laugh but it was all good, sound advice. I thought how lucky I was to have such guide – a mentor.

My fourth child was born on October 12, 1964. It was late that night when my wife asked me to telephone for the midwife to come as she was getting regular pains. I telephoned her and then started to light the open fire as it was a pretty cold evening. I placed the paper into the fire grate, put the sticks of wood on top, then placed my pieces of coal carefully and lit the fire. My hands were black with handling the coal and I was about to go to wash them when there was a screech.

"It's coming out. Where's the midwife? Tell her it's coming, quick – you'll have to help me."

She screamed, I went over to see what was happening and the baby was appearing with what looked like streaky black hair showing. More screeching.

"Try to help it out – it's stuck – it won't come out."

She was screaming pretty loudly and it was pretty scary. I was shaking like a leaf. My hands were black with coal but it was too late to go and wash them. I grabbed the head and helped to pull the baby out, and suddenly it was there in a great puddle of fluid. Its face was covered in coal muck and it all looked quite shocking. I laid the baby down and it coughed and spluttered and started to cry. Thank goodness for that, I thought. I wouldn't have known what to do if I'd had to smack it to make it cry. All I could do was to cover the baby and my wife over with a towel as best I could. I was really panicking at the thought of trying to cut the cord. Just at that moment the midwife appeared at the door.

"My, my, what have we been doing here?" she coolly said. "Go and boil a kettle and I'll sort everything out."

My heart was beating about a hundred and fifty beats per minute. I just thought, "Thank God she came in time." She came out to the kitchen about twenty minutes later and said, "My, my, Mr. Canning, you did very well. If ever I need an assistant midwife, can I call you?"

We called our son Eden, after Eden Kane, the pop singer.

I had decided to call my business Canning Conveyor Company. My artistic, creative mind came alive as I designed a logo using the letters CCC placed on two triangles connected by two lines, which represented conveyor belts, and approached a printing company to beg for letterheads to be printed very quickly so as to send off my agreement to Tarmac. A friend of mine, whom I had done sign writing for, allowed his secretary to do my typing. It all happened at breakneck speed – contract done, signed and delivered, transport hired, belts collected in a tipping lorry. It was easier to tip them off, as I didn't have any lifting equipment to off-load them. Suddenly my garden was full of massive rolls of belts.

I needed manpower. My brother Gud, my next-door neighbour, the bloke across the road, a lad from up the street, my brother-in-law, my Dad – anyone and everyone was roped in to help. My garden became a hive of industry. We learned how to handle belts, how to roll them, how to lift them, how to cut them. We learned how to repair them with self-curing rubber solution used by tyre companies. We learned how to vulcanize them by hiring the services of rubber-vulcanising specialists. We hired lifting tackle and we developed our own crude cutting machines. We learned about rubber adhesive from specialists.

It was a great learning curve brought on by sheer enthusiasm and by trying to cope with the speed of things. All the time I was delivering, not only to Bishop Auckland, but also, gradually, to other new buyers. I was approached by companies who wanted to market my belts, along with their other products and machinery, to industries like the steelworks and the quarries and the car industries. I visited a large company who produced coke (smokeless fuel) from coal. They carried hot coke on their conveyors, which actually cooked the belts, making them redundant after a very short period. I convinced them to use some of my second-hand heat-resistant belts, which I had bought from other similar plants, as they were half the price of their special heat-resistant belts and lasted just as long. I sold my belts to numerous stone and sand quarries and to concrete-making plants, which found it much cheaper to use a good second-hand belt than to buy new ones from the manufacturers. Also, it was much more convenient for them to phone me up in an emergency situation when a belt had broken down and they required an immediate delivery.

Things were moving along at a great speed. I had changed my small Commer van for a larger Bedford Dormobile, which was better for travelling around the quarries, buying and selling, and ideal for carrying and delivering.

My garden was a bog, a hive of activity: belts all over the place, men working, cars, lorries, cranes, in and out day and night, mud and sludge traipsing all over the road. It was a shit hole.

Good things and bad things seem to happen in phases and I was in for a few bad incidents, one of which was a tragedy of the worst kind.

It was 4 am. The phone rang. "Your Mam has died. Can you come over to pick us up and bring us back home?"

What do you say on receiving news like this? Nothing comes out of your mouth, only gasps for breath trying to accept what has just been said.

I was dumbstruck.

Dad said, "Are you there?"

"Yes, tell me what's happened."

"Just come, I'll tell you when you get here."

I couldn't help thinking, "Why did he have to break the news so bluntly?" I could only imagine that he was in a terrible state and it just spurted out. He could hardly speak and just said the plain basics. I could hear him sob as he put the phone down. After I had calmed down, I phoned Gud who said he was already on his way to my house.

The family were in Scarborough on their annual holiday, staying in a boarding house where they had stayed several times before. They were all there – Mam, Dad, Alan, Janet, Gerald, Richard, Irene and Linda.

Ten minutes later Gud arrived. He also didn't know what had happened. He had received the same simple message from Dad. Mam had died and we were to go to Scarborough and bring them home.

When we arrived they were all packed and ready for home. The girls just burst out crying and couldn't speak. Dad was in a dream-like state. His eyes were all swollen and he looked terrible, tired and old. Alan and Richard told us that she had taken to bed feeling very poorly and they had called for a doctor; by the time he arrived, Mam had passed away. The doctor called the undertaker and she was taken away. I can only imagine what they went through whilst this was happening. During that day they had all been enjoying their holiday and, next thing, she was gone! Gud and I had had our sobs in our cars, and so we had arrived trying to look strong and trying to console everyone and trying to organise everything. It was devastating.

I went up to the bedroom with Dad to see where she had died. I don't know why we did this. It was a thoughtless thing to do. Perhaps we were just hoping for a miracle. The bed-sheets had been cleared off and only the mattress was showing, which was a little wet. We both sat on the edge of the bed and cried. The landlady came into the room and pulled us both to her and said that Mam was the nicest person she had ever met, and that the good thing was that she had never seen her as happy as she was that day.

Why does it happen to the best people? She was only fifty-one. All through her life she had worked hard and had seen hard times. She was just beginning to enjoy good times when she had died. Why? Why didn't I do more for her as she did so much for all her family?

I have spoken about my guardian angel before but, from that terrible day onwards, I have had a strange feeling that Mam is still with us. Every time something good happens I suddenly think of Mam and often say Mam is watching over us. I know it sounded silly at the times I said it and I never expected anyone to take it seriously, but, a few years later, something amazing happened which was proof to me without question that Mam was still watching.

The Ugly Duckling

The post arrived – a letter from the county council – I was the ugly duckling.

"Get out of town!"

The neighbours had put in a petition to evict me. I couldn't blame them. I don't think I would have liked living next to a mucky pile of old conveyor belting and being disturbed by lorries and cranes. It was on the cards. I was surprised it hadn't happened sooner. My problem was, with everything happening so quickly and being so fully occupied, I hadn't put any thought into the fact that I would not be able to stay where I was forever, and I had not put any thought into moving. It was obvious that my time had come to an end in my council house garden. The letter from the council instructed me to leave. In fact, they told me that I was breaking the law. Really, I ought to have felt very lucky that they had not taken it more seriously. I couldn't understand why they hadn't made a big issue of it and taken me to court and fined me. Perhaps they were being kind or sympathetic or something. Anyway, I looked at it that way and thought, while they were being so kind, would it be worth asking them for help?

I wrote a reply to them asking if they could advise me what to do or where to go, and sure enough, they replied with good news. They told me about a property located in the centre of town, which used to be a large coal distribution depot called Fletcher's Yard. Apparently, Mr. Fletcher had halved the size of his coal-yard and was letting off the spare land in "lots" to small industries. I agreed to rent a piece of land about three times the size of my garden. This was perfect for me. It gave me plenty of room to spread out and had good hard standing for my "ins" and "outs" of heavy traffic.

I moved quickly. Half a dozen lorry loads, and my garden was clear and my neighbours were happy once again. The council was happy, and so was my wife, who was under constant pressure, being surrounded by big rolls of conveyor belting that looked like a herd of black elephants, and sludge and coal dust ploughing into the house every day.

Worksop was a changing town. It was surrounded by several coalmines, each employing two or three thousand people. Although these people lived in and around their own mining villages, the town was the centre of all things. It had a thriving twice weekly market, large shops, a police station, a Town Hall and cinemas. The major part of income for the traders of the town came from the mining folk.

Unfortunately, it was all changing. Several coalmines had closed down and for the other collieries, which were still working, the cards were on the table. Many miners were moving on to other areas to follow their chosen occupation, or they left the pits and tried to find other employment. Several re-training centres were set up to help miners adapt to other trades like bricklaying, plastering, plumbing, painting and decorating, and many of them tried self-employment. Worksop was slowing down and the council was looking at the new situation very seriously: the reason I, and many others, were offered or encouraged to take on vacant plots and encouraged to expand and create more jobs.

Although I didn't employ any full-time workers at this time I engaged several part-time men who already had regular jobs, but liked some spare-time work for a bit of cash in hand. This suited me fine as I couldn't guarantee regular work and didn't want to take the risk or responsibility of employing anyone full-time.

My new yard was perfect for my particular type of business. The longest part of the yard was about 200 feet, perfectly flat and partially sheltered by a high wall. On the floor along the wall side we laid pieces of old belting, which weren't good enough to sell, this created an excellent floor for working on. This type of belt we called "flooring belts," and it became one of our products. It was sold to factories, farmers and builders – in fact, to anyone who required a heavy-duty floor material that was tough and could take plenty of impact. This is just one of the many uses we found for old belting. I acquired a second-hand lorry and a second-hand estate car called a "shooting brake." I was now travelling all over the country, buying and selling, and the shooting brake was also ideal for fetching and delivering.

There was an increasing amount of paperwork to do and it became a bind to me. My part-time lady wasn't always available and so I had to employ an experienced office lady who worked two mornings a week to do my typing, invoicing, bookkeeping and general duties. The downstairs passage in my home was converted into an "office" with a desk, two chairs, a filing cabinet and a typewriter. I didn't spend much time in the office since my office work was now done very efficiently. The office became a ladies gossip centre as I learned several times when I arrived home unexpectedly and caught my "up the road" sister-in-law, my wife and my next-door neighbour tea-tasting and putting the world to rights. Nevertheless, I was now an efficient businessman with proper books, proper typed letters and a neat filing system.

I was about to meet my second mentor. My bank manager and friend Mr. Cruikshank advised me to seek the help of an accountant/auditor. At first I thought it strange as I thought I already had an accountant in my new office lady and I thought an auditor was something to do with music and, knowing that Mr. Cruikshank was very keen on classical music, I wondered if he was trying to get me interested in this subject.

I told him that the only music I was interested in was the Top 20 and that Johnnie Ray and Frankie Lane were about my limit. He nearly fell off his seat laughing. When all was explained, he telephoned and made an appointment for us to see a Mr. George Godley, a chartered accountant. This was another one of the most important turning points in my career. George became my advisor, guide, encourager and mentor. He sorted out my bookkeeping systems, advised me how to prepare proper invoices, how to quote, how to speak to customers, and he even taught me what an audit was and why it was done.

BOROUGH OF WORKSOP
BOROUGH ENGINEER'S DEPARTMENT

ANDREW T. BARDSLEY
M.I.Mun.E.   M.Inst.H.E.
BOROUGH ENGINEER
AND SURVEYOR

PARK HOUSE,
PARK STREET,
WORKSOP.
Telephone   30818.

15th November, 1965.

My Ref.   Your Ref.

41/61.   12089

Dear Sir,

<u>Unauthorised structures, Central Avenue, Worksop</u>

I refer to my letter of the 3rd instant and your reply dated the 5th idem with regard to buildings which have been erected without the consent of my Council during the last few weeks, on land apparently leased to you by a Mr. Fletcher of Worksop.

I have reason to believe that planning consent is unlikely to be given to this development because an application for a similar development was refused on the 22nd June, 1965.

It should also be noted that approval under my Council's building byelaws is necessary in this instance and because you have contravened these byelaws you will, unless the buildings are removed, run the risk of a summary conviction and penalty under the provisions of the said byelaws, apart from whatever action may be taken by the Local Planning Authority who, I believe, are aware of this unauthorised development.

Unless the buildings are removed within the next 3 weeks, the matter will be reported to the appropriate Committee of my Council.

Yours faithfully,

Mr. F. Canning,
3 Dudley Road,
CARLTON-IN-LINDRICK,
Worksop,
<u>Notts.</u>

`Get Out Of Town`

Maths was not my thing but George spelled it out to me in a simple way, which made everything interesting and made me want to learn. Had it not been for George I think I might have fallen at the first post – certainly at the first financial problem, of which there were many to come. I know he liked helping me and seemed to have a personal interest in all that I was trying to achieve.

I spent many hours with George. In fact, he gave me more of his time than he ought to have done – he was a true friend. Our meetings and discussions seemed to take on a regular format. We spent our time talking about work and war – bookkeeping and war – accounts and war – business and war.

George had been a prisoner-of-war in Germany and he enjoyed telling me about his "long march." The Germans had conquered Poland and had placed several of their POW camps there.

At this point in the war there was an advance by the Russians to take back Poland. The prison camps were full to capacity and the Germans feared that if the Russians took over the camps they would repatriate the prisoners back into the war to help fight against them. Hundreds of prisoners were forced to march out of Poland into Germany. These poor wrecks were marched continuously for hundreds of miles, only stopping by the roadside to sleep. Exhausted and starving, many of them died or were shot during the march, either trying to steal food or water, or by just becoming too exhausted to walk any further.

The stories he told me were horrendous. These poor men were forced to stagger continuously, mile after mile, in the worst type of weather, and were treated to the worst type of cruelty and deprivation, with very few clothes on their backs. Some of them didn't even have boots to wear.

I once had tears streaming down my face as he told me of a time when a farmer took pity on them and sneaked up to them in the dead of night. He gave some of them water and bread, only to be shot along with the soldiers who were eating the food. They were so ravenous that they had allowed themselves to be heard by the Gerries. It made me think how lucky I was.

I was then about the same age as George was when all this was happening to him and here was I enjoying life, eating well, riding about in my shooting brake, free to carry out my business. All is sometimes taken for granted.

Talking of taking things for granted. George gave me some sound advice, which I will never forget. He told me that it is quite easy, after a few successful deals, to become complacent and take things for granted. He said that a period of successes does not mean success is guaranteed. If the utmost care and thorough attention is not continuous then one bad deal could end the business. A lesson I will never forget.

Winter was coming on. We were getting cold and wet. We were like Eskimos dressed in our big coats, balaclavas and gloves. We had a couple of steel oil drums in which we burned bits of scrap rubber belts to help to keep us warm. The wet and damp made it hard work and it was impossible to do any sort of repair work on the belts when they were wet. We decided to build a shelter to work in. The high wall running along the side of my yard was an ideal place to build a shelter for working in. We built a simple wooden framework alongside the wall. We then affixed a roof which was slightly lower at the back and covered it with old conveyor belting so that the rain would run off into the empty yard next door. We moved the steel drums containing the fire to the front of the shelter and, bingo, we had central heating! It took about three weeks to construct this fantastic "factory." We had just about knocked the last nail in when I had a visit from a council official.

Planning Permission

I had broken the law, contravened the rules and put up a building without proper planning permission. I was summoned to appear in court.

"Bugger!" – I think I said something like that.

It was then I met the third of my lifetime mentors, a solicitor by the name of Mr. Robert Ilett. I needed advice. No, I didn't have planning permission. I didn't know what planning permission was. Yes, the building was contravening building regulations, but it kept the rain off us. Yes, the water from the roof drained into the next-door property, but there was no one in the next-door property. Yes, I was an idiot! I didn't give it much thought. We were desperate to keep warm and we needed to keep dry to carry on working. No excuse! The building had to be stripped down immediately. Another hard lesson learned: there is only one way to do things and that is to do it properly. George Godley reprimanded me and Mr. Cruikshank wasn't very happy.

Mr. Ilett came to see me at my yard and listened to my story. Once again, I realised I had another friend and advisor. Once again, like my other two advisors, he took me under his wing. He seemed so interested in what we were trying to do. He seemed to understand our problems and he, like Cruikshank and Godley, became my advisor and friend for life.

Mr. Ilett (Bob) was part of a very influential firm of solicitors in Worksop.

I had never been to a court before and it was certainly an experience, watching the solicitors battle it out and the Judge give his judgement. I must give Mr. Ilett his due. He put up a good case defending me as "a young entrepreneur trying to create a new business and in turn create jobs," but the law was broken and I had to pay the consequences. The building came down and we spent the rest of the winter working in the cold.

Work was becoming pretty hectic. Part-time workers would come and go depending upon the weather and their own personal circumstances. It was time now to employ a man full-time as a lorry driver and labourer, and I took on a man who had been helping me part-time for quite a while. We shared the work in the yard, the lorry- driving, and fetching and carrying. I enjoyed driving the lorry. It was such an experience to be what was called a "King of the Road," plodding along at a respectable speed, every other vehicle respecting your size and giving way to you. It was so pleasantly peaceful and safe. The driving seemed even easier when you had a full load of ten tons. There were some times, however, that were not always so enjoyable!

I often took my Dad as a passenger and he helped me during loading and unloading. We once picked up a load of scrap belting from a coal plant in Liverpool. Unfortunately, the stuff was just lying all over the floor and covered in thick black coal dust. We had no option but to roll it all up. It took about six hours of hard manual labour and no one at the plant would help us. We were exhausted and as black as coal. Luckily there was a man using a loading shovel on site who helped us load. We left the site and headed for the nearest transport café. We staggered in and sat at a table. The manager took one look at us and told us that he couldn't serve us, as we were too dirty. We drove about ten miles further, found another café, and staggered to the door, but it was closed. By now we were feeling a little jaded. Off we went again and after driving along another few miles, looking for another eating place, a tyre exploded. Dad had just about reached his limits and I was flagging. We were both starving and exhausted and I hadn't a clue what to do. I had never changed a lorry wheel before. We were miles from civilisation. It would be silly to walk to try to find help, so I decided to try to change the wheel myself. It was probably the worst decision I had ever made. With Dad's help, and a lot of swearing, we managed to get the spare wheel out of its housing. It weighed a ton. We could hardly lift it upright. The next job was to try to release the nuts off the punctured wheel, but firstly to find the wheel spanner. There was no spanner. In fact, even if we had found a spanner we didn't seem to have a jack, and even if we had found a jack, we didn't know where to fit the jack. I was in despair. We were so exhausted we flopped down on the grass verge to try to rest, and think what to do. Both of us dropped into a sleep, and were suddenly awakened by the siren of a police car.

It was probably a blessing as we were in a bit of a mess, and even though I realised I was now in trouble, at least there was help on hand. The policeman radioed a local garage, who came along with a repair vehicle and got us roadworthy again. We were escorted to the local weighbridge and found to be overweight. It didn't end there! It was overweight and I didn't have an official weight ticket. I was driving an HGV without an HGV licence, the lorry wasn't road worthy, as it didn't have proper wheel changing equipment, and the load wasn't properly secured. I was ordered to hire a driver to drive the lorry home, which involved another driver with a car to take the lorry driver back. All in all it was quite a costly experience, but we did manage to find a café that allowed us to eat!

Because of this silly incident I wasn't allowed to drive the lorry again, and so my employee took on the duty as a full-time lorry driver. Unfortunately, this man gave me my first experience of treachery.

I had managed to gain a contract with the South Western Electricity Board to remove all scrap and redundant conveyor belting from the whole of the South Western Region. They gave me a contract for twelve months, and apparently they had never given such an agreement before so this was quite a coup. I secured the contract at a price of £25 per ton. It was really the making of my business as the material that they disposed of, was, to me, first class second-hand belting. It was one of my best deals that, for several years, gave me a regular source of good material.

As part of the contract I was asked to collect a consignment of belts from a power station in South Wales called Fiddlers Ferry Power

Station. It was ironic that it had the name of "Fiddlers" as this deal introduced me into a world of deceit, dishonesty and intrigue, of which I had several experiences during the forthcoming years in business. But more on that in a later chapter.

It was my first consignment and I wanted everything to be done properly. I firstly visited the station to examine the consignment along with the manager of the power station, and I painted my mark "CCC" on each roll so that my driver could identify which rolls to pick up. The contract stated that the belts had to be collected by my transport and weighed on their weigh bridge and an invoice would be sent to me for £25 per ton.

My lorry driver collected the belts a few days later and brought them back to my yard.

A few weeks later, I was approached by a dealer who just happened to be the man who first took me to Hanratty's in Bishop Auckland. He said that he had a few rolls of belts in his yard for me to look at and to make him an offer. I had done quite a few deals with this man recently, and he said that he wanted to sell them quickly for cash. I drove over with cash in pocket. Lo and behold, the belts I saw were marked with my "CCC." My eyes nearly popped out of my head. All sorts of things were zooming into my mind. How on earth had he got hold of some of my belts? I hadn't sold any of these belts to him. I asked him how he happened to have these particular belts as they had my marks on them. Apparently, he said that a man (he gave me his name) had taken his lorry round to his yard and dropped these particular rolls off, and he was paid in cash. I told him that this man worked for me and that the lorry he was driving was mine. He said that if he had known then obviously he would have told me!

It was my first experience of sacking and my first experience of cheating. I would have many more of these devastating experiences in the coming years. He got off really lightly. I didn't want to inform the police as the man was married and had a couple of children. I gave him a bollocking and told him to leave. I got my belts back and I left it to the other dealer to sort it out with my now ex-driver.

Canning Luck

I am a great believer in fate, luck, coincidence or whatever you call it. Things always seem to happen for a reason and seem to have a second mysterious reason for happening. I got into a habit of saying, whenever something fortunate happened, that it was "Canning Luck" or, more recently, "Mam is looking after us." Even when anything unfortunate happened I could handle it pretty well, because I took it for granted that it was fate or that it had happened for a good reason. So many times something dreadful happened and, after the usual upset and miserable feeling, I landed firmly on my feet again. Take, for example, cases when certain people left my employment for some reason or other – it usually happened just at a time when I wanted them to leave or when I really needed to cut down my staff. Was it coincidence? Another typical example, just at a time when I had to move into larger premises, it just happened that other larger premises suddenly became available.

There have always been so many strange occurrences or anomalies or peculiar strange incidents in my life, strengthening my belief in fate or coincidences.

One day I decided to phone my client Mr. O'Leary of Ireland. I picked up the phone and was just about to put my finger onto the dial when Mr. O'Leary said, "Hello, Frank!" I nearly jumped out of my seat with shock. He had just at that very second dialled me, and I had just at the same second before the actual ring picked up the phone. I told him what had happened; he said it was scary.

Another similar incident happened recently. I located my gardener's number in my telephone directory and picked up the telephone to start to phone him and my wife handed me the other phone and said, "It's the gardener!" Quite often there are strange mind-reading occurrences between my wife and me. I will suddenly think about something, turn to my wife to tell her about it and she will tell me the same thing before I can get my words out. For instance, if the thought enters my mind to phone say, Roger, my wife will suddenly turn to me and say, "Do you think you ought to phone Roger?" This happens frequently and I always say to her that she is a mind-reader but I often wonder if I am a thought transmitter!

A strange thing happened when I was a young man before we had house telephones. I used to arrange a certain time with my girlfriend to phone her at a certain B.T. telephone box near to where she lived. One day I needed to make a general telephone call. I opened my little notebook with telephone contacts in and by mistake I phoned my girlfriend's B.T. box number. She was about to phone someone at exactly the same time and when the phone rang she picked it up. We were both shocked with the realisation of what had happened and of course we both thought that we were sending telepathic messages.

I once witnessed an unusual happening whilst painting the outside of a shop on the main shopping street at Worksop. Traffic roars past the shop continuously all day bumper to bumper. One day, mid-morning, there was silence – everyone went to their doors to see if there was an accident or road block or something. For some strange reason no one drove along that road for twenty minutes. What a strange coincidence! It was the talk of the town for months.

Fate, luck, strange happenings; OK, not all these unusual happenings have anything to do with my life or my business but nevertheless I find these things so interesting.

As I have said before, I am sure that I am being guided. I nearly always seem to do the right thing at just the right time and things quite often seem to go my way at just the right time. Perhaps it could be called optimism.

Looking back through my life, luckily, I always seemed to have finished up OK even after so many poor starts; my family's poor beginning in the old railway carriage, our poor home in Moorends, with little food and clothing, our continuous flitting, our home in the condemned pub in Oldcotes. When I think about it, even though we have lived through some of the most humble times, I personally have good early memories, even though it must have been hell for my parents and the rest of my family.

Even though many of my later business experiences have been traumatic, my wife has always said that I look through rose coloured spectacles. I wonder if this was because I was so intent on succeeding and going forward that I partially closed my eyes to the obvious problems that were happening all around. I certainly don't look for trouble even though I have had my fair share, but I would rather, if it is at all possible, try to solve a problem and shed it quickly, usually with a little help and advice: get it out of the way and get back to normal.

I don't know if it was rose coloured spectacles or living in fantasyland, but I remember quite often bragging that my ambition was to own a hundred companies. Some of the knocks I experienced in my later business life certainly brought me back to reality.

Over the next three or four decades I lived through a rollercoaster of experiences, and survived. It is not because I had a "first class Harvard business education" as my education is only second-class secondary school. I do think it is because I have had a lot of luck and something has been driving me along.

However could a person like me, with a poor education, and classed as a dunce at school, have evolved from such meagre beginnings to achieve such a successful and completely fulfilled life, without Canning Luck?

Business

I finished my first year in business on August 31, 1964. My accounts were prepared by George Godley, and consisted of two sheets of paper with a few lines of figures representing my "Balance Sheet" and my "Profit and Loss Account." These were beautifully bound in a grey-coloured folder and looked like an official document. I was called into George's office. He told me that we were having our first Annual General Meeting. I was dressed in my mucky overalls and boots, and was dirty and smelly, but George, unperturbed by my appearance, sat me down opposite to him in a leather armchair and talked me through it. The main two figures I was interested in were:

Turnover   £1538.4s.9d
Net Profit   £563.8s.5d

On the face of it I didn't know what this really meant. I didn't know if it was good or bad. All I knew was that I had had an exciting year and, according to George, I had done well. He was very pleased and I was very pleased by his reaction. He told me that I had earned a reasonable living of £12 per week and had given my wife £108; this equated to a family income of £14 per week which, on a regular basis, was what George said was quite a reasonable income. He said I had a good stock in hand to continue into the following year.
I was beginning to find new customers. Belts were coming in on a regular basis and sales were increasing. I was finding new types of markets and developing new types of products, which we could make out of scrap belts.

Every consignment of belting that came in was firstly rolled out, examined and sorted into various grades. Grade one were the best belts, which were in excellent, re-usable condition. Grade two were belts that needed repairing or cutting down. We used a type of self-curing rubber to repair the holes and grooves, which was a long and tedious process but, when properly done, gave the belts a second life.

F. L. CARLING

BALANCE SHEET as at 22nd AUGUST 1964

Liabilities

CAPITAL ACCOUNT
Cash introduced at 16th February 1964 90. 0. 0.
Add: Net Profit for the period ended 22nd August 1964
263. 8. 5.
613. 8. 5.
396. 17. 2.

Deduct: Drawings 16. 11. 3.

ACCRUED CHARGES 10. 10. 0.

£27. 7. 3.

Assets

STOCK ON HAND as estimated by the Proprietor 15. 0. 0.

UNEXPIRED EXPENDITURE 3. 17. 0.

CASH in Hand 6. 12. 5.
at Bank 1. 11. 10.
8. 4. 3.

£27. 1. 3.

We have prepared the foregoing Balance Sheet and the attached Trading and Profit and Loss Accounts from the Books and Vouchers of the Business and Certify that the aforementioned accounts are in accordance with the Books relating thereto and the information and explanations given to us.

John J. Philip
Certified Accountants.

4a Queen Street,
Worksop,
Notts.

Dated - 8th July, 1966.

'Balance Sheet'

145

Cutting down meant slicing off the worn edges, which were usually damaged by something scraping the edge whilst the belt was running. We could normally slice off a certain amount on either side, which would leave a narrower width that was still suitable for resale. Grade three were belts that were in short lengths of reasonably good quality, which we used for making other products. Grade four were belts that were beyond repair and could not be used as by-products. We sold this type of belt as floor-covering for factories and workshops.

During our dealings with quarries we were often asked if we could supply rollers and idlers for conveyors. The roller and idler trade is not dissimilar to the conveyor belt trade. It was quite common to find a pile of old idlers and rollers alongside a pile of old belting. The quarries didn't seem to bother about repairing them, as it was quicker to replace them with new. We started to buy the odd lot of rollers and idlers, took them back to our yard, stripped them down and rebuilt them again using the best parts. The parts which were unusable were sold to a scrap yard. The rebuilt idlers were cleaned down, repainted and resold back to the quarries. This operation in itself became quite an industry, and it wasn't long before a couple of men who were specialists in welding and oxyacetylene burning were employed full-time. It gave me a lot of pride when I employed my old coalmining friend Arthur, who had retired. He visited me many times to see how I was getting on in business and, as he jokingly said, he needed to get away from the housework! One day he arrived in his overalls and made himself useful in the yard, cleaning and painting idlers, and he ended up staying for several years until his health gave out.

It was better than washing pots, he said.

In a short time my yard was overflowing. It was a hive of activity. Different areas of the yard were designated for certain duties. The "runway" was for cutting and repairing. There was a place for unloading and stacking incoming belts, and a place for placing finished belts ready for resale. A place was allotted for making products and a place for stacking and repairing rollers and idlers.

E. A. in CAMBING

TRADING AND PROFIT AND LOSS ACCOUNTS FOR THE PERIOD 16th FEBRUARY 1964 to 22nd AUGUST 1964

	£. s. d.		£. s. d.
To Purchases	726. 9. 0.	By Sales	1538. 4. 9.
" Gross Profit carried down	826. 15. 9.	" Stock on Hand at 22nd August 1964	15. 0. 0.
	£1553. 4. 9.		£1553. 4. 9.
To Wages, Wife	108. 0. 0.	By Gross Profit brought down	826. 15. 9.
" Motor Expenses	97. 4. 10.		
" Casual Labour	30. 0. 0.		
" Carriage	2. 0. 0.		
" Repairs and Renewals	5. 3. 0.		
" Bank Charges	1. 1. 0.		
" Postages, Printing and Stationery	1. 12. 9.		
" Rent	7. 15. 9.		
" Accountancy Charges	10. 10. 0.		
" Balance being Net Profit	563. 8. 5.		
	£826. 15. 9.		£826. 15. 9.

'Profit & Loss'

here were half a dozen part-time workers and two full-time workers.

The business seemed to be doing well and I had finished my second year of trading, ending August 31, 1965. Once again I was in Mr. Godley's office and sitting in his brown leather chair. He handed me another beautifully bound account on two sheets of paper, with a few lines of figures and an envelope in which was his account. This time I looked more respectable and was dressed in trousers and shirt.

"You've had another good year. You've more than doubled all your figures. Well done," he said.

Turnover	£5670.14s.11d
Net Profit	£1225.8s.2d

He went on to explain the figures. Then we talked about the war. Then I mentioned to him that I really needed a bigger work yard as my existing yard was now brimming over.

A few weeks later George phoned me and told me that he had been talking about my business to a colleague of his who dealt with the council. He had heard that there were plots of industrial land available in Worksop for small businesses and that there were some vacant plots, which might be of interest to me.

I contacted Mr. Ilett to ask his advice, and he said he would "look into it" as he knew the right contacts in the Town Hall.

It wasn't long before I was signing a contract to rent a half acre site of industrial land. Apparently this area was an old waste disposal tip that had been covered with hard core and left standing empty for a few years to settle. It was now being "kindly" offered by the Worksop Council to small industrialists in half acre plots at very reasonable rents of £1000 per year. I think it was also a ploy to move all the "mucky" businesses out of central Worksop.

'Mucky Business'

When I arrived on the site, I found several other "mucky" local businesses were already established. There was a scrap-metal dealer, a British Road Services depot, an engineering workshop, a joinery business and a guy who bought old lorry engines and shipped them to Indonesia. I moved into my plot, which was like a bog. I couldn't deny that mine was a mucky type of business and it seemed to fit in quite comfortably with my new neighbours.

The first thing was to find loads of hard core to spread on the ground to try to make it a little more solid to work on. I put the word out to builders and demolition companies that tipping was available for a short period for half the price they were paying at the official tip for off-loading bricks, tarmac and hard rubble.

It wasn't long before lorries were lining up to tip their hard core on to my plot. I also did a deal with a local demolition man to bring along his JCB digger to spread and level the hard core. In return he could tip his loads free of charge. There were about a thousand tons tipped, levelled and flattened in about six weeks. The yard now looked as flat as a football pitch and I moved in. My experience in my old yard had taught me to plan the space very carefully by marking it out for every different activity. There was an added attraction to my new "spectacular" set-up, a shed for storing tools and bits of machinery, and for sheltering when it rained. Jokingly, I called this shed my "factory."

The new half-acre industrial land was called Sandy Lane Industrial Estate. It sounded so important. New letterheads, new energy. This was an exciting new beginning for my business.

I will never forget how proud I felt in my new, important, mucky yard.

Turmoil

Life is a series of ups and downs, so the saying goes. Just as everything looks good something bad happens; when you are at your lowest something good lifts you up.

Although I was entering a new and exciting phase in business, my private life was at its worst. My marriage was rapidly going downhill – we were continually at loggerheads. I didn't know what we were about, but it seemed it was all and everything. We seemed to get on each other's nerves. I blame myself for our way of life, which must have been hell for any woman to cope with. Perhaps if I had a normal regular job nine till five then everything might have been OK. Perhaps that had a lot to do with it.

We had a few holidays, the best remembered were when we went to South Wales where Vera's family lived. The South Wales trips were so much fun for us all. The kids were so excited about the journey. We all piled into the shooting brake. The cases and bags were fastened to the roof rack. I drove. Vera was in the passenger seat. We let down the back seats and formed a sort of bed made from cushions and pillows. All four kids and Mandy's friends piled into the back and snuggled up together, covered in blankets. God knows how they did it but they slept all the way, only waking up when we arrived at Aunty Hinda's house. Vera was always happy to see her sister Hinda and her hubby Eddie and their family. They were the most placid people ever. They seemed to inject a happy, calming feeling into everyone around them and I think it rubbed off onto all of us. The South Wales holidays were always so enjoyable and refreshing. However, as soon as we were home, the bickering started again. I thought there must be an obvious answer but I was blind or stupid and couldn't see the wood for the trees.

I gave it a lot of thought and reached what I thought was the answer. I tried to analyse it. We had had a shotgun marriage. Before we were wed we didn't really have time to get to know one another and decide if we wanted to spend the rest of our lives together. We had four quite active kids. We were not madly in love with each other. We were not very well off and had little or no security. For a long time we lived in a house which was a factory with dirt and muck everywhere. I was always away at work or travelling. To top it all, the inside of the house was an office. I thought that if I moved the office away from home there might be a chance. There were no funds available to afford a proper office, so I bought an old caravan and moved all the files, desk and chairs, etc. Now that all signs of the business, including the secretary, had been removed, the house was gradually brought back to normality. For a while things seemed to settle down, but not for long!

As time flew by there was no particular advancement in our relationship. I wondered if it was because of the old, bad memories of running the business from home, and we discussed buying another house to try to make a fresh start.

We bought a bungalow called "Shalimar." It was like a five star hotel compared with our "Airy" house. It had central heating. It was clean and modern and had a nice garden. It was a dream palace! The kids loved it and it wasn't long before they had settled into their nice, cosy bedrooms. We had the place redecorated and the kitchen modernised and wooden panels were fitted to the kitchen walls. I was so pleased that I took photographs of all the kids standing in front of the nice wooden walls.

I remember we were quite happy for a while. We had a few parties and had friends round for meals and drinks, etc., but one day we all got a bit merry and someone started fighting. He was very drunk. I intervened and we started to struggle and he fell through a big plate glass window cutting his head pretty badly. Blood was all over the place. He was rushed to hospital and had a few stitches.

This incident seemed to set off tremors again. Everything seemed bad and the bickering started all over again. In fact they seemed to be worse than ever. I sometimes felt that I wanted to get away, and sometimes I didn't want to go back home, and made excuses to sleep in the caravan.

I distinctly remember the night I left for good. It was the worst night of my life. It was the worst argument we had had in our lives. I don't remember what it was all about, but we were both screaming with anger. I jumped into my car and drove and drove for what seemed like forever. I didn't know where I was going and I touched 100 mph in places. I remember thinking that I didn't care if I had a crash and killed myself. I just kept on driving and finished up in Cleethorpes. I drove into a caravan park and saw a caravan for rent and that was my home for the next few weeks. I was in turmoil!

I had left home and this was final. All I thought about was my kids and how they would take it. Were they also in turmoil? I felt so wretched and I thought they must be feeling the same way. What would they think about me as a runaway father? Would they think it was their fault? I was going mad! All I wanted to do was to go home but I couldn't. I was on my own for the first time in my life and all I wanted to do was die. It was agony! In my wallet I had the photos of my kids standing against the wooden panelled wall. I spread them out on the table and cried. I cried so much that I think I drained every drop of water from my body. I think the photographs saved me.

I vowed there and then that whatever happened I would care for my family forever.

My decision to care for my family forever is as strong now as it has ever been, it has lasted forever and I know that my family and I have a very close loving relationship. However, I have never lost the deep, dark feeling of guilt for leaving them. It will stay with me all my life.

Back to Business

The business seemed to be carrying me along faster than I could cope. At the year ending August 31, 1966, the sales and net profit had increased, but I was losing out on production and organisation. I had a few regular workers and several casual labourers but they always needed supervision. They worked hard and in poor conditions, but their hearts were not in it and I was trying to better the quality of my products. My brother George (Gud) was spending quite a lot of his spare time working for me and I persuaded him to leave the pit and come to work for me full-time to look after the works. At the same time I asked Barry, a person whom I had taken out travelling with me on several occasions and who had done several travelling jobs for me, if he would like to try working for me as a travelling representative.

I supplied both of them with a vehicle and agreed to pay them a decent salary, but told them that we had not only to increase sales but also to increase production and quality.

One of the ways we increased our sales was by inventing and developing products.

There are many products made from old scrap conveyor belting and it was always challenging to try to think of a use that we could make in our own works. We had a delivery of oxygen from British Oxygen, and the deliveryman placed a square of spongy material on the floor for the cylinder to drop on, to avoid damaging the floor. The material wasn't very substantial and he told me that he normally got through one a day as the cylinders were heavy. I gave him a piece of scrap belting the same size and asked him to try it out. He was so pleased with it that he took it back to his depot to show them. I received an order for 1000 to be supplied to them in batches of 100 per week. We supplied them for many years.

A pig farmer approached me one day and told me that a pigsty was divided into two compartments, one for sleeping and one for eating, with an opening between for the pig to shuffle across. The openings had a sheet of canvas that was fastened to the top and hung down to form a sort of a door. Unfortunately, the canvas material wore out very quickly as the pigs' backs were rough. The farmer tried a piece of my scrap belting and said it lasted ten times longer. He asked me to make some for the rest of his pigsties. They were pieces of old belting measuring two feet wide by three feet high, fitted with five brass eyelets on the top for hanging. These became one of our good marketable products and over the years we have sold many thousands through our adverts in Farmers Weekly magazine.

We made cow mats, which were placed on the floor of cow sheds for the cows to stand on, hanging strip curtains for driving vehicles through, straps for supporting pipes and cables, mud-flaps for motor vehicles, knee pads, scrapers and door mats.

Another profitable invention that we manufactured out of old scrap conveyor belting was "fishing rings." Rings were stamped out of the old belts by using hydraulic presses. Each ring had a hole in the middle, making it a similar shape to a doughnut. The rings were used by the fishing industry, where they were threaded on to wire ropes, which were fastened to the bottom of deep-sea fishing nets, to form a long, flexible roller. The roller weighed the net down and rolled along the bottom of the ocean. These rings were made in many sizes and thicknesses, and were ordered by every fishing port in the British Isles. The small central pieces of rubber that were stamped out of the middle were sold to bowling clubs throughout the country: they were placed into the channel that ran around bowling greens for the bowls to drop onto, in order to make a soft landing.

Nothing is wasted. After the production of our many products, the very last remaining pieces of scrap belting are shipped off to several firms who grind them into rubber crumb for making cushion flooring, carpet underlay and for insulating ice cold containers.

At the end of my fourth year in business, ending August 1967, things were fine but hectic. The workload and sales had increased but, because of the extra wages and vehicles, we only broke even. Even so, Mr. Godley told me the decisions we had taken had been good strategy. He was happy with our progress and, providing we carried on in the same vein, we could do better the following year.

The following year we made a reasonable profit but it was a case of trying to keep ahead of the game. In other words, we were trying to cope with demand. The belting trade was always good, mainly because we were skilful and experienced at buying, and had secured some good contracts with the power stations, the NCB and the steel works to recover their scrap materials.

We were now handling more rollers, idlers, electric motors, conveyor drums and complete conveyors. We would deal with anything to do with mechanical handling. We could handle anything and everything that had been made redundant. Anything that was in reasonable condition we would buy at scrap prices to be renovated and resold.

Our contract with the South Western Region of the Central Electricity Generating Board (CEGB) was beginning to reap rewards. We had a call from Aberthaw Power Station in South Wales. The main station coal plant had been modernised and the old plant had become redundant. They asked us to clear the site as they required the land for further expansion. There was about a mile of conveyors, complete with belting. It was quite a large job and we were working on the site for several months. Gud and his men moved down to a boarding house and lived there until the job was finished, just coming home at the weekends. They firstly had to remove all the belts, which were all in exceptionally good condition; as they had not had their lifespan, we wanted to remove them in as long lengths as possible. On similar jobs, we normally just dragged them on to the floor and rolled them up, but the condition of these belts was so good that it meant we would have to take more care with them. We needed some sort of a mechanical reeling machine to take them off and reel them up carefully.

I put the problem to a contact of mine, Mick, who was a mechanical engineer and worked for a large engineering company. I asked him if he could devise a mechanical reeling machine that could be mounted on the back of a lorry to enable us to move it about the site from conveyor to conveyor. A simple machine was designed by his draughtsmen and was manufactured to do this job. It was driven by a diesel engine and was capable of reeling up long lengths of conveyor belting with ease.

These types of reeling machines are so successful that, after several modifications, they have become one of Cannings' products and have been sold to many companies throughout the world.

The Aberthaw job was quickly and efficiently completed. We also recovered about two thousand idlers, which were also in excellent condition.

It was another fluke that, at the same time as we were doing this job, we had an enquiry from another company in South Wales who required two thousand second-hand idlers. Their conveyor system was nearly identical to the job we were dismantling. We got the contract, and all it entailed was to carry the idlers back to Worksop, clean them and deliver them back to South Wales. Was it Canning Luck again?

It was probably because of our dealings with the quarrying industry that we were occasionally asked to quote for the design and manufacture of complete conveyor and handling systems. I wasn't an engineer and my company was not yet at a stage where we could manufacture jobs of this size ourselves. I have always classed myself as a "wheeler-dealer" and enquiries like this were too good to turn down. It was a natural course to subcontract these jobs to other engineering companies, who included a financial margin for us. Mick was employed as a mechanical engineer by one of the engineering companies.

We worked together on many contracts, and he told me that my "wheeler-dealer" attitude enabled me to grasp engineering opportunities more easily than he could. His words struck a chord with me and I thought that maybe we should be thinking about doing this type of work ourselves. I discussed this idea with him and we agreed on a plan. He said that he had always wanted to go into business and was very keen to become a partner if I was to form a new company to do this type of work. The idea was that we would build a new factory with offices and workshops, and would form another limited company, which we decided to call "Canning Engineering Co. Ltd."

The new building was to be a simple construction, large enough for handling this type of equipment, with doors big enough to get the equipment in and out. George Godley advised me that government grants were available for creating this kind of building with a view to creating employment. Everything was agreed and planned. Mick would stay in his present employment until the factory was built and ready for use in about twelve months' time. In the meantime, conveyor work was increasing and I had several engineering companies producing systems for me on a design and supply basis. At this time my workforce consisted of a travelling representative, a works manager, five workers including a delivery driver, and a full-time secretary.

Romance

It was mid-summer and my secretary was about to have a holiday. I was making enquiries about temporary office assistants when Barry told me that his sister Jane, who was training to be a schoolteacher was on summer leave and she could do with a bit of part time work answering the phone and doing some typing. I asked him if she could come in the following Monday.

I was on the phone talking to my Irish client Patrick O'Leary, when a little blue car pulled in at the gate.

She walked into the caravan and sat down in the chair beside me.

While I was on the phone, I looked at her and couldn't help noticing that her eyes were deep blue. I had the telephone next to my mouth and I thought I was still talking but all I could do was stare into her eyes and she was staring back at me. I was sinking into her eyes. I couldn't turn away.

"Are you there, Frank?" Patrick said. "Frank?"

I couldn't tear my eyes away and slowly put the phone down.

"Hello, I'm Jane."

I remember it so clearly. My heart missed a beat – never in my life had I looked into a girl's eyes like this, and never had I seen such magnetic eyes.

We kept looking at each other; she must have thought something was wrong with me.

"Hello, I'm Jane," she said again.

I couldn't stop looking at her. The phone rang. I didn't look at it; I just picked it up by habit.

"Frank, what happened? The phone went dead."

I suddenly came to my senses and finished my conversation with Pat O'Leary.

Jane seemed very competent, and by the time I had finished talking on the phone she had taken her coat off, tidied up, lit the gas ring and put the kettle on.

"Would you like a cup of tea?" she said.

That day was the dreamiest day of my life.

We talked and talked. I answered the phone and we talked. I wrote things down and we talked. I went outside, dished out a few orders and then we talked again.

I was completely smitten with her. It was like one of those romantic films – "and they saw each other across a crowded room…"

I had never had such an overwhelming feeling like this in my life before.

At the end of the day she went back to her car and drove away.

The next day, I remember every detail; it was like when you read and enjoy a special book and you can't get it off your mind. I arrived at work earlier than usual, and sat in the caravan window, staring at the gate entrance, looking for that little blue car. It was gone nine; I thought she wasn't coming. A quarter of an hour went by and she turned in at the gate. As she entered the caravan, I pretended to be talking on the phone. I said "Bye, bye," and put the phone down. Something was happening to me and I didn't understand it!

That day was the same pattern as the previous one. We talked and talked and she listened. It wasn't as if I deliberately told her things. It was as if she drew things out of me, things that I had never talked about before, things that worried me, things that I normally got twisted up about. She was so easy to talk to, and it was so refreshing. Whatever she said to me was so interesting. She was training to be a schoolteacher and I thought that part of their training was to be able to communicate with people. Many times since people have told me that they get the same feeling when they talk to her. It seems to be one of her gifts and she just seems to bring things out of you.

As the week went by I got more and more infatuated with her. I didn't dare say to her how I felt; it might have sounded a bit silly as I couldn't put it into words, and it might have frightened her away; so I just enjoyed and revelled in the wonderful feeling.

Each day I spent looking gooey eyed at her and lingering over all her words. I don't think I got much work done. Lunchtime came. I said that I would go into town to buy a sandwich and asked her if she would like me to bring her one back for her. I asked the sandwich maker to make me a chicken one with a bit of lettuce and a sliced tomato on top and cut it into triangular quarters. She had the tea made when I got back and I gave her the sandwich. She very gently put a tissue on the desk and opened the sandwich, unwrapping it very carefully. I felt like a little kid giving an apple to the teacher. She looked at it and said, "Oh, Frank, this looks so lovely. It's my favourite and it is cut into triangles just as I like it. Did you make it yourself?"

I think I blushed as I was so excited. I wanted to say, 'Yes, it was me', but I bit my tongue just in time. She must have thought I was a bit of an idiot the way I was acting.

I think it was at that moment that I fell in love with her, but how could I tell her? If I told her, would she walk away from me like the girl from the swimming club or Betty? All day Friday I was trying to pluck up courage to say how I felt, but I didn't even know if she liked me. Perhaps she was like this with everyone. I was in a bit of a state by the end of the day. Five o'clock came and she said that she had to go, and took my hand as if to shake it. She pulled me to her and gave me a kiss on the cheek. She kept looking into my eyes as if she was waiting for me to say something. I realise that at that point I should have said something, but I was afraid that if I said the wrong thing like "Can I see you again?" she would run away. She lingered for a minute. I had a lump in my throat. Then she turned away and left. I watched the car drive away. Suddenly I plucked up courage and ran after her, but she was gone.

My secretary came back the following Monday and for that week I was the most miserable person on earth. I remember her asking me if there had been a problem at work whilst she had been away. I couldn't get Jane off my mind. I lost interest in everything: all I wanted was for the telephone to ring and for it to be her; but I knew she wasn't giving me a second thought and was getting on with her life. I kept thinking, why didn't I make a move when she was looking at me? If she had slapped my face at least I would have known. Now I was in limbo.

Months later I was travelling with Barry. We were talking about Jane and he asked me if I didn't like her, as she had told him that she had been very upset when she left as she was hoping that I would at least have asked to see her again. How could I have been so stupid? I told him that she was always on my mind and that I, too, was upset that she hadn't indicated that she would like to see me again. Barry said that it was really a man's job to say things like that. I am stupid. I told him that I was crazy about her, but was frightened to take it further and asked him to tell her how I felt. He gave me a quizzical look, gave me her telephone number, and told me to tell her myself.

We made arrangements to meet at a Chinese restaurant for lunch, and it all started again – the talking – the eyes! I told her how I felt and she said she felt the same way. I told her I didn't know what true love was, as I had never experienced it before, and didn't realise it until she drove away that day, and that I had run after her – but she was gone and it was too late. We both realised that there was something very special happening to us.

We couldn't keep away from each other from then onwards. Although we saw each other regularly, I was still torn in half, missing the kids so much. Jane understood my dilemma, and after many soul-searching conversations she suggested that we part for a few weeks, to find out if I really wanted this sort of life, or if I wanted to go back to "Shalimar" and to the children and my wife.

The furthest I had ever travelled was to Glasgow on a plane with propellers, and on that journey I was violently sick and travelled home by train. Jane suggested that I go to the "other side of the world," away from everything and everyone, to a place where it was impossible to get in touch with anyone, in order to sort out my true feelings and make decisions about the future.

Thinking about the adventure comics I had read when I was younger and the Tarzan films I used to enjoy, my mind went a bit wild – "Darkest Africa!" At that time, travel to distant places was just starting and it seemed to me like a great adventure.

My tour was for three weeks. My itinerary was Heathrow to Kenya for a week on safari, then to Mombasa for a relaxing week, and then to Dar es Salaam in Tanzania for a sightseeing tour.

The plane was bound for South Africa and touched down at Nairobi airport to refuel. I was the only one to get off the plane and was met by a travel rep. As we walked across the tarmac I noticed black soldiers with rifles standing on the top of all the buildings. I had always thought it was only a joke about "Darkest Africa," but it wasn't a joke any more. I was feeling pretty scared and felt like running back to the plane. The airstrip was surrounded by tall palm trees, which looked like a jungle, and every hundred yards there was a guard posted. I wondered if I had arrived during a war or something.

The rep told me that the president of Kenya was about to arrive, thus the number of heavily armed guards standing around. It was a bit of a nerve-racking arrival but my hotel was the most luxurious hotel I had ever stopped in. It was the Nairobi Hilton, a high-rise circular hotel in the middle of the city. My room was on the top floor with wonderful views.

My safari started the next day. I was collected, along with a group of German tourists, and we were loaded into a convoy of jeeps painted with stripes to look "Africanised." Off we went on our first stage to a place called Treetops Hotel. It was an amazing hotel, built completely in the top of the trees overlooking a small lake. The rooms were a little small but built to the standards of any normal hotel rooms with en suite toilets and showers. There was a large dining room, which served as a viewing room with a complete wall of glass, which was see-through only from our side, so as not to disturb the animals.

We didn't sleep much that night as we were watching the magnificent, ever-changing views of different animals as they came to drink at the natural reservoir. As soon as one herd had finished drinking they plodded off; then another herd of a different type of animal arrived. It was very well organised! The animals didn't argue. They just took their own time, did exactly what they wanted to do, and then strolled off, leaving it free for the next herd. It was much too interesting to even think about sleeping. All the Germans were setting up their super expensive and very elaborate cameras with telescopic lenses, on very sophisticated tripods, to photograph the animals. While they had their eyes to their cameras, I whipped out my Baby Brownie and did a few snapshots.

As we travelled to the next stop, I began to feel intimidated as I was the only English-speaking person on the tour except for the guide, and he was more than occupied by the Germans, who demanded his full attention all the time. After three days I was fed up with speaking to myself and taking photographs. The guide seemed to notice my dilemma and made an effort to speak to me, but was always interrupted by the Germans. There was a car that followed us throughout the tour, going back and forth with supplies. I asked if it would be OK if I dropped out and went back to the hotel. The car took me straight to Mombasa. They had phoned ahead and my early arrival was expected.

Once again the hotel was luxurious. There were English people staying there and everything was wonderful and relaxing.

After a few days of relaxation, I caught sight of the most beautiful girl I had ever seen. She had pure white hair, brown skin and a very sexy figure. I noticed that she seemed to be on her own and we occasionally looked at each other. The next day she gave me a very welcoming smile and spoke to me.

She was Swedish. Her name was Suzy. She was an airhostess for Swiss Air and staying at the hotel between flights. We got on very well with each other. She told me her story and I told her mine. I told her about Jane and the reason I was taking a separate holiday. I just couldn't understand why she seemed to like me: I wasn't a tall, dark, suave, handsome man and I didn't have a wealth of worldly experiences to talk about, but we got on like a house on fire.

Here I was, on the other side of the world, in a superb location, relatively single, befriended by a very beautiful, sexy Swedish girl. It was every man's dream.

One evening after sunbathing together she phoned me on the room phone and asked me to come to her room to put sun cream on her back. This was the type of thing one read about in Ian Fleming books. I couldn't believe my luck. The door was off the latch. I went in and she was sitting on the bed with a towel around her. She said that her back was sunburnt and handed me the sun cream. She turned slightly and lowered her towel.

Wow! I smoothed the cream on to her back, my mind racing. I had come to the other side of the world to sort my mind out. This gorgeous, dreamy Swedish girl was asking me to rub cream on her back. She was waiting for me to make an approach and for some reason I was holding back. It was crazy. How many times had I been with a girl trying to succeed and something had happened to stop my approach. Here was a dream come true and I was shying away. All I could think about was Jane! Look, I am only a normal man. At this point in my story I could make up a wonderful tale of rampant love and no one would ever disbelieve it, but I finished creaming her and put the towel back over her shoulders and said that I must go. She stood up and kissed me on the cheek. I said "Bye" and returned to my room. Believe me, I was torn!

The following two days we went sightseeing, snorkelling and had all our meals together. I often think what I missed and sometimes kick myself for not taking the chance. After all, I always thought I was an opportunist!

Once back home, my mind was settled. I had made my decision: I would do as much as I possibly could for the welfare of my ex-wife and my children; I would try to see them and help them as much as possible; but I was absolutely sure about my relationship with Jane.

Shortly afterwards Jane and I were married.

A Stressful Year

The year ending August 1970 was a big year. The accounts now consisted of six sheets. George, who was still spending a considerable amount of time with me, seemed very pleased and gave me a lovely compliment. He pulled his spectacles down to the end of his nose, looked over them and said, with a very serious look on his face, "What have you been doing?" I am sure I blushed. "You've made a profit again. You are keeping the Inland Revenue very happy!"

He had a little titter and then spent the next two hours explaining the accounts to me.

Sales   £53,460.9s.2d
Net Profit   £6012.5s.4d

We must have been doing well but the accounts still didn't interest me. The figures I remembered mostly were the most important ones to me: Sales and Profit. All I knew was that I was working flat-out, and all I thought about was work, and how to get through all the work.

George was very patient with me and took his time trying to help me to understand what the accounts were all about as he read through them, carefully explaining each item to me.

I was paying Corporation Tax and Interest on my loan.
Auditor's Fees
Depreciation
Hire Purchase on Vehicles
Rent and Rates
Electricity
Telephone
Travelling Expenses
Hire of Equipment
Insurances

Wages and National Insurance
Crane
Machinery
Van
Lorry
Caravan
Office equipment
Advertising

I realised what he was trying to tell me and tried to take everything in. It was slowly making sense. I didn't think I would ever like to be an accountant as I liked making money and didn't like accounts, but it was slowly making sense.

He looked through my sales ledger and explained that I was dealing with a good spread of customers, and explained about the pitfalls and benefits of giving credit, and bank loans and overdrafts.

My head was swimming. My God, where was it all going? Only six years of business and I was starting to suffer from stress!

The problem was that not only was I driving my business forward, it was driving me, and I was also struggling to keep up with it and understand it. There was no master plan, now called a "business plan" – it was just a matter of taking on whatever happened and trying to do it properly and make a profit.

I had read a few books about business, and they all looked at strategic planning and forward thinking. I couldn't always identify and associate what I was doing with these books, but I must have been doing something right, probably by guesswork! I was just trying to cope, keep abreast of it all and keep my head above water. I learned hard and fast but only because I had to. When I had to do something my brain would suddenly open up and take it all in. There was no way I could do it by studying or taking a commercial course. Also, I just didn't have the time. It was a case of trial and error. When an enquiry or an opportunity happened to come along, I got on with it, took the initiative and took a chance. Some you win and some you lose. If I didn't do this, then all would be lost. That's what my business was and is all about. That's what I had got myself into. That's how I ran my business. This is what I had always wanted and now I had it, all I wanted to do was to get on with it and become successful. After all, how could I possibly fail – I was being guided by my mentors, George, Bob, and Mr. Cruikshank and, of course, my Guardian Angel – Mam - kept her eye on me! Nothing could possibly go wrong!

I had taken out a loan of £5000 and, with the help of a government grant of £1500, the factory was built and all ready to take the plunge into engineering.

Mick's wife phoned me. She was in a terrible state. She wanted me to come over to her house in Melton Mowbray to tell me some bad news – she couldn't even say it over the phone.

Mick had died.

I thought Mick had seemed a little unwell just before and he seemed to be depressed and losing interest in our plans and the project. Who knows why things like this happen? His wife couldn't find an explanation.

A friend of Mick's, Errol, whom I had met many times before, said that he would be keen to take on the project. In fact, he told me that he was ready for a move and he and Mick had discussed our project many times in the past. It was a great relief to me as all the plans we had made for the new engineering company over the previous twelve months were just about to be put into practice.

Errol became my new partner in Canning Engineering Co. Ltd. We had fifty per cent each of the shares. The factory was owned by my company and Canning Engineering Co. Ltd paid a rent to use it.

Errol was a qualified engineer and had worked for the same company as Mick. He was very experienced and knew a great deal about our association and our type of work. He was to run the company. My part in the action was to try to get work from clients I was already dealing with and to introduce contacts.

Things were getting more and more complex. I realised that I needed other people on whom I could rely to take on some of the responsibilities. I had reached a stage where, looking at it from anyone else's eyes, it would have been quite sensible to say that we had a reasonable business and we did not need to not go any further in our development. We could happily manage what we had, try to do it well and cut out the silly, extraordinary drive forward. But that wasn't me!

I have always driven myself, and everyone around me, to a state of madness. I consulted my friend Bob, my solicitor, to ask his advice about directorships and shareholdings. After many meetings and discussions it was decided that the next stage forward was to appoint Barry and Gud to become Directors. They were each allotted five per cent of the shareholding. Barry was made Sales Director and Gud was made Works Director. The idea was that if they were Directors they would take on more responsibility and help to take the company forward.

For quite a long time, I had been living in hotels and lodging with various people. I decided to rent a flat above some shops. This, I thought, would make it easier to entertain the kids when I saw them. We could watch TV and play games and I would not have to take them to the cinema or go for drives every time. It also made it easier for me to "settle down" as I seemed to have been living out of a suitcase forever. Unfortunately, I didn't see the kids as often as I wanted to. They occasionally came to see me at work. The lads enjoyed doing a bit of work for pocket money, such as clearing up all the bits of scrap metal and scrap nuts and bolts from the yard, and putting them into large, empty paint tins and weighing them in at the scrapyard next door for pocket money. Mandy was now a young lady and had surrounded herself with her friends, in particular a special friend called Cliff.

The stress of not being able to see the kids as often as I wanted and being so hyped up with the business and working all hours was causing me severe health problems. My main symptoms were what I called "wooden tongue." My mouth, jaw and tongue were in pain. My tongue became stiff and it affected my speech. I couldn't pronounce my words and sometimes couldn't even speak. My doctor advised me to steady down and prescribed some tablets called Valium, which slowed you down and helped to combat stress and depression. I felt like a drug addict; it was a constant battle to carry on, drugged-up, half asleep and forcing myself to cope with the pressures of business.

It was Christmas. The firm had broken up for a week's holiday. This was our only true holiday, when all other firms in the country were also on holiday, and one could forget work and relax. We had a company party in a pub and everyone got sloshed. I went to bed that night and stayed in bed for a week, all through Christmas and the New Year. I phoned for the doctor, who said it looked like ME. He called it "London Flu," as he said he had seen it happen to city bankers who were stressed out. He explained to me that sometimes when sufferers from this complaint took a holiday, they broke down in sheer exhaustion. Nowadays it is called Chronic Fatigue Syndrome. I was unable to get out of bed and the thought of meeting anyone made me feel worse. I often seemed to have the "wooden tongue" whenever I felt stressed out, but continued to overcome it with more tablets – a couple of Valium to calm me down and a couple of Diatalgesic (DGs) to rev me up. I couldn't carry on without the tablets.

Canning Engineering Co. Ltd was formed and was soon established in our new factory. We were now in the engineering business. It wasn't long before we were struggling for more space. The main stockyard around the new factory became full of belts and conveyor products. The engineers needed the whole of the office block for their own office staff and drawing office, and most of the stockyard for their engineered products. It soon became manic. We were overcrowded and sharing offices.

It all began humbly in Langold back garden

A WORKSOP engineering company which had humble beginnings in a Langold back garden will now be able to increase its work force and production ... and seek new markets abroad.

The heartening news was given yesterday week when extensions to Canning Conveyor Co. Ltd. and Canning Engineering Co. Ltd. were opened on the Sandy Lane industrial site by Worksop's Mayor, Coun. Hubert Bell.

Canning Conveyor Co. Ltd. managing director Mr. Frank Canning said during 1971 the two companies had employed 20 men and saturation point had been reached in the existing premises.

The firm had approached Worksop Borough Council for more land and had been allotted a 2½-acre site adjacent to their factory, he said.

Work on the new warehouse, packing shop and office block started 12 months ago.

"These premises are now complete and will enable us to handle and store our products more efficiently, increase our sales and give better working conditions to our ever-increasing staff," Mr. Canning said.

He paid tribute to all the employees who had worked so hard to bring the company up to its present standard, especially Canning Engineering managing director Mr. Errol Mason.

Mr. Canning also thanked the Borough Council for the help he had received.

He gave a welcome to the Mayor, town clerk Mr. Russell C. Pharaoh and Planning Committee chairman Coun. Fred Cooley.

It was indeed a pleasure to be opening a new factory on the industrial site said Coun. Bell.

The idea of having such a work area had been adopted by the Council to cater for industry as local pits were run down, he said.

"But the Council's campaign has not been as successful as we would have liked," said the Mayor.

"I am pleased to say, however, it is improving and with more land coming into the Council's ownership we shall be able to put it to new and diverse industrial purposes in Worksop."

The Mayor wished Canning Conveyor Co. Ltd. and Canning Engineering Co. Ltd. a prosperous future.

When firms had two factories working to capacity it was on the books there would be more, he said.

"I am glad to be able to open the new factory of a firm which started in a Langold back garden," said Coun. Bell.

"Anyone who has done what Mr. Frank Canning has done can be referred to as successful."

The Mayor also referred to the improved conditions for employees.

"I am sure your confidence in your workmen will not be misplaced," he told Mr. Canning.

"I am pleased to offer you the sincerest wishes for the future and we are proud to have you in Worksop.

"I hope you will remain here and go from strength to strength."

Nearly 100 people associated with the engineering companies were at the opening.

Outlining the history of the firm, Mr. Canning said it was first registered in September 1965.

The basic idea was to buy used conveyor belting, renovate it and then sell it back to industry. Although early processes were satisfactory they were crude and time consuming.

The company progressed rapidly because the product it offered was good and yet cheap, said Mr. Canning.

They worked from a half-acre site on the Sandy Lane industrial area, but saturation point was soon reached and it was obvious more space and premises were needed.

After being asked to also supply conveyors and equipment, plus all other types of low-cost renovated machinery, a bigger labour force was engaged and it quickly became apparent healthier working conditions were required.

A £10,000 factory was completed in 1970, and by this time the firm's turnover was increasing annually by [?] per cent.

Because demands for new equipment were constantly being made, Canning Engineering Co. Ltd. was formed in January 1971, Mr. Canning said.

"This company's task was to design, manufacture and erect new conveyors, hoppers, silos and steel fabric[?] for the quarrying industry covering the whole of the country," he said.

Saturation point had again been achieved and that was the reason the company had been forced to build the extensions.

It was now his intention to seek markets farther afield.

"We are looking both in this country and abroad," Mr. Canning said.

"We intend to form our own exporting department because in addition to our regular exports to countries on and around the Mediterranean, we have had enquiries from South America, India, Japan, Africa and the continent.

"We shall take on more salesmen and be able to cope with the anticipated influx of new customers."

The Mayor, Coun. Hubert Bell, congratulates Mr. Frank Canning, managing director Canning Conveyor Co. Ltd., at the opening.

'Grand Opening'

Luckily, just at the time we were becoming desperate the council offered me another half acre plot on the same site. I told them that a half acre plot wasn't large enough for my requirements, and asked them if they could offer me more space as it seemed that the plot next to this had not yet been taken, but they told me that all the plots were spoken for. I didn't accept this and, with my solicitor's help, we bought the lease from the person who had put his name on the adjoining plot; this upset the council. I now had my full one-acre plot but, unfortunately, I was in the council's bad books. Plans were drawn up to build a new office block, workshops and a warehouse for the main conveyor business.

The design included an office block with a reception, sales office, two administration offices and a toilet block. Adjoining this was to be built a special workshop, which was more like a long "tunnel," which was to be used for rolling out and repairing long lengths of conveyor belts. Adjoining this workshop was a warehouse, which was to be used for stocking the finished products prior to sale. There was also to be a large stockyard.

Another stroke of Canning Luck made available a "tunnel."

We were stripping out a conveyor system from a power station in South Wales. The conveyor was housed in a building about 12ft high by 12ft wide and about 200ft long. After clearing out the conveyor I realised that the building was, more or less, identical to the plans for the tunnel that had been designed for our new workshop. Fortunately for us, the whole of this particular part of the power station was due for demolition.

The demolition contractor was more than pleased to sell it to me as it was more economical for him to dismantle it in large pieces and place it onto my lorry than to scrap it. It was a good deal for both of us. It was transported to our site and re-erected to make a splendid workshop.

We finished our buildings and we were so proud of them that we organised a grand opening ceremony of the premises. The Mayor of

Worksop gave an exhilarating and flattering speech and unveiled a brass plaque to commemorate the day. The town council officials, who had forgotten about our previous misdeeds, were invited along with several of our best clients, and a good time was had by all. Wine, cakes and back-patting.

Expansion Madness

The following four years moved along fast and furious as we expanded. We bought another small company that traded in rubber products; we took over a one-man vulcanising company from a man who didn't like the responsibility of running his own business. We separated the buying and selling of quarry plant from the engineering company and formed a company called Canning Plant Ltd. Our works dismantling contracts became another division that was handling large volumes of scrap metal, which we were selling to various scrapyards across the country. We were also ploughing many tons of scrap metal into our neighbouring scrapyard so it seemed an obvious and good reason to buy this business. After this purchase there were only two remaining factories on our site that we didn't own. As soon as they became available, we bought them and converted one into an engineering workshop and the other into a warehouse.

A toy manufacturing company based at Leicester, called Palitoy, was in the process of modernisation and expansion, and they asked us to clear out one of their toy inspection departments, which consisted of several conveyors. When the department closed everything was left just as it was, and we had to clear the site. There were toys scattered all over the place: Action Man, Pippa Dolls and Carrie Dolls, all in their boxes and many of them still in perfect condition.

Jane had always talked about having a little toyshop and this was an ideal opportunity for her. We rented a small vacant shop in Worksop, converted it into a toy supermarket and for the first year she seemed to sell nothing but dolls. She called her shop Playday.

We also invested in a café/taxi business.

One day, Mr. Cruikshank asked Errol and me to call in to see him. He informed us that a large engineering group wanted to buy a conveyor manufacturing company, with good potential for expansion, good profitability and experienced management. More important, they were interested in talking to us!

Errol had said many times that he needed to expand his factory but we didn't have the capital reserves to do so. He really needed to double the size of this operation, in order to cope with the size of the jobs he was becoming involved in, as our small factory just wasn't allowing us to take on any larger jobs. It was too good an opportunity to miss. The business was sold and was moved to another larger factory. Errol joined the new firm as Managing Director.

Our existing factory was now to be utilised solely for the renovation of used plant and quarry equipment. A new engineering division was created. A new man, Michael, who was very experienced in this type of work, was employed to run this new division.

As the business flourished and expanded, my problems of trying to cope with the finances of the group and trying to make the right decisions were increasing tenfold. I was still as ambitious as ever and would look at every opportunity that came along.

The business was rolling along like an express train. I needed continuous support and help to understand the finance and planning. My three mentors were always available to help and advise me, but I found that I required more daily assistance – someone within the company who could look at the company as a whole and not just on an ad hoc basis.

I discussed my feelings with Bob, who fully understood my dilemma. He suggested that I talk to a business consultant who could probably advise on finance, accounts and management on a more regular basis. He introduced me to Rex, a Financial Advisor, whom he had previously worked with. I went out for lunch with Rex and he suggested that he came in a couple of mornings per week to start with and I could talk to him any time to discuss problems. The first thing Rex advised was to appoint a full-time accountant/office manager. Interviews were arranged and we appointed David.

Canning Conveyor Co. Ltd. was founded in September 1965 and in the early days its main activity was trading in conveyor belting.

Its original employees worked in a field, in the open air, and in all kinds of weather. But even in such arduous and basic conditions the customers requirements were fulfilled, and the hard lessons learned were good grounding for future years of successful trading.

Over three decades of development now see the company located in a fine complex of industrial buildings and offices.

Years of experience supplying the mining, quarrying, mechanical and civil engineering, fishing, farming, and film making industries, have made Cannings a leading name throughout the world.

Our trade is divided up as such - one third to direct users in the UK, one third to other retail outlets and vulcanising companies in the UK, and one third export.

Whether the demand is for a simple belt fastener or a mile long belt conveyor - from a single roller to the design, manufacture and installation of a complete handling plant, Cannings are able to supply with excellent professional efficiency.

177

The thing that struck me about David was his sincerity and thoroughness. Over the forthcoming years David became one of my most loyal and conscientious employees.

As Rex gradually became more involved in the life of the company and our expansion programme, he informed us about a local company that was about to close. This was an old-established building company called G.G. Middleton & Sons Ltd. During its existence it had been a very strong and successful family firm. The management had been passed down through the family for generations. Apparently the last surviving member was very ill and two long-term employees were managing the firm, but they were not prepared to buy the company. One of them had suggested to Rex to ask Cannings if they might be interested.

We bought the company and appointed the two managers to run it. Middleton's also had a subsidiary company called W.S. Roe and Sons Ltd. who were plumbing and heating specialists. Middleton's became a very valuable subsidiary for many years under the leadership of Stephen.

I was on my way to my dream of owning a hundred companies!

After another reshuffle, a new management team was formed. We had regular management meetings under the guidance of Rex, who also became secretary of the meetings.

The new formula was:
I was chairman
Rex – Advisor
Bob – Non-Executive Director and Legal Advisor
David – Accountant and Company Secretary
Barry – Sales Director.
George – Works Director
Michel – Engineering Manager
Barry – Scrapyard Manager
Stephen – Middleton's Manager.

Each person would give their reports and forecasts of their individual department's good or bad news. I felt that we were now going in the right direction; things were being discussed properly and decisions were correctly made. There seemed to be a glowing light at the end of the tunnel and the future looked exciting.

Malta

I was becoming more and more involved with exporting and importing. My aim was concentrated mainly on Europe, the Mediterranean countries and North Africa. We were receiving many enquiries from Malta from a Maltese father/son business, who had a contract to do engineering work in Libya. Alex and his father firstly visited us and purchased a container-load of conveyor belting, rollers and crusher parts, which were exported Libya to be used on the project they were working on. After several visits from them and several successful deals, they invited Jane and me to visit Malta to meet their families and see their factory.

Malta is called the "Friendly Island" and we certainly found it so. We were drawn to it, not only because of the marvellous trade we were doing with them, but also because of our strong friendship with Alex, his family and many other Maltese people, which is still as strong now. We visited Malta so many times that it seemed like our second home. We became very close friends with them and took every opportunity to visit them as they did us.

At this time, there was an embargo between the UK and Libya. The UK was not allowed to do trade with Libya because of political problems concerning Colonel Gaddafi, the Libyan leader. Regardless of this, most of the equipment we sold to Malta was forwarded on to Libya to the engineering contract of Alex and his father. Apparently Libya was so short of our type of equipment that our dealings with Alex became more and more frequent.

One day Jane and I were in Malta, walking along the seafront after a nice meal and a bottle of Soave. We were both talking about how nice it would be to own our own flat along this particular front. Although it was dark, the bright moonlight picked out a block of flats that we were walking past.

A voice came from one of the upper balconies. "Would you like to buy my nice flat?"

It sounded like the voice of a man and I immediately thought it was Alex messing about. We looked up and could just make out an old lady, standing, looking over the balcony. She said, "I could hear you talking about buying a flat and mine is for sale, if you would like to buy it."

The flat was on a second floor of a block of four. It had a big balcony overlooking the bay and it was called "Mon Refuge." The name itself was enough to entice our interest.

I had an instant good feeling and thought to myself that Mam was watching us.

We were given a tour of the flat and the old lady said that her legs were bad; she had difficulty climbing the stairs and would like to move to a ground-floor flat. She said that she wanted to sell immediately. Without any hesitation we said, "Yes, please."

The flat became our office, our haven and our refuge for fifteen years.

I have personally never felt more at home than when in Malta. It was the most perfect place to live. The people were so kind and friendly, especially to the English. Many English people had settled there. We found a special place close to the flat called Luzzu, which is the Maltese name for a fishing boat. Luzzu was a section of the beach that had been adapted as a small leisure complex. It consisted of a restaurant/café, a sunbathing area, with beds and umbrellas, and a pier to which were tied several motorboats and small sailing boats. It provided ski and sub aqua facilities. It was a paradise and being just a small stroll from the flat we spent quite a lot of our time and often ate there, staggering home after a few bottles of Soave.

One evening I strolled down for a late-night drink and sat talking to the owner, Joe, who confessed to me that he wanted to sell as he felt he was getting too old and wanted to retire. My mind started ticking over. After a few beers, the odd brandy or two, and another bottle of Soave, my mind was firmly set on becoming Maltese.

Jane and her sister Valerie, who had been staying with us at that time, had been looking for me for the previous two hours and I heard them calling. "Frank, coooee."

Poor Jane thought I had fallen into the sea and drowned. Although I had been drinking and was well and truly sozzled, I managed to explain that I was going to buy Luzzu. She and Val looked at each other and rolled their eyes. I could see what they were thinking as they carried me home.

"No, not another one of his crazy investments!"

I was hooked. During the remainder of the holiday my thoughts and plans were made. Jane would manage the restaurant as she had had previous experience running a cafe. Mandy would become a "Redcoat" and social organiser, as everyone is attracted to her vibrant personality. Andrew would become manager of the bar and the beach area, hiring out the beds and chairs and things. Jay and Eden would take charge of the boats and the skiing and sailing. All that remained was for me to appoint a general manager to run the business back home, or sell it! We would all emigrate and would live happily ever after. What a wonderful plan!

The dreams were soon shattered when I found out that the owner wasn't really the owner: he was just a part owner, and the other part was owned by an Englishman who had taken everything out of the business. The business was in serious financial trouble. The assets were already in the hands of the solicitors and anyone who might be thinking of taking it over had firstly to pay off the debts and, by Maltese law, he had to appoint another Maltese partner who had to own more than fifty per cent of the business.

Malta sun and wine give you such crazy dreams. Perhaps that is the reason I felt so much at home there!

It was during our negotiations for buying Luzzu, when Jane and I were studying the documents and I was trying to read them out loud, that I kept floundering as the words kept jumping around.

Jane told me that the reason for this was probably because I was dyslexic.

What a revelation! It was stunning news to me. It answered my many self-doubts. Perhaps I wasn't such a dunce, after all.

I have always had this problem and, as I have mentioned earlier, my teacher used to think that I was a dunce. Dyslexia wasn't "invented" then and wasn't understood as it is today. Jane just happened to have had experience teaching children with dyslexia, and spotted it when she realised that I had so much difficulty reading small, typed print out loud.

When I was young, sufferers of dyslexia were thought of as dunces, or even backward. Jane told me that sufferers "think" in pictures and in 3D, and have a problem with printed words as they are only in 2D.

My problem was recognising numbers and letters such as b or d or p or q, for instance. I also find lines of words move upwards or downwards. Often a word from a lower line appears on the line I am reading.

An example happened recently when I was reading a newspaper, which I thought said that a certain TV programme was to be shown on a certain Friday. I told Jane and she read the article and noticed that the word Friday was on the lower line. To combat this problem I have always found it easier to read if I put a ruler beneath the line I am reading. I also developed my own method of calculating figures by using imaginary pictures such as squares. Fortunately there is no problem now, with the use of calculators and computers!

The British Dyslexic Society says that sufferers often compensate by behaving badly or becoming withdrawn – in my younger days I was always in trouble and was very shy. It certainly makes one wonder!

Skateboarding

Skateboarding was at its peak and practically every kid in the country had a skateboard.

Our local council had a problem!

There was a very long, steep hill on the way to Langold Lake and the kids were using it as a skateboard run. They stood on their boards and skidded down the hill at breakneck speeds. There was a spate of accidents as kids fell over and bounced off the concrete. Broken limbs and blood were frequent. The council were also annoyed that the kids were climbing back to the top of the hill by walking up the grassy verge, turning it into a sludgy path.

Someone at the council thought that it might save the grassy verge if we laid a path of scrap conveyor belting alongside for the kids to walk on. The rubber path soon became the skateboard track. The kids decided that it was smoother than the road and when they fell off they didn't hurt themselves as much.

The council official said that this was a saviour, as a proper skateboard track would have cost about £5000 to build. It not only saved money but, if the skateboard craze ended, we could just take up the belts, without any problems, and everything would be back to normal.

I thought this might be a golden opportunity to sell more of our scrap belting.

I contacted the council and asked them if we could fit another similar track on an old disused railway cutting, free of charge, to use as a prototype. It was immediately approved by the council as it wasn't a permanent structure, it would help to avoid accidents and, perhaps most importantly, it wouldn't cost the council a penny.

WHAT THE PAPERS SAY ...

WHAT A BELTER...

OF TO THE RUBBER HILLS

Skate track a success

Morning Telegraph Reporter

A skateboarder council was bowled over...
The "nail-tops" track at Langold Park...

Crowds pour in to use the 'soft'
Langold skate rn
Rubber
track

Evening Post Reporter

Park where skaters
bounce if they fall

Lindsay Council...

On the right track for a craze

A NOVEL cheap skateboard track material...

cheaper
and
safer

Council's belting skate board
idea is a runaway success

Falling
about
with
praise

Rubber skate
track orders
pour in for
Worksop firm

By neil Worksop staff

A WORKSOP firm has been inundated with orders for rubber skateboard track...

BELTING IDEA
FOR LOCAL
SKATEBOARDERS

Skateboard
track is a
'belter'

We constructed what we called a "Cresta Run." It was a 200-yard switch-back run, which started off from the top of the railway bank at one side, ran across the level floor and up the other side. It was about 15 feet wide and took about two days to fit. Even as we were fitting it the kids were waiting, skateboards in hand.

It was an instant success. We planned an opening day and invited a skateboard club and all the local kids to attend. A few simple competitions were organised and a few prizes were arranged. Several newspapers were invited and were very keen to attend as skateboarding was big news at that time.

That day was mad!

There were as many as two hundred local kids, reporters and photographers from several newspapers including *The Daily Mirror, The Daily Express* and *Sheffield Star* – even *The Times* had a small report on their front page. It was a phenomenal batch of free publicity for Cannings. There were photos of masses of kids, and even a picture of dog on a skateboard whizzing down our Cresta Run. One newspaper included pictures of prizewinners being presented with cups. It filled the newspapers the next day. It was also covered by television. One report said it was a revolution for skateboarders, as when anyone fell off they bounced back. What a punchy, gimmicky line!

We were inundated with enquiries from all over the country and it was "all stops out" to keep abreast with it. We created another division of the company, called Canning Leisure Products, and employed two sales and administrative staff to handle the enquiries and orders. A team of site-fitters, under the supervision of George, was engaged practically full-time fitting the tracks. Each time a track was fitted a stream of publicity followed from the local press. It was like a snowball rolling along, getting bigger and bigger.

The simplicity of it all was the key. All that was required was a natural grassy bank. The grass on the bank was cut as low as possible and rolled with a heavy roller. Then belting was secured at the top and rolled down the hill. The joints were sealed with a special rubber seal and, hey presto, the job was done! The most prestigious track we fitted was in the Royal Greenwich Park just below the Greenwich Observatory. Someone joked that we might be able to put "By Royal Appointment" on our publicity.

It was an exciting time and although the tracks worked very well as a stand-alone, I thought there was still room for further development. The material, after all, was just dirty black conveyor belting. I approached the company BTR Greengate, who were a large manufacturer of new conveyor belting and who specialised in developing several types of special belts for unusual applications. I discussed with them the possibility of producing a type of belting which had less friction and could be made with a brightly coloured top-cover to make it look more like a sports product. They came up with a specially formulated, low-friction belt, coloured red. The price was also very reasonable, as it didn't have to have the very tough interior plies which were put into heavy industrial belting. The final benefit was that during the development experiments they had found a way to print a logo on the surface. This set my mind racing regarding the possibility of advertisements.

I had already been in discussions with the British Safety Council about the safety angle on the tracks and, at a meeting, the Chairman said that his grandson was an ardent skateboarder and often used the "in" word "radical," meaning good or exciting. He actually asked if we would call the material "Track Radical." Greengate then produced logo labels which were vulcanised into the top cover every ten feet or so with the words "Track Radical – The Skateboard Track With Added Bounce."

I'm quite sure that if there had been a programme on TV like *Dragons' Den* the Dragons would have all wanted to invest in it!

The next step was to go forward with the advertising idea. I had discussions with a company who were responsible for producing the advertising around Wembley Stadium and other similar sporting venues, and asked them if they might be interested in selling advertising space on our skateboard tracks. Because of the amount of free publicity we had already received, they realised the potential and were very keen to go forward with the project. Within a few days they had confirmed interest from a sweets manufacturer and a popular beer company.

It was going like a dream. The next idea was to approach the councils and pleasure parks and tell them that we would like to fit a skateboard track free of charge, full of brightly colourful advertisements. Then, we would remove the track after twelve months and replace it with another brand new track, full of fresh adverts.

Our income would come by a proportion of the fees from the advertisers, who would have twelve months' exposure of their advertisement, contracted to be renewed annually, and we would use the old track material for manufacturing our other products. After the initial cost of buying the rolls of printed belts from Greengate, and laying and recovering the tracks, there would be a good return on our investment.

The advertising people said it was a "coup." The managing director of Greengate wined and dined us in the Directors' dining room, assuring us that their rolling presses were ready to roll. As usual my mind was racing ahead – multi-millionaire, private helicopter, penthouse apartment in Monaco.

After receiving definite interest from several councils I was awaiting their confirmations, but they never arrived. I couldn't understand why, until I phoned one of them.

"Just look out of your window," he said. "Do you see any skateboarders? The skateboard craze has died a sudden death!"

True enough, like most crazes, as quickly as it started it finished.

We made some money over the skateboard year, but I didn't become a skateboard millionaire.

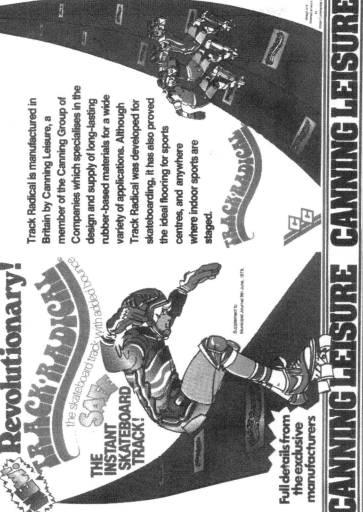

Revolutionary!
TRACK·RADICAL
...the skateboard track with added bounce

THE
INSTANT
SKATEBOARD
TRACK!

SAFE!

Track Radical is manufactured in Britain by Canning Leisure, a member of the Canning Group of Companies which specialises in the design and supply of long-lasting rubber-based materials for a wide variety of applications. Although Track Radical was developed for skateboarding, it has also proved the ideal flooring for sports centres, and anywhere where indoor sports are staged.

Supplement to Municipal Journal 9th June, 1978.

TRACK·RADICAL

Full details from the exclusive manufacturers

A Division of the Canning Group of Companies Ltd.
Sandy Lane Industrial Site, Sandy Lane, Worksop, Nottinghamshire.
Telephone: Worksop (0909) 86166. Telex: 547398

CANNING LEISURE CANNING LEISURE

CANNING LEISURE CANNING LEISURE

189

It was so disappointing, but I was used to highs and lows. As one idea dies, another appears.

I had noticed that the tracks we had fitted using the new, red, low-friction material had become very slippery with continuous use. I noticed that, if anyone fell off their skateboard, they slid to the bottom of the track. In fact, after a while, as some of the kids got fed up with skating down the tracks, they put aside their skateboards and the tracks became slides.

As we still had several rolls of the red material in stock, I wondered if we could change the usage. We developed a new type of children's slide. My sales lady thought of a very catchy name: the Jumbo Safety Slide. "Jumbo" because it was big. "Safety" because the slider could not fall off as it was at ground level, and there had been so many accidents whilst playing on high-rise slides. The only way anyone could fall off was by sliding off the sides, but they would just slide onto the grass in complete safety.

After many weeks of ideas, development and trials we developed a flexible side- arm, which fitted to each side of the slide and adapted to the natural contours of the hill on which the slide was fitted.

We were old hands at publicity and approached the BBC, who had previously covered our skateboard tracks, and told them about our revolutionary Jumbo Safety Slide. They invited me to visit them at their studios in Wood Lane, London, to talk about a possible inclusion in their programme *Tomorrow's World*.

Filming took place in a park in Mansfield. Word had been given out to the local kids about the filming day and they arrived in their thousands. I think all the schools closed down in Mansfield that day. When the kids arrived it was like a madhouse.

The first bit of the filming was taken on an old-fashioned, steel, high-rise slide, showing the possible pitfalls of falling from the top, or getting fingers trapped, or shooting off the bottom of the slide.

190

Presenting The New Concept Contour JUMBO SAFETY SLIDE ©

By the makers of Track-Radical rubber skateboard tracks

All Rubber Slide

Specially designed to make use of banks and slopes of any length

For Children of all ages

The Ultimate in Safety

RESURFACE YOUR OLD DANGEROUS SLIDE.

JUMBO SAFETY SLIDE IS 100% COVERED IN CNR4 – SPECIALLY DEVELOPED RUBBER WHICH IS NOW AVAILABLE FOR RESURFACING OLD SLIDES PERMANENTLY AND QUICKLY

★ SUITABLE FOR ALL TYPES OF SURFACES ★ NO DANGEROUS SCREWS OR NAILS ★ EASY TO FIT ★ SPECIAL ADHESIVE SUPPLIED

FULL DETAILS AND FREE SAMPLE OF CNR4 FROM THE EXCLUSIVE MANUFACTURERS

CANNING LEISURE

A Division of Canning Conveyor Co. Ltd.

Sandy Lane Industrial Site, Sandy Lane, Worksop, Nottinghamshire S80 1TN
Telephone: Worksop (0909) 86166 (4 lines). Telex: 547398

©COPYRIGHT 1978 CANNING CONVEYOR CO. LTD. PATENT PENDING

11

Then they went to another part of the hill to film our men fitting a mock-up of the Jumbo Safety Slide.

Finally we went to the real slide, which had been previously fitted and was prepared and clean and tidy, ready for filming. A camera was set half way down the slide to catch the kids whizzing down. There was quite a queue at the top. The kids' excitement was by now bursting as they had been kept away from the slide for nearly half a day during the pre-filming. They were taking a bit of controlling and some of their teachers were feeling a little impatient by now. A camera was set up near to the starting post and the director raised his arm and shouted, "Action." A wild mass of kids dived onto the slide in one big mad lump! Head-first, upside-down, back-to-front, some on top of each other, some somersaulting. It was one continuous stream of crazy, wild, screaming lunatics, all enjoying themselves. The director said later that he had never seen anything so hilarious in his life and would keep the film to show on *Candid Camera*. The parents and teachers were asked to calm them down and organise the kids to go down a few at a time. Eventually he got what he wanted.

It was shown on *Tomorrow's World* on November 22, 1979.

Once again, after a flurry of orders had been placed, the basic concept for our slide was redesigned by the bright sparks of the slide-manufacturing industry, who developed their own version of a flexible hill-mounted slide, made from stainless steel, which was much more stable than ours and, of course, cheaper. This type of slide is still seen and is popular in most children's playgrounds.

Other leisure projects like golf mats and sports flooring kept the mind alert and added excitement to the job.

Then it was back to reality.

For a couple of years things were looking good with the engineering department. Michael certainly knew his stuff regarding crushers and screens as they were his speciality. He would buy a giant mobile crushing plant, which would be stripped down, rebuilt, repainted and sold onwards. I suppose this is a common activity with second-hand machines such as lawn mowers, cars and bicycles, but to see a machine arrive that is as large as a three-bedroom house, stripped down by half a dozen engineers using cranes and heavy lifting equipment, each part repaired where necessary, shot blasted, painted and refitted, and then to see the finished article roll out, looking in pristine condition, is a magnificent sight.

Eden, my son number three, had a bad accident on his motorbike and lost the use of his right arm. He had just started working as an apprentice in our plumbing company.

It was devastating to think that such an accident could lose the use of an arm for life. He was only sixteen years old. He hit an oncoming car with his right shoulder and it severed the nerves in his arm. The doctor told me immediately that he would never use his arm again. I told him that it was pessimistic to make such a forecast at such an early stage, but he told me that this sort of injury was common with motorbike riders. I can only imagine what Eden went through. It must have been devastating for such a young person to have such terrible news. It was devastating to me also, but I assured him that I would support him as much as possible. After he had recovered he tried to carry on his plumbing work, but it was practically impossible to do plumbing with one arm. I took him into the office to train as an office administrator under the guidance of David, the accountant. He attended a college course on Business Studies. I admired the way he managed to cope with one arm and eventually, over the following years, he became an important and influential member of the company.

Our House

Jane and I thought that it was time we moved out of our small flat into a house. For several months we were floating around looking at properties. Some, she liked and I didn't. Some, I liked and she didn't. We must have looked at twenty houses. We decided to give it a rest and leave it until something we both liked caught our eyes. Then, one Sunday, we were just driving along when we saw a "For Sale" sign. The sign was prominent but we couldn't see the house. We drove on for a while, then decided to turn back to have a look, just out of curiosity. We turned in and drove very slowly up a tree-lined drive to a beautiful house.

We both looked at each other and said, "This is it."

We knocked on the door and an elderly, rather posh lady answered and looked us up and down with an air of snobbery.

"Can we look at your house, please? We think we would like to buy it."

She looked down her nose at us as if we were beggars. We were both very casually dressed in jeans and scruffy jumpers. She must have thought we were a couple of scruffs and I can't blame her for looking suspiciously at us. She said, after a little thought. "I will show you round the garden, but you can't come into the house without an appointment."

We walked past the fishpond and round to the back garden, through the orchard, and over the beautifully tended lawns. We said, "Yes, we are definitely interested. Could we please have a brochure?"

She gave us a brochure, shrugged her shoulders and we thanked her and drove away. We stopped at a lay-by. I said to Jane, "I think she thinks we're gypsies and can't afford it."

We looked at the brochure and Jane said, "She's right. We can't afford it!"

That night we studied the price, studied our finances and decided that it was really beyond our reach – but we just knew we had to have it.

I phoned Bob and he started the ball rolling early next morning. By midday, apart from the paperwork, it was confirmed. Bob worked fast. That evening we visited the house again. This time we were in our good clothes and, this time, the lady opened the door and greeted us with a big welcoming smile and a handshake.

Elsdale House was now our home.

I have moved into more houses than I can remember but I think that this is my last move.

Traitors

I have suffered several cases of gross disloyalty and dishonesty during my years in business, which were so distressing and upsetting to me and damaging to the company that I will list a few of the worst cases in this next chapter, in order to get them off my chest.

The first incident, as I mentioned in an earlier chapter, was when my lorry driver sold some of my rolls of belting to another dealer for cash. There were two more incidents of trusted employees claiming cash for fictitious petty cash receipts. All were sacked.

An old school friend of mine, and a friend of his, called at my home one day to tell me about a business idea they had thought of, and they wanted me to advise them on how to start up.

They wanted to rent a small café in the centre of town and use it as a café/snack bar and a base for a fleet of taxis. The idea sounded fine to me and, after a few long discussions, we agreed to have a three-way partnership. The two partners would run and drive their taxis, one of their wives would run the café, and I would help to set up the business and advise them on finance and the purchasing of cars and so on.

We called the company Zulu Taxis and Restaurant. The idea behind Zulu was to use African colours on the cars, similar to the ones I had admired during my African visit, and we also used an African influence for the café décor and on the menu.

Things went fine for a few months until one of the partners informed me, very discreetly, that the other partner and his wife were not booking in all the cash they were earning. After the usual bitter enquiries, arguments and sackings, the cars were disposed of and Jane offered to run the café for a while until it had paid off its debts and become profitable again. Once achieved, Zulu was eventually sold.

Back at the main company, everyone seemed to be working hard and the companies were prospering. I thought it time I tried to reward my people, who were working so conscientiously and getting seriously involved in their work. I wanted everyone to feel good about their jobs and to have an opportunity to develop within the company. I devised a profit-sharing bonus scheme from which all the responsible people had a percentage of the true profits. The basic reasoning behind this profit-sharing scheme was to encourage effort and reward loyalty. In most cases it was graciously accepted and encouraged responsibility and activity, but I became disillusioned since, in some people, it seemed to encourage cases of self-importance, dishonesty and treachery. I don't know whether it was because the bonuses made some people greedy, or because the rewards made them believe that they were better than they really were. From that day on I was continuously bombarded with requests for more in the form of higher wages, better company cars, and more benefits. Certain people seemed to think that they were the "star attraction" in the company and should be rewarded accordingly, and that their efforts should be acknowledged. One director even requested that his "exceptional efforts" should be written into the Company Board Minutes. These people thought that the company's successes were due to them alone. I personally think the bonus scheme created this situation and brought out the worst in certain individuals.

The UK Department of Trade and Industry was fiercely encouraging and advising smaller companies like ours to try to do business abroad and, as we became more and more involved in foreign dealings, I appointed agents for Ireland, Germany, continental Europe, Malta and North Africa. I was also keen to encourage exporting and importing, as the competition in the UK was getting fierce with new "cowboy" companies starting up in opposition to us.

My Engineering Manager, Michael, had told me that he and his wife were thinking of taking their holidays in South Africa as they had friends living there. He said that there was a possibility of business out there for our company, and asked if I would like him to promote our company whilst out there. This was just the sort of initiative I was trying to encourage. I was so pleased with his drive and ambition, I told him that I would fund his part of their holiday, if he took time to represent us whilst he was out there. Also, if any business resulted, I told him that he would be rewarded. On his arrival back he gave me a list of names and addresses of the companies he said he had approached.

Over the next few weeks he became very quiet and secretive and began acting oddly, almost as if he had something on his mind that was bothering him. On several occasions I walked into his office and he would suddenly put the phone down and turn red in the face. I thought something was strange, and then he told me about where he had been on certain days but these accounts were proven false. I suspected something was amiss.

My Canning Leisure man, Stephen, was a very good friend and confidante. I told him of my suspicions and he suggested I "tap" Michael's phone. This sounded like a great idea but it was illegal. Stephen said that he knew someone in BT and would ask for advice.

After many meetings with the BT officials and their legal people, they found a way round the dilemma. It was possible to direct all Michael's calls from his phone onto a twin receiving phone somewhere else, but it would mean fitting a special open speaker which would allow the calls to be listened to without picking up the additional handset. The chosen receiving phone was to be located in our toyshop in the middle of town. The problem was that I had to sit by the phone all day to listen to his calls and this was just not practical.

Stephen had a brainwave. He suggested moving the machinery into the attic above the boardroom, which was above Michael's office. He would also fit a tape recorder which would be activated by Michael picking up the receiver and putting it down again. It was an ingenious system which was easier for me as I didn't have to sit there for hours every day waiting for calls. All I had to do was to climb into the attic whenever it was convenient and listen to his recorded calls. We arranged to install the equipment one night when no one was around. It took eight hours of work to fit and test. We had to lead the wires from Michael's phone into the wall, up through the boardroom wall and into the attic. It was quite a messy job. We were to have a management meeting in the boardroom the following morning and there was a lot of cleaning up to do. Stephen was in the attic and I was sitting in Michael's office testing the phone. Suddenly, I heard an almighty crash.

Stephen had come through the ceiling.

I rushed upstairs to see his legs dangling down, through the ceiling. Plaster and dust was everywhere.

Panic! I didn't even ask him if he was OK. All I thought of was all the mess we had to clear up in just a few hours before the management meeting, which was to be held that day, and which, incidentally, Michael normally attended.

Stephen telephoned his wife who was asleep. He begged her to come to help us clean up. I telephoned a friendly builder and begged him to come over immediately and to bring his van with the necessary plasterboards and tools. It was about 7am when we were done and cleaned up, with just one hour to spare before people started arriving for work.

It had been all sweat and cursing, but we managed to get away with it just in time. I opened all the windows to clear the smell of plaster and sweat. Jane had brought me a change of clothes and calmly I sat at my desk when everyone arrived for the meeting. No one noticed a thing, but I was knackered.

The phone worked perfectly and all his calls were recorded.

Apparently, Michael had spent his time in South Africa setting up a business to import a special type of material to make firestone bricks for furnaces. The recordings caught him making arrangements for shipping, transportation and to build a factory in Dewsbury to process the raw material. We heard discussions with his lawyer, his bank and his dealings with the estate agent regarding his new factory. We heard everything. We even heard him talking to, and arranging to meet, his mistress during his lunch breaks.

We arranged a special management meeting and my solicitor drafted out a series of questions for me to ask him in order for him to incriminate himself and to provoke a confession from him.

I firstly had to ask everyone if they had any new ideas for the company to invest into. I went round all the people at the meeting in turn; they all said "no." Michael was the last one to be asked. When he said "no" I asked him if he had any knowledge of the firestone brick industry and did he think it would be worth looking into. His answer was negative. I went on to ask him if he knew of a certain man and mentioned his contact's name. He went blank. I then asked him if he had been in contact with this man. He went a bit white. I mentioned certain dates and certain people's names, and he began to shrink lower into his chair. I then said, "Michael, it has come to my knowledge that you think I am a bloody idiot and when you told Mr. so and so this, you also said that I was a 'daft twit.'

By this time Michael had nearly shrunk under the table. I then passed it on to Bob who read out the accusation and told him to leave the company immediately and to leave behind the company car, papers and briefcase.

I often think about it and one day perhaps I will write it as a TV drama.

Michael's briefcase was full of evidence but we didn't take it any further. He was a very experienced and intelligent man with a great future ahead of him, but he just became greedy. He could have resigned and set up a business on his own without any problems, but he decided to try to do it at the cost of my company. It was such a shame.

200

A few years after this incident, I used a similar method to catch out my Works Manager who had been regularly taking advantage of me.

Bobby was taken on as a general labourer. It was shortly after he had started his employment with us that I spotted his exceptional interest and enthusiasm. I kept my eye on him and thought that he had a little more about him than to carry on as a labourer. He was always asking questions and trying to reorganise to do things more quickly and efficiently. After a while he was promoted to foreman and, shortly afterwards, he became in charge of stock. This job also entailed ordering and arranging deliveries.

Things went fine for a couple of years. He seemed to create more responsibilities for himself and eventually the Works Manager left and he took over his position.

I had spotted him and I promoted him. Perhaps he performed so well for me that I looked at him through rose-coloured spectacles, but I didn't look deeply enough into his character. My problem is that I cannot judge people well and am easily "taken in" by people's thanks and flattery, which he gave so freely.

The usual things started to happen. He put the telephone down when I walked into his office and lied about his whereabouts. Word came back to me that the lorry driver had asked questions about why he was delivering other people's equipment on instructions from Bobby. I sensed that something was happening and sought the help of a private detective. They put a "tap" on his phone, which was a much simpler modern surveillance device than the one I had used before. His telephone was simply wired to a tape recorder that was placed in a drawer in my desk.

Bobby was involved in another business and he and his partner were delivering parts and equipment all over the country using my company vehicles, my time and my fuel. They were hiring cranes and charging them to me. They were buying steel structures and welding equipment and supplies, and then charging them to me. He became really greedy and over-confident when he started ordering things for my company which included a commission for him.

A meeting was arranged between the private detective and Bobby. He confessed and was sacked. Later, the cheeky devil even tried to sue us for unfair dismissal!

If I had charged him for the amount of time wasted by me and the detectives it would have cost him thousands but, once again, I was too soft. I felt like flattening him for abusing my trust in him, but the detectives told me that I would have been in serious trouble if ever I had even touched him. It's certainly a crooks' world.

Another very disturbing and costly case was when two of my most trusted employees left to set up in business on their own in direct competition; but before doing so, one of them actually took with them hundreds of copies of papers from our files. My accountant informed me the next day that our copying machine had registered that hundreds of copies had been made during the night after they had left. The first and easiest thing they did was to go to all my best contacts and offer more money for belting. After that, it became an auction of ever-increasing prices. That was the end of several beautiful contracts. Over the following few years we had a continuous battle with them and, eventually, their company finished.

The next one to get off my chest involved two more of my trusted employees. It involved my Works Manager and my Engineering Salesman.

An unsigned letter had been handed in addressed to the Board. It said that these two people were "on the fiddle" and were doing business privately. They were both sacked after the usual depressing enquiries. Immediately afterwards, they both started up in the same type of business in direct opposition to us.

It must be that this type of business that attracts these sorts of people. It is so easy to start up, buying and selling second-hand bargains and, even though many people have tried to copy, not many of them seem to be able to do it properly. Many have failed and many have gone bankrupt, and some just seem to mess about earning a bit here and a bit there. All they succeed in doing is to make life more difficult for my company, and it creates a bad image of our industry. Many people have set up as conveyor belting dealers, thinking that it is easy money, but not many survive. Some work from the back of a van, many have ceased trading and some are going bankrupt even today. It's easy to make a quick buck but to survive in any industry takes guts, determination, integrity and honesty. The second-hand conveyor belting business is a "wheeler-dealer" type business, likened to a scrap-metal merchant, or a second-hand car dealer. One doesn't have to be the Brain of Britain to trade and make a few bob, but to do it properly takes a little more and the people who are prepared do it properly can become successful.

Recession 1980

This was real-life drama, not a storybook or a TV programme. The details of how the recession of 1980 affected me, my business and everyone involved in my business has not been altered or dramatised in any way.

The next few years were a learning curve for all companies on how to survive. For me, it was an education on how I, and other people, change when faced with extreme difficulty.

George Godley had warned me many years earlier about complacency. After so many years of relatively good trading and good luck, his "warning bells" began to sound. The recession affected not only the running of my "empire" but, for many years afterwards, also my confidence and my health. Most of all, it made me realise that being in business wasn't always about fun and rewards. There is another side to business!

In the year ending August 1981, we suffered a loss. Sales were down and our charts were showing a gradual downward trend. The whole country was in a recession.

Companies all over the country were closing down. There was a special daily item on television giving lists of names of companies that had closed down. Personally I think this only created despondency. It didn't help anyone as it only made people fear the worst. They became more negative and frightened that their world was coming to an end. Coalmines, steel works and the bigger industries were also either slowing down or closing down.

My company was slowing down but it was still trading. In reality, it was only surviving because other companies were trying to conserve and, being short of cash, they sought cheaper spare parts to keep their equipment working. The main part of our business was directly involved in wheeling and dealing in redundant plant and cheap second-hand belting. Many companies, which in the past had only bought new, were now also trying to conserve and so, if they had to buy spare parts, they looked for good deals and reverted to searching for good, second-hand, refurbished spare parts and equipment. Because of the many closures, there were more second-hand plant and systems becoming available to us. But it was becoming a balancing act: we had to create funds firstly by selling before we could speculate in buying; but we had to buy before we could sell. The companies we were selling to, were hard up and tried to hang on to their money as long as they possibly could. This in turn made us short of cash and thus made it hard for us to take advantage of buying opportunities. It was a vicious circle.

Although our sales levels were down, we were still able to steal a good section of the trade because of our type of stock and our stock buying policy.

Although the recession was spreading generally throughout the country, we were fortunately in the right place, at the right time, regarding the type of work we did and the types of products we traded in. This helped us to stay afloat during this depressing period, and allowed us to keep slightly ahead of our competitors and many other types of businesses that were struggling to survive. The closing down of giant companies like the Corby and Scunthorpe steel works was tragic but, for us, it was indirectly helping us to keep afloat. We were in the salvaging business and were able to make good use of the various items that these works were disposing of. I suppose we could have been described as "vultures" picking off the remains of the dead.

There were little or no orders for new equipment as capital spending was at an all-time low. The few orders we got for new equipment were for little or no profit. Most engineering companies were working for nothing just to keep trading.

Our building company was also struggling as building work, especially council work, had dried up. Our scrapyard was standing still. There was very little demand for scrap metal and therefore little or no reason to buy scrap.

Even though we were fortunate enough to be in the second-hand trade, we were suffering generally. We had to make rash survival plans, which involved cutbacks and redundancies. The solution sounded pretty ruthless, but the end result was survival. It was based upon taking certain courses of action at the end of each month or each quarter, based on savings, by introducing short-time working, reducing our workforce, cutting back expenses, and mothballing some buildings and divisions. It affected everyone from the shop floor up to top management. I remember having one of our crash management meetings when I told everyone that, by the end of the following twelve months, if the economic climate didn't improve, there might only be myself and a belt-cutter left. I would be working seven days a week as I normally did, but we would still be in business. They laughed, but never a truer word was said!

We started another trading year in September with several carefully worked-out cutback schemes, such as shorter working hours, and we made several hard, cost cutting decisions. But things didn't improve.

During December, I called another crash meeting. I said that we had to cut back twenty-five per cent of all staff and we also had to close the doors of some of the buildings in order to save money. It was a very heated meeting and no one wanted to accept my plans. The managers wanted to save their own people, but also feared that their own jobs might be at risk. We made harsh decisions to be put into practice at the start of work after the Christmas/New Year break. After an overheated and argumentative meeting each manager agreed who should go and how we should cut back on the expenses incurred by trying to keep some of the factories and workshops open. We looked at transport and even more delicate things like expenses, allowances and salaries. All salaried staff had an immediate reduction, even the three directors, including myself.

I remember that particular Christmas and New Year as a nightmare. We had already arranged a bash at my home and all our employees were invited, including several of the ones who were to be made redundant in two weeks' time, but didn't know it. Everyone got well and truly drunk. I will never forget the guilt I felt when they joined hands and drunkenly sang, "For he's a jolly good fellow," knowing that some of them were going to be laid off.

I spent hours and hours writing my words on how to tell each person. It was one of the most miserable things I have ever had to do. I had a list of the people who had been chosen by their managers and I had a list of managers who were also to be made redundant, and they had no idea. They had thought that they were safe.

The day dawned after a sleepless night. I asked my Business Consultant, Rex, to sit beside me throughout the proceedings. He was a pretty hard man and I needed someone like him to be by my side to support me: he might be able to control the situation if it got bitter. The Engineering Manager was also asked to sit with us.

One by one they were called in and given the bad news. Three engineering men, four general yard workers, two office staff, an office sales person, two site workers, a works foreman, and the two Canning Leisure people were made redundant.

There were tears, sour looks and heated disagreements, all covered up with a wild promise that when things got better, I would try to take them on again.

When that was all done, I told the Engineering Manager that he too would have to go and finally I told my Business Consultant that I couldn't afford his services any longer. I had a very careful speech written out to cover his redundancy and his reaction was shock and disbelief.

I noted that day and will remember it always. I kept thinking, "How could I do this to people?" That day, I didn't want to be me. I didn't want to be Frank Canning any more. I would have willingly changed places with any of the people I was making redundant. The total responsibility was on my shoulders; I had to do this dreadful thing. This is the other, dark side to business!

I went home to recover. I just drove away and left everything. I didn't even tell anyone where I was going. I just went home and wept, and finished up screaming like a madman. It's a good job my house didn't have any neighbours.

My nerves were completely wrecked. I took three Valium tablets and I remember Jane kept trying to wake me up when she came in from work. I just couldn't come round.

I spent the next day planning my strategy to get through my business life with the remaining people I still employed.

Over the next couple of years there were more redundancies, and some of our staff left to set up their own businesses in direct competition against us. There was reorganisation after reorganisation. The scrapyard was wound up. The plumbing company was sold. It was all very stressful. Sales were up one month and down the next. Enquiries were either two or three together or none at all. Things were often way above my head. The accounts showed a crazy mixture of refunds from losses of other companies, which only accountants understood. The main company was funding the other divisions and companies, and it was also guaranteeing their overdrafts. There were readjustments of tax allowances. The holding company was using group losses to reduce its tax bill and was also guaranteeing their debts. It was a quagmire of accounts and manipulations. My accountant, David, was at his wits' end. Thank goodness he was experienced enough to supervise all this but his health was also waning.

We were tested up to the limit but I was determined to survive at all costs. If we crashed then that would be the end of my business and the end of me. I was determined that I would never go back to the pit.

It was like a roller coaster, up and down, headache after headache. We seemed to survive from one day to the next.

After my head telephone salesman left I took over the sales desk and realised that most customers had not been contacted since they last placed an order. In the past, the sales staff had seemed to simply administer orders as they came in, but now it was a time to actually try to get orders. With the remaining staff, we set about phoning every customer systematically. We mailed our stock lists and contacted every customer methodically.

The engineering division was relying solely on renovating second-hand equipment, as orders for new fabrication work were nil. The building company was at an all-time low and was struggling to find work.

Our son was born on October 10, 1983. His name, Christopher, was not in recognition of any film star or pop idol, but was for no other reason than it was instantly thought up by my wife, Jane. We were both convinced that he was going to be a girl and she was going to be named Katie.

When Christopher was born he was a little crumpled-up because of his position in the womb. On his arrival, the nurse picked him up, wrapped him in towel and, before she took him away to be cleaned up, she asked his name. Jane said, "Katie."

The nurse said, "But that's a girl's name." She handed him back to Jane. She cuddled him and said, "Hello, Katie."

"Jane, it's a boy," I said as I opened the towel to show her his manhood. "There, he's a boy."

At this point the nurse wrapped him up again and was about to take him away when she asked once again what his name was. Jane said the first name that came into her head – Christopher.

She couldn't have chosen a more perfect name. He is such a gentle, kind and considerate person that his name suits him perfectly.

Films

Having always been a film fanatic and, in particular, enjoyed science fiction films, I think everyone at work was fed up with me raving on about the latest "Superman" film. I must have sounded a bit childish at times when babbling on about them. I often caught their eyes rolling when Superman was mentioned. I've been his fan ever since I drew the picture of him at school and I used to read the *Superman* comics.

I was working late at the office one evening. I was on my own. The phone rang.

"Good evening," said a very posh voice. "My name is Brian Auckland Snow. I am the Art Director of the new film *Superman III.*"

I coughed and spluttered, trying not to laugh. What immediately came to my mind was a very popular TV programme in which Noel Edmunds set people up with silly schemes and I thought it might be something like that, or something the office people had planned to try to set me up. I thought I would go along with it.

"Yes, what can I do for you?"

He explained that they were designing a scrapyard, which was to be constructed in Pinewood Film Studios, in which Superman fights the "baddies." He said that our company had been recommended to possibly help, as we were involved in conveyors. It sounded hilarious. I could hardly control my giggling. He asked if we could visit the studios to discuss the job, and could I phone his secretary in the morning to make the necessary arrangements?

I was still giggling when I arrived home. I burst through the door with my arms pointing forward and said, "Superman, ha ha!"

Jane just looked at me with a wry look on her face. She must have thought I was drunk. After I explained about the call she said it must be the people at work who were trying to wind me up.

Next day I arrived a bit late, expecting everyone to be looking through the window and laughing. I entered the room and shouted, "Superman." No one laughed. Someone muttered, "Dream on!" Everyone looked at each other with glazed looks on their faces and carried on working.

I told them what had happened and they said it must have been a genuine enquiry.

My phone call to Pinewood confirmed it. My legs were shaking with excitement. I made an appointment to visit them the very next day.

I travelled to Pinewood with my son Andrew, who was also a film fanatic. We met Brian Auckland Snow and Alan Booth, the Construction Manager, who was in charge of building the sets. We discussed the job and they gave us drawings of the layout of the set, scenes and requirements. They then kindly gave us a guided tour of the studios and the construction workshops.

It was like a dream for two film fans like us. We had a glorious day. The *Superman* sets were magnificent. They had created a massive Science Fiction set, which consisted of a computer that stood as high as a house, with gigantic tubes, lights and spring-like coils that looked like electrical conductors. This was all built inside a massive cave in the side of a replica of the Grand Canyon in the USA. All was constructed in a studio called the 007 studio, which was as big as a football field. It was magical. It all looked so real and it was hard to believe that the solid mountain rocks were really made out of plaster and plastic.

No expense is spared in the making of film sets.

My engineers detailed the job and quoted a price for them to hire our equipment at a weekly rate. The price was also inclusive of four of our men to deliver it to Pinewood Studios, erect it on the set and to be there on hand to run the equipment during filming. Our scene was a full-size scrapyard for crushing cars. The yard was supposed to be in America and for this they had imported hundreds of scrap American cars from the States to make the scene realistic.

We took full advantage of this wonderful opportunity, and found any sort of reason for someone from the company to visit the set to watch the filming over the next few months.

One day I visited the set with Jane. We were walking towards the scrapyard and we bumped into Superman himself, Christopher Reeve, dressed in his blue and red Superman outfit.

He had just finished filming and was walking away from the set towards his caravan. As we passed him Jane said, "Hello."
He smiled and said, "Hi."

I could have kicked myself afterwards for not stopping him and shaking his hand, as he seemed such a pleasant man.

This film was our introduction to the world of movie-making.

Because of the success of the film, and the success of our work, we became involved in many more film jobs, including *Indiana Jones and the Temple of Doom, Alien 3, Who Framed Roger Rabbit?, 101 Dalmatians, James Bond – Die Another Day, and Charlie and the Chocolate Factory*, to name but a few. I also introduced us into becoming involved in similar television work.

I was once visiting the *Roger Rabbit* set and was sitting on a box watching the filming when a little fat man sat beside me and said, "Phew! How many more times are they gonna do it?" I turned round and looked at him and saw it was Bob Hoskins. He was such a friendly chap, and told me what they were trying to do and that they had filmed it six times that day already. We quite often bumped into famous stars.

Roller conveyor carrying aliens. Filmed at
Pinewood Studios © Twentieth Century Fox.

Above Left to Right
Stormbreaker computer's on conveyor

One day I was walking round a set with my two grandchildren. They were filming *Indiana Jones and the Last Crusade* with Sean Connery and Harrison Ford.

They were high up on some scaffolding on the set where they had created the inside of a cave, in which they were filming a scene looking down into a crack in the rocks into which Indiana had fallen. Suddenly Stephen Spielberg himself looked down at me and waved. I was startled and my witty granddaughter jokingly said, "I think you will be in his next film, Granddad!"

Spielberg must have thought I was someone he knew. Later on, during a break, Sean Connery gave my grandson his autograph.

The film *Alien 3* was about a distant planet on which they were mining for a precious metal. We supplied a conveyor for this planet, which was built in the studios at Elstree. During the manufacturing stages of the conveyor the local newspaper got to hear about it and interviewed us. The report jokingly said: "During the manufacturing of the conveyor, all the doors and windows in Canning's factory were sealed and the roof and roof beams were thoroughly inspected every morning just in case there were aliens lurking. The manager told us that all the engineers were equipped with stun guns!"

Andrew spent months working on the *Charlie and the Chocolate Factory* set, where he supplied and supervised the running of all the conveyor systems for the chocolate factory.

Film and TV work have long played an important part in our business activities. We always find it so fascinating and take every opportunity to visit the studios to see the magnificent sets and, of course, hopefully "bump into" film stars!

Surviving the Recession

To put the early Eighties into a nutshell, we were suffering from the effects of the recession, but still in business and surviving. Shortages of staff, a general lull in trade, and the fact that all the surviving companies were fighting to get the same jobs made the following few years hectic and testing. We were trying to be more effective but, at the same time, trying to do three jobs at once. The competition was not helping as they were 'buying' work. In other words, surviving companies did work for little or no profit in order to stay alive.

One month we were riding high and the next month it was hell awaiting the next order, but even after such a struggle we still made a little profit.

Our continental agent, Charles, who was located in Amsterdam, introduced us to several new continental companies who supplied us with lifesaving stocks at good prices, which helped us to keep afloat. Charles's main activity was to find and buy. During the next few years he created buying opportunities in Italy, Germany and Holland, and it was probably due to our good foreign purchases that we were able to keep ahead of the game in second-hand belting. The manufacturers of new belting were trying to grab every opportunity in the UK. Cost prices were so high that there wasn't much point in trying to market new belting here at home.

Eden and the office sales lady were handling sales whilst I was away travelling abroad. George was looking after the works. Tony was in charge of engineering. David was trying to keep abreast of admin and accounts. All were stretched to the limit.

I was in Holland, with Charles, negotiating buying a large consignment of conveyor belts, when the person we were dealing with received a telephone call. He gave me the phone.

"Your Dad has died."

My receptionist couldn't wait to tell me the bad news and it couldn't have arrived at a more inopportune moment. I wasn't sure how I was supposed to react, but I had to leave Charles to finish off the negotiations himself while I went into the other room to break down. Luckily, Charles was an excellent negotiator and an excellent deal was done.

When I arrived back home the next day, I was met with more bad news. Tony had handed in his notice. I think he couldn't take the pressure of trying to find work and manage the engineering division at the same time. I asked Andrew and the Works Manager, Karl, to consider trying to manage the engineering department between them and they seemed very enthusiastic about the challenge. I tried to give them some encouragement but, by explaining to them that times were hard, and it would take a miracle to survive, it wasn't really the thing they wanted to hear.

My health started to go downhill. I became depressed and considered selling the business. I finally came to the conclusion that trying to run a business like mine, and trying to survive from one week to the next, was an endless battle of misery. It had always been my motivation that had driven the business along, but I felt for the first time in my life that my motivational skills were gone. I felt trapped. I talked to my solicitor and remember him jokingly saying to his secretary that Frank was having his period pains again. I consulted my accountants but they advised me to rethink as, in that climate, it would have been foolish to think that there was a buyer out there waiting to take on my problems when everyone else in the country was trying to survive also.

We reached Christmas 1986. I was trying to keep up appearances in order to encourage enthusiasm, even though it was tough going. We decided to have a company "do" to try to boost morale, and booked the Masonic Hall for possibly a hundred people including all employees and spouses. I put the organising of this party into the hands of my two office ladies. Unfortunately, they were little troublemakers. As if we didn't have enough to cope with, they decided to try to make the party a flop. I only realised then just how

216

mischievous and evil people can be during times of stress and struggle. As I have always said, when things are good, people are good, but when things are bad, then the worst comes out, probably because normal people cannot cope with these sorts of pressures.

The hall had been booked, plus a disco and meals for a hundred.

There was a lot of funny gossip about for the following few weeks and I couldn't make out what it was all about until someone told me privately that no one wanted to go to the "do" and that they didn't want to tell me in case it upset me. I *was* very upset as everyone had always enjoyed the company bashes and we were specifically doing it that year to try to boost morale. I was going crazy with worry. I couldn't believe that no one wanted to go. I started asking questions and found out that the two office ladies had, for some silly reason, told everyone that there was to be a brass band and that only the builders were invited. I questioned the ladies and they told me that it was only a joke, but I told them that if they knew that everyone had decided not to go, then why hadn't they tried to sort it out? I was very angry with them and told them to do so immediately and that I would never trust them again. Both of them finished up crying. I don't believe it was a joke, as they would not have let it go so far. I honestly believe they were up to no good; they had decided that their days might be numbered and conjured up this little trick.

The party went fine and almost everyone attended. Everyone commented that they really enjoyed themselves. But the little trick had ruined my Christmas break. On the first day after the holiday, I asked both the office ladies to come into my office and asked them what it was all about. They tried to tell me it was all a joke and tried to cover it up with sweet innocence. I gave them a verbal warning and there were more tears. I will never understand why they did such a crazy thing. I have my suspicions but cannot declare them. A short time later, one of them left to join the opposition. At the next crash meeting the other one was made redundant. I was unable to communicate properly as my wooden tongue was at its worst. Valium and antidepressant tablets were put to full use.

It was the end of another year. Although we were still trading and still making a small profit, I was living on my nerves. I felt trapped in a company that I was finding impossible to run and I didn't have the strength to try to carry on. I was also fighting competition from the people whom I had trained. I wanted to get out but my advisors had told me that the company was impossible to sell in the present economic climate. My home was guaranteeing the overdraft and during all this I was trying to handle the sales and purchases. I felt as though I was on my own. It was crazy. My doctor told me that I must have a break otherwise I would crack up. Jane booked a holiday to the flat in Malta and I think it saved my life.

The Dream

Every time we went to the flat it usually took me two or three days to unwind and come back down to earth. Then, I was at peace with myself and able to relax. However, this particular time it seemed slightly different.

On our previous visit to Malta we had taken Dad with us. This was shortly before he died. On arriving this particular time we couldn't get him off our minds. We were even jokingly remembering him spreading out his tablets across the table in the order they had to be taken: breakfast, lunch, dinner and bedtime. We even found the old sunhat he wore whilst he was there. We were forever quoting him and his idiosyncrasies.

We were on about our fourth day when I told Jane that I kept thinking about Dad and she said she had felt the same. She also said that she kept thinking about him sitting in his favourite chair looking out to sea. I couldn't settle down and I couldn't seem to come back down to earth, as I normally did, after a few days. I thought it must be because of all the troubles we had been through with the business.

That night I had a dream.

This is the content of the dream.

A telephone rang. I picked it up and a voice said, "Hello lad, it's me, Dad."

"You can't be my Dad because he is dead," I said.

"I will prove it to you that I am your Dad," he said.

"Jane had something wrong with her leg when she was very young, and it's a secret. How would I know that if I wasn't your Dad?"

He then paused.

"Put me on to Jane," he said.

I gave the phone to Jane. She spoke to him, then gave the phone back to me and said, "It's definitely your Dad. Speak to him."

"If it is you, where is Mam?"

"Don't worry, everything is taken care of. She has been watching over you but she has gone into transition," he answered.

"Are you on your own?"

"I'm fine. If I wanted her to come back she would."

Do you want her to?" I asked.

"No, she's fine where she is. Everything is fine. I'll look after you now. Look after Jane and everything will be fine."

When I woke up I remembered every detail of the dream just as if it had really happened in true life. I even wrote it down in my diary.

I was very thoughtful that day, thinking about the dream. I couldn't get it off my mind.

That evening we went out for a meal at a restaurant. During the meal Jane asked me why I had been so thoughtful during the day. I said to her, "Did you have something wrong with your leg when you were very young?"

She was very surprised and said, "How do you know that? No one except my mother knows. How do you know? I haven't ever told anyone."

I told her about my dream. We were both totally amazed. It was impossible for anyone to know about her leg, but Dad had told me in a dream. We talked about it for the rest of the holiday and, from that day on, neither of us felt the presence of Dad in the flat as we had done before. The dream convinced me that there is something else that we don't understand and I accepted it as proof that Mam or Dad were watching over me.

Recovery

It might have been fate, or it might have been that I just had a good rest and had been given a confidence boost after the dream, but things did slowly and surely start to improve. I felt as though my spirits had been lifted.

As I have said before, the key to my business was the buying. I have had many disputes with my financial advisors and accountants about stock levels, but I have always pointed out to them that our business is different to most others. We were dependent on our stocks on hand.

The type of trade we were in works like this – quarries, in particular, work on a very tight budget. Their stock is the materials they produce, whether it is crushed stone or sand and gravel, or concrete. Their stockpiles of finished materials are there to be sold and all their efforts go into selling it. The machinery that produces this material is less important as they know quite well that they only have to pick up the phone and all the conveyor belting and roller dealers will come running. There are many companies "just around the corner," waiting for instructions to serve the masters. The one who wins the order is the one who can offer the product "off-the-shelf" with "immediate delivery" and, of course, the best price! Thus stock levels are very important. When we have good stock levels we get the orders. Like most other companies, our building and engineering divisions work differently and carry very little stocks. They only buy whatever is required for any particular contract. The main company business, which is involved in this demand-and-supply system, has to carry vast stocks, and the stocks have to include many thousands of different types, in order to supply everyone's individual requirements.

Most quarry companies' finances are tied up in their stocks of saleable materials, not in stocks of spares. When one if their conveyors or a piece of equipment is about to break down, or is in need of a new belt or roller or spare part, the engineer will phone a particular company which they think could give them the best deal, meaning off-the-shelf, immediate delivery and an instant on-site fitting service. The company they phone would have to give the engineer an immediate assurance, whilst on the phone, that they can supply to his terms in order to get the order. If the answer is, "No – I haven't got it in stock, but I can get it for you soon," then the order is lost; the engineer will phone someone else.

It is so simple: If you've got it, you can sell it.

Our success has always been in carrying huge stocks of *everything*. The key is to try to finance these vast stocks, but the art is to locate these items, and buy them at the right price.

After the years of struggle we were finally finding a little stability, but this had only come about by making the hard and sometimes cruel decisions. We were thankful that we were still around when a wonderful opportunity came along.

Charles had been following up the possibilities of business opportunities in Eastern Germany due to the opening-up of trade after the fall of the Iron Curtain.

The doors had been opened and the free countries of the West were flooding in to have their pick of business with the now ex-communist states. Charles was in touch with a large industrial machinery distribution depot in Bankenburg, near Dresden, East Germany. It was a major storehouse for the whole of the Eastern Bloc. Charles was able to speak German, and had been told that vast stocks had been released for sale in exchange for Western currency.

The journey from Frankfurt to Dresden took about twelve hours. It was pretty awful. The roads were OK until we entered the Eastern Bloc; then they became cart tracks. We were both very weary when we eventually arrived and booked into a hotel. The only way I can describe this hotel is something like a pre-war prison. The beds in the hotel looked and felt as though they had been salvaged from a dungeon. They were bunk beds, which were fastened to a wall by means of hinges and were lowered down to be slept on. There was no en suite bath or toilet; everyone used a community bathroom at the end of each corridor. The food must have also been created from a prison menu. Still, we were not on holiday and we made the best of it. Next day we were picked up by the officials from the depot. My image of workers behind the Iron Curtain materialised. They all wore the same sort of clothing: dark blue pinstripe suits, which looked as though they were made from serge. They were all pale and stern-looking and thin. They took us into their office, which was very sparse: a desk, wooden chairs and only oilcloth to cover the floor. We were the first buyers to arrive there.

The men talked to Charles, who could converse with them in German. It all seemed very tense, as if they were frightened to speak freely, and their serious faces were showing signs of stress. After the initial, very formal introductions, Charles turned to me and said that they were only used to strict formalities, and it seemed that they were always under some sort of observation, and that was the reason they appeared so edgy. I told Charles to try to put them at ease as we wouldn't get very far if they were too frightened to speak to us. Charles was a very witty person and a man of the world, and it wasn't long before he started talking to them about the Reeperbahn, which is the red light district of Hamburg. As he was talking to them he kept turning round and explaining everything to me in an animated way, which made me laugh, and then he repeated the joke to them and it started them off laughing too. After a few more dirty jokes, we were in stitches and everything became more relaxed. They were asking him all sorts of questions about life in a free country. They then pulled a bottle of vodka out of a hiding place behind a wooden panel in the wall. With glasses all round they became our friends and, with invites to the Reeperbahn and an invitation to see the sights of London and to see the Queen, they were at our mercy.

They now welcomed us with open arms. They not only wanted to sell everything to us, they also wanted us to supply them with things. There were shortages of everything, and Western clothes, jeans, shoes and chocolate – things that we took for granted – were in great demand. They wanted anything and everything, and Charles took lists of what they wanted and promised to deliver them. I don't know what became of this but, knowing Charles, I think he probably followed it up later. I remember, later that day on our way back to the hotel, I noticed quite a few vans with West German number plates parked up at the side of the road, selling things like jeans and shoes to crowds of excited people.

Their stockyard was like a city. At one time there had been over a thousand people working there, but now it was handled by just a few people who were employed solely to dispose of everything in exchange for foreign currency, which they desperately needed.

Everything imaginable was available for us to buy but we were only interested in the conveyor belting. The stocks were unbelievable. I have never seen such an amount of stock. There were hundreds of rolls of belts of every width and type and description. It was like an Aladdin's cave. After we had picked off all the types and sizes which we were desperate for, and that we could possibly afford, I became so greedy that we went round the stocks again, and picked out quite a lot more than we could possibly afford, thinking that it was a one-off opportunity, I was quite prepared to put my house up as guarantee once again in order to purchase it all. There was so much for sale but I think we only bought a quarter of it. Charles heard later that the rest of it went to other countries like the USA and South Africa. We also agreed a pretty good buying price as they had no idea of present free country values.

I don't think the Worksop people will ever forget the sight of twenty-five large foreign lorries lined up on the main road to our works waiting to be unloaded.

After it had all been unloaded into our yard, I remember looking through my office window and thinking, "Thank you!"

Over the next couple of years other beautiful buying opportunities came along.

There had been a terrible storm in Northern Spain. A Bilbao factory that manufactured conveyor belting had been flooded. The news I received was that the factory had been under twelve feet of water, which completely covered the stock of conveyor belting and, after the water had subsided, the stock was waterlogged and the insurance had paid up. The belts were to be got rid of as "damaged stock." They were quite pleased that some "silly" people like us were prepared to buy them. We had seen this problem before, and knew that it was only the outside edges of the belts which were damp. We also knew that the inside reinforcing was made of nylon EP plies and they were water-resistant. It was just a matter of slicing off the damp edges and we had perfectly good reusable belts for sale.

These deals seemed to be a turning point. It was a great "pick me up" financially, emotionally, and mentally. Things slowly started to recover over the following year.

My Malta agent, Alex, telephoned me to say that he had a firm enquiry from Libya. Although the UK had put an embargo on trading with Libya at the time, the Maltese people were free to work there and do business with them.

The enquiry was for two giant mobile stone-crushers/screeners. We located two in Northern Ireland. These massive machines weighed about twenty tonnes each. These machines are put into use at the rock face of a stone quarry. Large lumps of stone are placed into the crusher and are smashed into smaller lumps, which are then separated by vibrating screens and stockpiled into various piles of stone, all in one operation.

Alex brought the Libyans over to examine them. We needed this sale very badly; so it was all hands on deck to try to secure an order. There were six of us involved in this deal: two Libyans, Alex and his father, my engineer and myself. We decided to hire a private plane to fly us over to Ireland quickly and efficiently. We also wanted to try to impress the Libyans with a personal luxury flight.

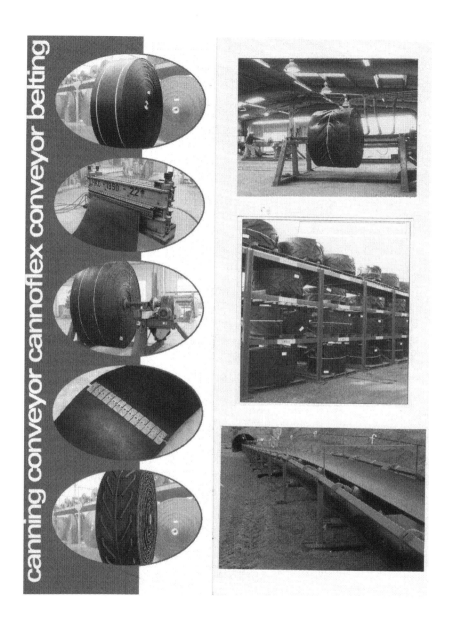

canning conveyor cannoflex conveyor belting

After a long, tiring day travelling from one end of Ireland to the other, the Libyans were happy with what they had seen and said that they wanted to buy them. We set off back to the airport. Then, true to Arab tradition, the bartering began.

Every time they spoke they seemed to have another reason to lower the price. They pointed out the dirty condition, the rust, the worn tyres, a missing bolt, the dilapidated engine. Anything they could think of was thrown at us. I was thankful that Alex and his dad were with us as they were used to bartering with the Arabs and they seemed to be able to do it naturally. I'm sure we would have lost out if we hadn't had them on our side. The price went from £30,000 each to £28,000 each, then to £26,000 then £25,000, then up again and then down and then up. It was so exhausting listening to them! We finally agreed on £25,000 and then, suddenly, for no reason, it went down to £20,000. By then, I was thinking the worst. I was frustrated, but the Arabs seemed to continue bartering non-stop as if it was the only proper and natural thing to do.

We were journeying back to look at the machines once again. We decided to stop at a café to eat. We were sitting at a table outside the café trying to decide what to order. The Libyans were still haggling over the price. Suddenly, a siren sounded and a couple of Army vehicles pulled up immediately in front of us, and proceeded to put up a roadblock.

This, I have learned since, was standard procedure during the Irish Troubles to do "spot searches." Four armed soldiers jumped out of their vehicles with machine guns pointing all over the place.

The Libyans, who have naturally brown faces, suddenly turned white. They were shaking with fear. They thought they were about to be shot. One of them grabbed my arm and stuttered out some words in English. I was amazed that suddenly he could speak English.

Small firm lands a giant contract

R...D bargaining and red-carpet treatment have helped a small Worksop firm to land a £25,000 order from Libya.

The Canning Conveyor Co., of Sandy Lane, who buy and renovate industrial equipment, are also hoping to land more orders — worth £250,000 — from the Middle East.

The contract is for two giant stone-crushing machines, each weighing 25 tons, which will be driven across Europe to Libya.

Canning's 38-year-old managing director Mr. Frank Canning set up the deal in Malta in the summer when he was asked by a Libyan delegation to find the machinery they needed.

"We brought them to England and the insisted on going to Belfast to see the machinery we'd bought for them. We were bargaining with the Libyans over lunch in the centre of Belfast when they saw the military vehicles and it dawned on them where they were.

"They seemed to be quite apprehensive about their safety and the deal was settled very quickly." said Mr. Canning.

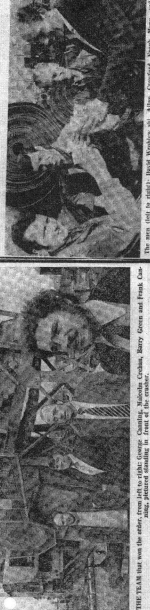

THE TEAM that won the order, from left to right: George Canning, Malcolm Crehan, Barry Green and Frank Canning, pictured standing in front of the crusher.

Tiny firm gets £20,000 order

The men (left to right): David Wroblewski, Allan Crawford, Frank Mann and George Canning.

By a staff reporter

TINY Worksop company with big ideas — and only four workmen — have landed a plum £20,000 contract.

Tea breaks are out for foreman Mr. David Wroblewski, of St. Cuthbert Street, Worksop, plater Mr. Frank Mann, of Clinton Road, Orchall, Retford, and welders Mr. Alan Crawford, of Cavendish Road, Worksop and Mr. Alan Canning, of Market Square, Retford.

Home life, too, is taking a knock as the men work ten hours a day.

"We are having to pull out all the stops but we've a great team and we'll get the job done in time.

To speed-up production, break-ups have been abolished ... the men are at their cuppas from a vending machine and ... white they work — and meantime, Mr. Mason and director Mr. Frank Canning are desperately seeking more platers and labourers who have to posses one key quality; a capacity for hard work.

seven days a week, to meet the contract with the giant Roadstone Corporation.

Led by their 31-year-old managing director, Mr. Errol Mason, Canning Engineering Ltd, are prefabricating bunker and conveyor equipment for a quarry in Foreign.

Vital to get by to assemble the plant on the site — and have it completed by December. Said Mr. Mason today:

'Libya Contract'

229

"OK, OK. Get us away quick. Deal done, deal done. £25,000 each. Yes please, thank you, please." They quickly jumped back into the car.

The soldier looked in the boot of our car and nodded to the driver and off we went.

"Deal done, quick, quick," the Libyan kept saying.

I think the soldiers would have been really chuffed with themselves if only they had known what a favour they had done us.

The Letter of Credit included transportation to docks, loading and shipping, and had a whopping profit for us.

I seemed to be travelling all over Europe with Charles. We appointed more agents in Italy and Holland and we became sole UK distributors for the conveyor belting manufacturers S.I.G. of Italy and Phoenix of Germany. This, along with our other spectacular buying opportunities, was slowly getting us back on to a more stable footing. I had learned my lessons the hard way and now I was feeling a little more confident, but still treading cautiously and trying not to become complacent.

There was an obvious positive feeling within the business. We had survived the recession! Many, many companies had fallen but the ones who had survived, like us, had learned valuable lessons and were stronger, leaner and better equipped to go forward.

A few years later Charles died. He was such a talented man, a very astute wheeler dealer who could speak most continental languages fluently and had the ability to deal and convert most European currencies into British pounds almost immediately. But he had a drink problem and enjoyed gambling. When he was working and travelling about Europe wheeling and dealing, he was fine, but when the continent recessed for their normal month-long summer break, he became bored, depressed, drank himself silly and gambled all his money away in the casinos.

Canning Conveyor Co. Ltd. was founded in September 1965 and in the early days its main activity was trading in conveyor belting.

Its original employees worked in a field, in the open air, and in all kinds of weather. But even in such arduous and basic conditions the customers requirements were fulfilled, and the hard lessons learned were good grounding for future years of successful trading.

Over three decades of development now see the company located in a fine complex of industrial buildings and offices.

Years of experience supplying the mining, quarrying, mechanical and civil engineering, fishing, farming, and film making industries, have made Cannings a leading name throughout the world.

Our trade is divided up as such - one third to direct users in the UK, one third to other retail outlets and vulcanising companies in the UK, and one third export.

Whether the demand is for a simple belt fastener or a mile long belt conveyor - from a single roller to the design, manufacture and installation of a complete handling plant, Cannings are able to supply with excellent professional efficiency.

a little about the company

231

Many times I had to help him to pull himself out. I even brought him back to my house to help him to sober up. I once had the unfortunate task of buying him out from a casino in Italy. He had lost a lot of money and didn't have any means of paying. The owners of the casino said that they had locked him up as he was fighting drunk, and they would not let him out until his debt was cleared. Unfortunately, the drink killed him; but he left us with a host of continental clients, some of whom we still do good business with, twenty years later.

The kids were becoming more involved with the management of the company. There seemed to be a more serious and wholesome feeling running through the firm. I think we were all looking and hoping for continued stability and security.

Andrew was now fully qualified as a mechanical engineer with a B.Sc. degree in Mechanical Handling and was running the Engineering Department. Eden was now fully involved in the Sales Office and the buying of new belting and rollers. Jay was becoming more involved in representation and site work. David had become the Company Secretary and was totally responsible for accounts and admin. We had a force to be reckoned with and were looking ahead with vision.

Middleton's Builders were picking up good contracts and had moved their operation into one of our Sandy Lane buildings.
Jane had started back at school as a teacher and Christopher was a pupil at her school.

Mandy was then a wages clerk with a large retail company, but already we were talking to her about joining the firm at a later date.

Heart Attack

I was travelling in Germany with Karl, the joint Engineering Manager and Bernd Kusel, the Sales Director of Phoenix, the company who supplied us with brand new conveyor belting. We had completed our business and finished the evening off with a wonderful meal in a fish restaurant in Hamburg. We were walking back to our hotel when I had pains in my chest. Bernd very kindly called a taxi to take us back to our hotel. Next day I travelled home but kept feeling the pains. I thought it was bad indigestion from the meal and drinks we had the previous evening. By the time I arrived home I was in continuous pain. The only way I could relieve it was to lie on my chest on top of a hard coffee table. Jane telephoned our doctor, who gave me an injection and called for an ambulance to take me to hospital.

It was a heart attack.

The pain subsided after a few days in hospital. The tests confirmed it was indeed a heart attack. After a week they allowed me to go home. As soon as I got home the pain started again and it was worse than ever. Jane called the doctor once again and he sent me straight back into hospital. Some of the people I had met before were still in the same ward when I arrived. They jokingly said, "Welcome home!"

I was wired up and looked and felt pretty grotty. I had survived another heart attack. After about a week of continuous pain, the doctors said that I was to be taken to a specialist hospital in Sheffield to have an angiogram. My own doctor visited and explained to Jane and myself the procedure and possible risks. It frightened us both, and because of the possibilities and risks I decided to make a will "just in case." Bob was immediately alerted and came along to the hospital with his secretary as a witness, and I signed my will. It must have been pretty traumatic for Jane, but it had to be done as I hadn't ever thought about such things as wills before this time.

The angiogram was done by injecting a black dye into the main artery, which is located in the groin. As it flows through the arteries, it is recorded by X-ray and transmitted on to a TV monitor, which I was able to watch. I watched the liquid flowing through my arteries. It was quite an unnerving experience. I joked that it looked like a map of England and the liquid stopped flowing in Sheffield, Doncaster and Nottingham. The only reason I was joking was because I was so scared. In fact it was no joke at all!

It seemed to be quite a long wait before we had the results. Jane was with me when the specialist arrived with his report.
"You have three blockages and we would have to do a triple bypass as soon as possible," he told me.

I told him that I didn't believe him. I said that it was only a few days since I was travelling in Germany feeling as fit as a fiddle. I was shocked. I am afraid I got angry and disagreed with him, accusing him of mixing up the X-ray results whilst they were so busy, and said it was someone else's results he was looking at.

The specialist wasn't very happy with my reaction and snapped back at me saying, "Mr. Canning, we do not get our X-rays mixed up. You can refuse to have your bypass if you so wish, but if you have another heart attack, I am afraid you might not survive."

After we had calmed down, he explained the procedure. Apparently the heart surgeon opens up the chest by cutting down the centre of the ribcage. The heart is then exposed. Tubes are connected from the main arteries to a blood-pumping machine, which diverts the blood from the heart in order to stop the heart beating whilst the operation is carried out. Whilst this is going on another surgeon takes out a good vein from the inside of the leg, which is to be used to make the bypasses. The bypass operation then takes place. The three (in my case) blocked arteries are located and a small hole is pierced at either end of the blockage. A piece of the leg vein is then cut off and stitched over the small holes at the front and back of the blockages, so that, when the heart is restarted again, blood flows freely, bypassing the blockages. After the three bypasses are done, the heart is restarted and the chest is stitched back together again.

I was allowed to go back home for a few days until a bed was available. The few days were thought provoking and worrying. Jane and I were both thinking the worst. To top it all, Christopher's rabbit died and Jane thought it was an omen!

The time came. Andrew took me to the hospital the evening before, to sign in and book into my room. That evening I was prepared: my chest was shaven and I was given a sedative to help me to sleep. Next morning, I was woken at 6am and given premedication. After that I didn't care what they did to me. I remember joking with the porter who was wheeling me into the operating room, telling him that he was a bad driver, and I asked him if he was sure he had actually passed his driving test. The doctor put a needle into my arm, and next I woke up trying to pull the oxygen mask from my face.

Jane kept a diary of the next two weeks. She went through hell, as she had to travel every day through the worst snow we had had for years. She sat beside me all the time I was in intensive care. One day she was telephoned by the surgeon, and told to get to the hospital as soon as possible as there had been a complication; they told her that they didn't know if I would pull through it. I was having trouble with my heartbeat and had fainted. They couldn't regulate my heart and, fearing the worst, they telephoned Jane. She says she drove to Sheffield through the snow at 100mph. I was very ill for quite a while, as my heart would not beat properly. Every time I tried to eat or drink my heart started to beat rapidly as if I was having a fit. They called it fibrillations. Most of the people who had bypasses at the same time as me were up and walking about, but I seemed to be taking longer to recover.

All my kids visited me, which I found very comforting as they made me laugh, even though laughing was a bit painful with all the stitches. I eventually returned home but it took me a long time to recuperate. With Jane's care and attention I gradually regained my strength.

I have heard of people who have had serious operations saying that they have been given a second chance at life. Well, I felt just like that. Slowly and carefully I gained my strength, and began to walk about the house and eventually strolled into the garden. Spring was beginning and the sun started to shine and warm everything up. I remember it so well. I felt renewed and somehow different. The nagging jaw-ache and wooden tongue had gone. I felt fresher, lighter and actually younger. Everything was different; the garden looked more colourful; people seemed to be happier and everyone seemed to smile a lot.

During the previous few years, since the beginning of the recession, I had found it difficult to cope. I had felt trapped in my own creation, and had been living on medication and every new day seemed harder than the last. It seemed as though I had a shadow hanging over my head. Every day was a dreadful drudge. I now felt as though I had been set free. I was a new man. I explained this feeling to my doctor and he told me that, although I had been through a stressful time in my business, I had also suffered from bad health because of coronary heart disease. He said it had affected me in certain ways and the wooden tongue and jaw-pain were typical symptoms of stress and angina. I had also been treated for hypertension, and the combination of the tablets I had been taking, severe stress and my business problems had aggravated the health problems I had been suffering. My bad heart was the final warning. The bypass operation had enabled my heart to work better than it had done for many years, thus the "new man" feeling.

I received a mountain of get-well cards. It truly surprised me. Apart from Jane and my family, I thought that most people looked down at me because of the things that had occurred in my business. I had a feeling, quite wrongly, that I was looked at as that horrible person who sacks people at will and slave-drives everyone else. I sometimes thought I was the next thing to the devil. However, the cards, visitors and telephone calls over the next few months boosted my self-esteem. I will treasure those cards and good wishes forever.

It took a long time for me to get back to normal. I had time to rest and time to think. Having time on my hands for the first time in my life, I became engulfed in my art work. My paintings came to life. I was told by an artist friend that the thing that had been missing from my artwork was "feeling and depth," and this could only come from contentment. For many years my mind had been fully occupied with marital problems and driving myself mad with business, thinking about the next job, or the next meeting, or the next day. I could never relax and completely concentrate on my paintings. Then, suddenly, having time on my hands, I could see things in their true perspective. My floral paintings suddenly seemed more vibrant, colourful and exciting.

Although I had painted all my life, it had only been a matter of putting paint on to paper. I now felt as though I was creating something meaningful. People showed an interest in them and even wanted to buy them. My first commission was from a teacher colleague of Jane's, who saw an unfinished painting on my easel and asked if he could buy it for his wife's birthday. I was thrilled to bits and said that he could have it, but he insisted on paying. He also suggested that I have an art exhibition as he thought other people might like to see my artwork.

I was kept up to date with company matters and business dealings by Andrew and other visitors from work. I felt that they seemed to have taken the business on with renewed vigour and seriousness. Their reports filled me with admiration for them and I felt confident that they were looking after things. It could have been because I wasn't hanging around the office or tearing around like a madman and acting as if I was carrying the whole world on my shoulders. They seemed to be taking everything in their own stride and coping very well.

Several things had happened during the time I was convalescing.

Karl, the joint Engineering Manager, had unfortunately died, also of a heart attack, whilst on holiday, and Andrew had taken on the role of General Manager. Everyone seemed to accept him as "a natural" for this new role and respected his position. He didn't have any superior air of authority but carried out his role with the calm sincerity he has always been known for.

Stephen, the Manager of Middleton's, had asked if he could buy the building company. He was really the keystone to this business and I was quite happy to let him have it as it was a problem I no longer wanted. The company was sold to him and he continued to rent the premises from us for many years afterwards.

David had taken on the full responsibility of the accounts and administration.

Eden and Jay were fully involved in managing the Sales Department.

I returned to work for the first time three months after my operation and walked into what seemed a very different place. Everyone appeared busy and to be carrying out their duties in an efficient and calm manner. After a brief chat with everyone and a general look around, I agreed with Andrew that I would come into work every morning for the time being. I must admit that I had to hold myself back. I thought that, if I didn't attend work full-time and was not in charge, things would go drastically wrong, but it was just the opposite. Months went by and, apart from the usual and expected anomalies, things ran very well indeed.

One day Andrew visited me at home and said that he had been talking with his brothers and they all agreed that it was not necessary for me to come in every morning as everything was under control. He suggested that I come in one or two mornings a week or whenever I wanted to, and if there was a problem or a meeting scheduled then he would call me in. Although it was only a suggestion I realised that it was for the best and this must be the way forward. At first, I felt hurt. It took me a long time to come to terms with the thought that the business could carry on without me. I don't think anyone could ever understand how I felt. The business was like another of my family and suddenly it was being taken away. There was a very strange, hollow feeling and I forced myself to keep away from the business for quite a while until I came to terms with it. On my first visit to work I realised that my sons Andrew, Jay and Eden, and David my accountant were quite capable of running the business without me hanging around. The fact that I wasn't there put them in a position where they probably felt more confident in themselves to make the right decisions. I also felt they could do it even better and easily if I wasn't around so much. After all, they were all experienced, young, and full of enthusiasm and energy. I am so proud to be surrounded by such dedicated people.

Over the next decade, under Andrews's management and with the involvement and dedication of Eden and Jay, and loyal staff and employees, the company surged forward in great waves. Reorganisation, new sales purges, new products, larger and more complex engineering work, skilful buying from many parts of the world, and creating more profitable exporting opportunities has taken the company forward.

David retired and a new Accountant and Company Secretary, Jeremy, was appointed.

A new, fully qualified and experienced Engineering Manager, Ian, joined the company.

Soon after, my daughter Mandy came to work for the company, starting in the office as an assistant to Jay and Eden. She quickly became responsible for what is now called the Roller Division.

So the business goes on: It grows; it matures; it becomes a force to be reckoned with.

I visit every now and again and try to get up to date with company happenings and the systems and routines of progression, but find it is beyond me. I used to write everything down on bits of paper and to communicate with clients by word-of-mouth and telephone and telex. I had the first hand-held adding machine, which I thought had come from another planet. It is now far beyond my understanding. The world is now joined together by computers. Computers take orders, computers make payments, and engineering drawings are done on computers (CAD). I recently watched my engineers and Construction Manager talking to other engineering designers at the other end of the country. They were altering and solving the problems of a contract at another site somewhere else whilst they were all sitting in an office, drinking coffee and looking at a wall-sized computer screen on which was showing the complete engineering project - nuts and bolts and the lot. I was truly amazed and full of admiration. I then walked into another office and watched my son and daughter receiving and processing orders, organising work, stock, modifications and transportation, and invoicing and quoting sales terms on their computers whilst supping their coffees. They then sent computer messages to other people in other offices with instructions and code numbers etc. Progress! One day my daughter jokingly said to me, "Come on, Dad, sit in that chair and do a bit of work. Show us how you did it."

I made a good excuse and a quick getaway and told her I was late for an appointment.

Thanks to these people with their skills, experience, enthusiasm and achievements, the company and its procedures and its methods of work have advanced far beyond my dreams.

Upon Reflection

It has been twenty three years since my heart attacks.

Life is so different. I am what is called "semi-retired," which means visiting work only occasionally, usually for Board Meetings, but sometimes as a courtesy visit to say "hello" to everyone, and to see what's happening.

The company is now an excellent, well run, profitable organisation with a glorious future ahead of it.

During my time in harness the company has been through many ups and downs, successes and failures. It has had a fair share of crises, and also a fair share of luck. But, through it all, it has safely expanded to become an officially rated "medium sized company." It has overcome recession, treachery and despair, but has also experienced happiness, and success; it fulfils most people's ambitions.

My ambition of owning a hundred companies was just a pipe dream. Perhaps, if I hadn't had such silly ideas, life might have been a lot easier, but I don't think I would have felt truly fulfilled. I might not have had my heart attacks, but I think life might have been pretty boring.

I seemed to have whizzed through my life on a gigantic big dipper, either flying high in the sky enriched with wonderful joy and excitement, or diving into the depths of hell.

By writing this book and reliving my life, I have learned a lot not only about myself, but also about other people. During my business life I must have employed more than a thousand individuals and, by plodding through my memories and experiences, I realise that I have experienced the best and the worst of individuals, and I have learned something from each of them.

Some of the downfalls and crises I have experienced have been created not just by the recession, but also sometimes by the people I have employed and trusted, and sometimes because of my immaturity and lack of management skills. As I have said before, I am not a Harvard Business School graduate: I am only a graduate of the "school of life." But this is no excuse for bad management. Good management requires a good business education and training coupled with a fair amount of good luck and a driving ambition. I had a lot of good luck and a driving ambition but also a streak of madness.

After forty-five years of employing people I think I am a more resilient person. I used to be "taken in" by false admiration, false friendships and false smiles, but now I find that, having been kicked in the crotch so many times, it takes me a long time to trust anyone. I mistrust compliments. I often have to ask other people's opinion as to whether a person is genuine or not.

Learning how to cope with my business was a hard lesson and I still don't know if it made me into a "better" person or into my own worst enemy. Although on the one hand I have had my share of disappointments, deceit and disloyalty, I have also had many honest and loyal associates, and I have gained many long-term, loyal and genuine friendships.

I still can't understand the reason I drove myself along at such a mad pace, always chasing my ambitions and reaching for the impossible. It could have started when I was living in Moorends, eating my jam sandwiches and drinking out of a jamjar. Or it might have started when I had to go to school in an army combat jacket. Upon reflection, however, I'm sure my poor upbringing had nothing to do with it: being poor didn't bother me or my brothers and sisters, for in those days we were as happy as larks and as contented as lambs.

It might have started when I made my animal figures out of plywood, painted them in bright colours and sold them in the village shop and received actual cash for them. Perhaps it was an early childhood desire to try to help Mam, as I always realised that the best way to help her, was to share whatever I had with her. Then again, when she died, I remember feeling really guilty that I hadn't helped her enough.

It could have been my desperation to escape from the coalmine – but my crazy ambitions started way before my pit days.

My first marriage breakdown could have been because I was too young, and my ambitions got in the way, or, perhaps, I had way too many ambitions to settle down – having said that, I settled down with Jane and have had forty years (and counting) of happy married life.

What was the motivation? What was the reason? There must be a reason, but, perhaps, the only way I will ever find out is to lie on a couch and be psychoanalysed.

Afterword

Over the past twenty-three years, since my heart attacks, through the sincere diligence and efforts of my children, loyal staff and employees my business has matured and become streamlined, sophisticated and has gone from strength to strength as a world-wide trading and engineering company.

I am presently the Chairman and a non-executive Director. I can define my present role as a listener and advisor. Whenever any of the family get together, I listen to business developments and problems, and try to advise, but what they are doing now is way above my head. I mainly give consolation, admiration and support.

Bob is still a non-executive Director and mentor and his advice remains immeasurable.

Presently the company has a superb close management team under the leadership of Andrew, who is the Managing Director. He is fully experienced in all the aspects and activities of the business. He is a cool, calm and careful leader who has gained much respect from everyone. He also handles the company promotions, and the TV and film contracts. One of his recent claims to fame was to supply all the conveyors for the film *Charlie and the Chocolate Factory*, after which he was given a photograph signed by Johnny Depp saying, "Thank you, Andrew, without your help we could not have made this picture."

Jeremy took over from David as Company Secretary and Financial Director. He has updated and computerised all the administration and office systems, and runs the office finances and accounts with precision, perfection and friendly authority.

Eden is in control of the buying and selling of products. He is a hard, conscientious and ruthless dealer, and is always in personal contact with all his clients. He recently received a compliment from one of our South African customers who jokingly and respectfully called him the "One-Armed Bandit." He regularly visits and deals with clients in Thailand, China, Africa, India and many, many other countries throughout the world. His latest brilliant deal was to supply a hundred tonnes of second-hand steel cord belting, the heaviest ever made, which he purchased from a dealer in Holland and was delivered by airfreight to Nigeria.

Jay and our latest talented employee Stephen, are responsible for running our engineering works. Jay is a hard but thorough representative and a thoroughbred entrepreneur. He is heavily involved in the Engineering Division and helps to secure many important contracts. He also controls the site work. His entrepreneurial ideas have provided the company with many new products, such as a revolutionary conveyor drive unit, the Canning Super Drive, unique Polymer rollers, a unique type of conveyor clip-on cover, and a unique safety handle for conveyor rollers. Working along with Steve, who is a high profile and experienced engineer they have, between them, exceeded the company's expectations by opening up large new workshops and gaining large orders for our engineering products. There are both noted for working eight days a week and twenty-five hours a day!!!

After only seven years with the company, Mandy is in charge of the Roller Division. Her sweet-talking cannot be avoided. Customers will phone her just to chat about their holidays and the weather before finally giving her a big, fat order. Her most recent claim to fame was when she phoned to tell me that she had broken the sales record for rollers on that particular month. I said, "Good girl. Well done, it's pork pies for everyone this week!" Everyone is given a pork pie whenever a record is broken.

Christopher gained a Degree in Auto Engineering and a Master's Degree in Finance at Leeds University. A foreign exchange company in Canary Wharf, London, employs him. His claim to fame is to have been promoted to Market Analyst after only twelve months with the firm.

Jane is my wife, my life and my mainstay. She directs me, pampers me, feeds me and keeps me young. She is a natural homemaker and often cooks an exquisite meal for the whole of the family – kids, grandkids, great-grandkids and spouses. She is my adviser, my controller, my chief cook and bottle washer. Her latest venture is to try to teach me how to use the vacuum cleaner, but it is a little too difficult and technical for me at my age. (Well that is my excuse anyway!) Jane never forgets a birthday or anyone's special day and is loved and respected by everyone.

My claim to fame is having a family of five happy children, eleven beautiful, happy, grandchildren (a football team) and eleven gorgeous, happy, great-grandchildren (the second team) and still counting: the most wonderful family anyone could ever wish for. I envy and admire them all so much. I am the proudest man alive. Not only do I have four brilliant kids, who are happily involved in running my business, I also have a most amazing son happily working in the big city as a financial genius. I also have the most loving, caring and understanding wife, who is happily slaving away looking after me. I am truly the luckiest and happiest man in the world.

I am now enjoying my dream ambition as a cartoonist. In my spare time I paint flowers and am an illustrator of magazine advertisements and books. I sell most of my floral paintings and have created and have had published, with the help of my wife Jane, a children's picture book. Painting large backdrops for our two local theatres fill my spare time. (Luckily I won't have time to learn how to vacuum!!!!)

I truly believe that, like the song in The Sound of Music, "I must have done something good" for my Guardian Angel to reward me with such a fulfilling life!

Why did I write this story? Because I want my family to know what really happened. They must be fed up with me telling them. I see them roll their eyes as they think to themselves, "Here he goes again, the old bugger!!!! "

Wait a minute! Just thinking! Just had a brilliant idea to start another business – an art shop in every town in the UK, circulating the stock of artworks around every shop, every month, to change the displays . . .I'm getting a little stressed at the thought of it... Oh forget it! ......Where's my pipe and slippers?

End of Part Two

Part Three
Brothers in Boots

During my research and the collecting of facts and information about the early days of my Mam and Dad, I contacted several of my cousins and older uncles and aunties, explaining I was involved with writing their stories.

To my astonishment I learned that several of the older generation, who have sadly passed away, were writers and diary keepers. Old files, records and manuscripts suddenly appeared. They tell of amazing episodes, adventures and experiences in the lives of these now long-gone people. There were boxes full of old diaries, notebooks and dusty files, some typed and some hand-written on any old bits of lined writing paper. Some were so faded they were hardly legible, some were in hand written scribbles, and some were carefully recorded in perfect English and actually typed on old fashioned, but faded, foolscap papers.

Most people at some particular time in their lives look back and remember what an extraordinary and wonderful life they have lived. They probably think that only they and their close family know anything about their lives. When they try to talk about it, especially to a younger generation, they usually find that others are not very interested because they are all too busy living out their own extraordinary and wonderful lives.

As the older generation start remembering the things they did, they might think that someone in the family - some distant relative - sometime in the future just might be interested in hearing, or even reading about their individual wonderful activities.

Normally these thoughts drift away and are put into the back of the mind as more important everyday life takes over.

Occasionally, one of these folk might decide to put their memories and photos together and write down some of the wondrous and exciting things they did in their lifetime, thinking it ought to be recorded for prosperity. Their writings and photos eventually become a nuisance to their offspring, and are usually stuffed into a file which is moved about the house from one place to another because of redecorating or the occasional clean up and clean out.

In time, the file ages, begins to get dirty and starts to fade – it is then stuffed into a box and ends up in the attic. The writer gets older and the box forgotten. He or she eventually dies and the next generation decide to move to fresh fields. The box suddenly reappears, covered in dust and cobwebs. At this time, it might be looked at, but, because of the speed and activity of normal life, it could be binned as a bit of old rubbish, spiders and all, or dusted down, put into a fresh box and taken back to the attic.

With a bit of luck and after many years, it could again reappear and be resurrected by some distant relative who is curious and inquisitive and has a little time on their hands.
"What's all this?" they might think. "Life in the coal mines with a candle! Joining the army! Fighting the Germans! I might read this one day when I've time. Got to get the kids off to school now!"

The box is sellotaped up, spiders and all, and stuffed into the back of the wardrobe where it hibernates for the next ten years.

Life gets busier, the kids grow up and digital technology takes over. The family needs more room for the kids to store their sports equipment and school files, and to do their homework. The computer, computer games and iPads take priority. A chest of drawers, a larger desk and a swivel chair are needed: it's time to turf out the old wardrobe!

One of the older kids, who might be a bit of a scholar, studying history at university perhaps, might open the box, eyes glistening with interest and enthusiasm, and think "Wow! This is treasure! This was my great granddad who was born in 1879 and started work down the pit at twelve years of age. His son fought the Germans in the Second World War; another son was in the Eighth Army fighting Rommel in the desert; another great uncle was in the Royal Navy on the mine - sweepers!!! Wow!"

All these stories, diaries and photographs had been hidden away for all those years waiting to be found, hopefully by someone who was interested enough to read them. They were taken out of their boxes, safe at last, were carefully scrutinized, read, retyped and photos enhanced.

I was kindly loaned similar treasures, which had been shuffled about and doing the attic rounds for many years. Old files, dirty pieces of foolscap papers, diaries, yellow faded photographs, all bundled into sellotaped cardboard boxes, and an old well-worn briefcase which was full of wonderful, exciting, courageous and sometimes tear-jerking stories.

These are some of the stories I excavated and copied in their original writings: dots, commas, warts and all. It would be such a shame if they were destroyed. These stories should be recorded properly, as one day someone might wish to know where we came from and what wonderful people our ancestors were.

Granddad Canning's story

Taken from an old typewritten foolscap manuscript

"Life of a Yorkshire miner. The good old days"

Miners have often been regarded through the nature of their trade as a small, stumpy race. But be that as it may, I was one of the wee ones and smaller than most at that.

Many times I have heard cracks about the good old days, but any old miner with just a grain of common – sense and a small element of truth would not wish for their return. Admittedly beer was a penny a pint and cigarettes ten for two pence, in fact half a crown would see one a long way. Despite this however, I am reasonably jealous of the way of life, which has now become the lot for the mining fraternity. Furthermore there is a vast improvement of relations between management and men and the trade unions. Let us never forget the men who really made the final phases of these good things really possible, I refer, of course, to the late Herbert Smith and A.J.Cook, who in turn were very nearly crucified by their fellow workers. My pride goes a long with many thousands more old miners for our part in paving the way towards this great achievement of better wages, better living and better education. Even though, I contend that I myself was the victim of a devilish plot leading to my being victimised with subsequent loss of the present miner's pension, I bear no ill wind of anyone connected with the industry, although I am sorry to see miners bread and butter being often endangered by petty disagreements between management and men. When I say I am a Yorkshire miner I mean just that, because the present day mining community is very cosmopolitan indeed, workers hailing from England, Scotland, Ireland and Wales – Germans, Jamacians and Jews – and despite great resentment from some parts of the coal field we may in due course have Hungarians and Polish as well.

My birthplace was East Ardsley near Wakefield and I was born on July 9th 1879. Amongst my earliest recollections was my Grandfathers funeral, when, not only had my parents had to dig themselves out of and into the house on account of the heavy snow, but they had to shift snow galore before the hearst could be got reasonably near the door.

Up to nine years of age when I commenced school at the charge of a penny a day there was little else to memorise except maybe the heavy proportions of household chores which were freely bestowed upon us. Jane Smallwood daughter of Sgt. Smallwood was my first teacher and was reputed to be very timid so you can imagine what a great thing it was for us lads when she panicked at the sight of a mouse, jumping on her desk and screaming for help, to be quietened only by the arrival of people from nearby houses. It was whilst in her class that through boyish pranks in the playground I was severely crushed by bigger lads in the corner of the ground. The worst to my mind was the intense bleeding of the nose and the only first aid equipment in those days was the cold water tap.

In our village the amenities for sport and pleasure were very few poor indeed, there being no such thing as playing fields and miners welfare services were not even thought of then. However the streets of Ardsley were linked into Wembley in winter time and Headingly or the Oval in summertime. Cricket was our great sport and very often a costly one with broken windows very frequently and the parental thrashings which followed very painful. "Spare the rod" was not adhered to by our parents.

We were eventually removed from the streets on account of protesting mothers fed up of rocking their babies in vain and a terrible outcry from the men engaged in night shift work. We weren't really sorry because very often the stench from the midderns had a very frustrating effect on us. After a great deal of persuasion and a little bribery we finely enlisted the help of a gentleman farmer who kindly loaned us a bit of ground where we could pursue the arts of cricket to our hearts content. Eventually a team was formed and after clubbing up our coppers for many many months we eventually went to Wakefield to Harry Huley's store and bought a complete cricket outfit, and I swear tom this day we were the pioneers of cricket at Ardsley who now have a flourishing team in the Yorkshire Council. In the team there is always someone who stands out from the others, our own personal hero was none other than Walter Bedford a fast bowler who eventually played for the Yorkshire Colts turned professional for Heckmondwyke and Doncaster. Another product from the mining communities was Freddie Truman, a great credit to Yorkshire and England alike.

Wagonettes

To play truant was equal to a criminal offence with heavy punishment to follow. I wonder how many remember the birch rod. No school was complete without one of those instruments of chastisement. I have had my share of punishment because I have played truant many times to go potato picking or other farm work for three pence a day plus a little food and drink, believe me we earned our coppers, as farmers in those days were hard bullying task masters although they all went to church on Sundays. Our famous motto of "If tha does owt for nowt do it for thissen" was very hard to stand by especially where farmers are concerned.

One of my most loveable memories and greatest joy in my life was to ride on the wagonettes. These were drawn by two horses and I would stand on the step and collect the fares which I would hand over to the driver on reaching out destination, the Crown and Fleece, Leeds, or Brunswick Hotel, Wakefield. I'm not blowing my own trumpet when I say I was a favourite with the wagonette parties on account of my small stature. From the driver I used to receive threepence and as much meat and potato pie as I could consume. I must admit that often the threepence included feeding the horses and polishing the brasses on the harness. Horses used to look a real picture in those days, in fact, more money was spent on those animals than on some of the children in our locality, what with gaily coloured ribbons to plait their tails with and big bottles of Brasso, it used to cost a pretty penny. Out of the threepence, I used to get four ounce of mixtures from Wakefield market and hand the remainder over to my mother who put it to very good use – there was no such thing as family allowances then. I remember somewhere about this time getting a thrashings for accepting a copper for running an errand for a neighbour. This was an offence punishable by the strap.

Home life, real, insomuch that anyone suffering from sickness or other adversity there always seemed to be a willing hand held out, they were, considered darned poor neighbours if they didn't assist with baking and washing. These were real drudgery jobs done without electric washers and top grade soap powders. Every woman and girl knew the rudiments of these tasks from a very early age and if my memory serves me right one could not buy bread from the shops. It would be unfair to leave males out of this because at a very early age they were taught the art of black – leading and cleaning cutlery (mostly a Saturday afternoon job) cleaning fire irons was a real sweater. Women were really houseproud, there was really nothing else to do. Probably the old adage of "early to bed early to rise" originated in those times.

1887
Whilst still at school another great occasion was Queen Victoria's Jubilee. This called for great celebrations throughout the country and in our own little village it was a day never to be forgotten. All the halls, schools, and chapels for miles around were commandeered for teas, concerts and festivities.

This was a famous year also for the introduction of gas into Ardsley. Before this, paraffin and candles had been the order of the day. Many years lapsed before families like ours could afford such a luxury. There were many improvements carried out by the gas company but there were still numerous deaths up and down through misuse of this new fangled idea. The trouble was to come when the mantle was introduced, what with draughts and banging doors it became a most expensive and dangerous article.

Ardsley
For those who have never seen the old back to back let them be thankful. Two up, two down, with a passage leading to the back where the communal lavatory and ash pit reigned supreme. There was always plenty of vermin in, these surroundings, fleas, flies, rats and mice, and the stench in summer time would knock one's hat off. I have watched with interest the vast improvements of the sanitary system and I know I am telling the truth when I say that similar conditions still prevail in many places, particularly in a group of villages a few miles from Doncaster where in this year of 1959 the only means of sewage are the old fashioned cesspools.

However to continue in this morbid mood my mind goes back to those elderly folk who often lived in cold dark basements on a mere pittance of half a crown a week "Poor Law Relief" or else it was over the hill to the workhouse.

The Old Hall, Ardsley used to be our post office and on receipt of a telegram a flag used to be hung out of the window indicating that a boy was required to deliver it to whom it concerned. Payment for delivery was halfpenny locally and sixpence if taken on foot to places like Tingley or Morley roughly two miles away. Putting out the flag was a signal for many a battle it being a case of the fittest surviving. Eventually this system was eradicated, it being left to the school headmaster to appoint the privilege to his most progressive scholars. This, to many minds was just a big twist.

One of my playmates was the youngest son of the Old Hall family, we became firm friends when I was casually employed as a bootblack. This was very tiresome work indeed considering the fact that the highways and byways were in bad condition, just rustic lanes which were more often ankle deep in mud. One incident I cannot omit was that during a snowball fight in the playground a terrible accident occurred when a snowball hit our teacher in the eye resulting in it being taken out, and although it was the end of her teaching career there was no prosecution although she declared she knew who the culprit was. There was no more snowballing in our schoolyard for many a year.

Every year in September we had a magnificent fair (Yorkshire folk call it a feast) which covered two or three fields known as a common, and was written about in various almanac's and suchlike. Apart from the usual roundabouts and fortune tellers there was boxing booths, sword swallowers, marionette shows, hot pea stalls, a fat lady and an hokey pokey (Ice cream) stall in charge of a moustached Italian. "Tony" as the Italian was known was not only an ice cream vendor but the owner of a performing bear and a barrel organ. The bear appeared to be a little on the vicious side and always had a big muzzle on his mouth, I have omitted the fact that "Tony" also possessed a monkey. During one street performance the monkey bit a portion of a boys ear who had apparently been tormenting the animal. When news reached the boy's father of the incident there was nearly a riot, only police intervention saving "Tony" from certain death. Alas, the troupe left Ardsley minus one monkey.

Morley Park was opened to the public in 1889, a memorable occasion when a young lady parachuted from a balloon and drifted at terrific speed toward Wakefield. Assuming from the number of wagonettes present there must have been a terrific crowd present.

We had to make our own amusements and it was not uncommon to see crowds of young men playing marbles and skipping, fancy seeing them do that today except maybe on a professional basis. One chap used to pull me up and down the street on an old pudding tin, the faster he went the more my behind burned.

In 1889 a new craze started, that of smoking scented cigarettes. We were quickly warned by our parents that each cigarette smoked was just one more nail in our coffin, however this did not stop a lot of sly and indiscrete smoking and when Woodbines were introduced later at five a penny smoking became world-wide with the exception of women of course. For women to smoke it was an unpardonable sin even though it was a common sight for gypsies to smoke clay pipes full of evil smelling twist.

As a child my favourite holiday was Whitsuntide, not only for the various church and chapel activities but it usually meant a new rigout of clothes which were really ready for when the holiday came. There used to be a lot of cutting down of trousers, from Father to son and further still if trousers retained a decent standard of wear. Being a member of Ardsley Methodist Free Church I was always glad to listen to the magnificent organ played by Mr. Jim Arnold. People came from far and wide to hear him render Handles Messiah. Occasionally old timers would roll up with their violins, oboes, piccolos, concertinas and euphoniums. To retrace my steps a while ,the new rigout previously mentioned consisted of a velvet suit with lace collar and cuffs, actually we were turned out like little dukes .Processions in those days were terrific events and the organisers were no mugs.

It was about this time that the miner's demonstration which I understand was a poor effort, so many miners were afraid to attend for fear of losing their jobs. May I say that at my early age I can remember miners getting killed and severely injured and still it goes on.

In the Pit
Sooner or later all good things come to an end, my schooldays terminated at a ripe old age of twelve, although I should consider myself lucky as my Grandfather once said they were working at eight and nine years of age when he was a lad. The time has now arrived when I was supposed to boost the family income in earnest and as we were of the mining fraternity that seemed to be my only outlet.

My father took me to see the manager at Robin Hood Colliery two miles from Ardsley, but he was loathed to engage me on account of my size but eventually he agreed on production of my school leaving certificate. I was now virtually a pit lad and it was with very mixed feelings that I wended my way back home to anxiously await that arrival of Monday morning. Mother didn't know whether to laugh or cry but she immediately commenced checking up what I should require for this auspicious occasion. First a coat with two large pockets (a quart glass bottle) n and a pair of clogs. Mothers chief worry, and she fretted somewhat over this, was the thought of me walking all that way at four o clock in the morning, but it had to be done because the factory act which later eliminated certain hours of work was then unknown.

It was with a sinking feeling I arrived at the pit head on Monday morning, every new starter gets it although I was amazed how fresh I felt considering I had had a practically sleepless night. A short journey to the pit bottom where I contacted the deputy who was to introduce me to my work. He didn't seem very enthusiastic when he saw my size and was doing a lot of muttering under his breath. Now Robin Hood was a candle pit and the deputy took me to a store – house and issued me with five candles and a lump of wet clay as big as a coconut. Then he introduced me to a boy who was to be my mate for quite some time, his name was Johnny Breed and I must admit I liked him from the start and he proved a real pall and workmate all the time he was with me. Johnny showed me how to work the clay into a kind of holder either to stand on the floor or put on moving tubs. Our jobs was pushing, or as they call it in Yorkshire, tramming tubs. This we did with our heads or hands grasping the tub rails at the same time, like thousands of old miners I still bear the mark of the trade – flat foreheads and persistent headaches. The rigours of tramming in the dark underground passages is nothing new to most miners but doing it by candle light is something which only ye ancient miners have experienced. Many were the times I lost my light during the process and many are the times I have been cursed for causing delay in productive endeavours. It was the same old routine day after day but the sweated labour seemed to be making a man of me, one thing was terribly apparent though, this kind of job was not helpful in increasing ones stature. Twelve months slipped by very quickly and one day the manager who engaged me came on our district and on spotting me he said to the deputy "How do you get on with this little chap?" "Fine" Replied the deputy "He is one of my best lads and I think he is worth another tanner a day," Well" said the manager, "If you feel like that I'll make it into a bob." I was eager to get home that day to impart the good news that I was now the happy recipient of two shillings per day. Comparing this with what some of my grandchildren get today for pit work, well, it makes me think. Talking of grandchildren, at the time of writing I have twenty three and nine great grandchildren. Some of them are engaged in underground work at Askern, Bentley and Firbeck.

A new phase in mining life now became my lot, that of shift working, Days, afternoons and nights. My first shift on night's coincided with bonfire night and I waited for my friend Barnabas Robertshaw who was eighteen to accompany me to the pit, he failed to show up however so I went my lonely way up notorious Thorpe Lane. There were no lamps and only one farm house with stone quarries either side. Many people had been way laid in this lane and it was nothing fresh to see crowds of searchers after someone had been attacked. Frightening thoughts ran through my head and I can't recall whether I walked or ran but I did eventually reach the pit with time to spare. It was with a sense of foreboding that I worked that shift, I sense that miners really get, call it sixth sense or premonition or what you will but it was there. Next morning when I reached home I knew why I had been unhappy at work. It appears that Barnabos along with some other chaps had been larking about and met with serious accident. Apparently they had been dipping sticks in a lime vat and fighting with them and throwing them at each other and one hit Banrabos in the eye which eventually had to be taken out. That finished his carere in the pit which leads me to say that I soon finished at Robin Hood colliery because my father got employment for us at Ardsley Colliery which was practically home.

At this new pit things took a turn for the worse, what with new mates and different methods of working everything seemed topsy turvey. How I longed to be back at Robin Hood where I had been treated with respect by nearly every one. Tramming at this pit was tramming with a difference so steep were the inclines it needed a superb effort to budge the tub let alone shore it, on the return journey it required two lockers in a tub which will give you a fair idea of the steepness of the place.
The two colliers whom I was tramming for were only in their early twenties but both had long black beards, a common sight in those times, however I couldn't do anything right for these two chaps the only words they knew were " where you bin" and " look sharp back." What a contrast to the other pit, anyhow I soon had ample time to think over the differences because after working just six months at Ardsley I was struck down by rheumatic fever. Whilst my illness was at its peak my father swore and declared it was the end of pit work for me. Gradually my strength came back and I felt myself making a grand recovery which set me off gallivanting on the wagonettes again. This continued for quite some while until father decided I should be better off working so back to the pit I went.

1893 was a red letter day for me, it was then that I made an application to the local brass band for an instrument.

They set me up with an old brass cornet and one of the bandsmen gave me frequent lessons and it didn't seem long before I was playing round the bandstand with the other fellows and when I received my uniform I felt fine, a real British bandsman. This year I also saw the first two wheeled cycle come into Ardsley, the type with solid tyres. Coinciding with those events was one not very good that of the miners strike which lasted thirteen weeks. There were days of hunger, anger and privation and apart from the local soup kitchens I cannot recall what we lived on. Some chaps were so desperate that they resumed work against their colleagues advice and were instantly labelled "blacklegs." Every miner knows what a "blackleg" is but when a man is torn between the devil and the deep blue sea it is marvellous how far he will go to sustain his wife and children. The strike affected most of the collieries in Yorkshire and one day the strikers commenced a march from Castleford being continuously strengthened by miners from Pontifract, Sharleston, Snydale, Featherstone, Normanton, Altofs and Methley, these were met by another contingent from South Yorkshire and by the time they reached Ardsley they were about two thousand strong. First they went to the colliery gates and fetched the manager and marched him to his home and stood him on his wall outside his house and made him declare that no more men would work down his pit until the strike was ended but that didn't stop some of the miners creeping back to work. On the very same day a terrible tragedy took place, two boys were digging on the tip, they had holed under quite some way when the lot caved in on top of them and despite immediate help they were both dead when released. After thirteen weeks the strike ended, much to every ones relief, but it took months and months to pay off debts which had accumulated. There were many bankrupts as well the only man who seemed to come out smiling was the now almost forgotten pawn broker.

Sailor Dick

When I attained the age of sixteen I finished at the pit commenced work at the West Yorkshire iron works as a plate layer at three shillings a day. This was interesting work with much to learn. Various gangs worked here on different jobs and one day the foreman of a gang who made tracks for barrow wheelers came to my foreman to borrow two men to go on another job. His name was "Sailor Dick" and I took an immediate liking to him, the feeling must have been mutual because he asked me if would like to stay with his gang at four pence extra per day. One day he came to me and said he had a special job for me, a job which needed a small person. This was in connection with the pulleys on top of the furnaces, my job was to go up with the barrow wheelers and oil the pulley wheel axel. All went well on this job for twelve months when one day during the process of oiling someone signalled the lift away. I was already between the pulleys and could feel one rubbing on my back, luckily Sailor Dick saw my predicament and immediately stopped the lift, believe me he was blazing mad, it was a serious matter, but like a lot more things it got hushed up, but Sailor Dick always supervised the job personally after that.

At eighteen years of age I tried a fresh job with the Great Northern Railway fitting shops. Here I worked in the blacksmiths shop and despite numerous severe burns I thoroughly enjoyed the job. Whilst I was here we had a big job from the U.S.A., twelve engines all packed in cases had to be cleaned and fitted together, it was the first and only time I ever saw engines fitted with cowcatchers on the front except of course on films. I was still in the band and still making good progress and we had the pleasure of playing at a reception given to our cricket team who won the cup given by Wakefield and District challenge League.

My elder brother Simeon who was working at Hemsworth Colliery came to see the family one week end and persuaded me to go back to the pit with him, after signing on I went to live with him at his home at Kinsley, where the famous rugby player Billy Batten was brought up. Here my wages showed a marked improvement and it wasn't long before I had the opportunity of getting my father and younger brother a job which subsequently led to them getting a house at Hemsworth, then I moved in with them.

Then came the Boer war with very disturbing news at times of our lads being hemmed in or surrounded by the Africans. Our great leaders at that time were General French, General Buller, Lord Roberts, and others. It was a joy for all of us when it ended with the burning of Kruser. After that most homes had pictures portraying the Relief of Mafeking and Ladysmith.

Kinsley Band
We had got nicely settled in our new home aand work when I joined the Kinsley Band, that was in 1901 and I hadn't been in long before I was elected secretary. I worked hard during that year for the contesting season the following year. Success was immediately at the first contest at Wharncliffe we gained second prize in the selection and at Parkgate two weeks later we achieved the first in the march. In all we won seven first prizes with a march named President. Quite a number of successful engagements followed when we were struck by a bombshell. The sponser of the band since its inauguration in 1890 demanded the return of his money which he had paid for instruments. A public meeting was convened to try to enlist help from surrounding folk. Perhaps they were aware that they had a good band because the response was great, apart from a few donors it was subsequently voted that a small stoppage should be made

from the Hemsworth miners to assist in paying off the debt and helping with the upkeep of the band.

I was married at Hemsworth church in 1902, on Christmas day to be precise. Six weeks later there was an over-wind at the pit which put us all out of work for seven days. They say ones troubles start with married life, well, this was a good beginning.

In the meantime I had taken a spare time agency for Pioneer Life Assurance Company, I found that by a little hard work this was a paying job, the ready cash being rally acceptable. Another serious matter befell us, Hemsworth miners began agitating for a new price list for the two new seams Barnsley bed and Haigh Moore.

There were numerous strikes and finely through the parties concerned being unable to reach an agreement the pit eventually shut down. The band went to pieces and after a general meeting it was decided to call in all the instruments and leave them in charge of the landlord of Kingsley Hotel.

Worse was to follow, in 1905 the colliery company served eviction all the tenants living in the pit houses. Men women and children were without a roof over their head before one could say "Jack Robinson." Eventually all the children were moved to and cared for in the top long room at Kinsley Hotel. One chap, a particular friend of mine created a memorable scene, he was one of a musical family who provided music on dancing occasions. It was raining heavily at the time and this chap Bob Batty and his family with all their goods and chattels piled up beside them got all their instruments and commenced to play "Home Sweet Home" believe me that was the occasion for a tearful scene. After a few weeks the village began to look a shambles it was amazing to see the hundreds of visitors in wagonettes who came from far and wide to see the colony of tents and to extend their sympathy with the children biletted in the hotel. One day the famous Kier Hardie accompanied by suffragettes rode into the tent colony to give his advice and blessing, he became a regular visitor to Hemsworth in the years that followed.

Insurance Agent

As I mentioned previously I was a spare time agent for the Pioneer Life Assurance and it was a lucky break for me when they offered me a full time agency at Bradford. I accepted the offer knowing full well that it would be uphill all the way and that my wife and two sons would all be on strange ground. We left Hemsworth with great rapidity and moved to our new house at Oak Lane Bradford. Settling down wasn't as bad as we had feared. My wife found out that we could live quite cheaply here, to quote one or two items, joints of beef at 3 ½ pence per lb. silver hake at 3pence per lb. and to crown it all the variety was bewildering. Furthermore the beautiful parks surrounding Bradford were just what the doctor ordered and we had a choice of entertainment in the evenings. This was my lucky day, my business increased unbelievably so much so that I was selected to go a huge dinner and party arranged for six hundred of the societies agents at their new offices at 67, Dale Street, Liverpool. Each agent received a beautiful invitation card requesting him to attend the above affair and to a huge spread at the Bears Paw Restaurant, Lord Street, Liverpool. I have omitted to say that the date of the great festival was Wednesday 19th June 1907.

It was a great feeling of pride that I set off from Bradford with a fellow agent on Tuesday morning and we stayed the night at the Waterloo Hotel Liverpool, all these things may I add, had been laid on for us by the society. Up early next morning we were taken on an organised trip round the docks where we were shown round a magnificent ship the "Luciana." To my mind this was sheer luxury what with the thick carpets and pivoting chairs I had seen nothing like it previously, or since if it comes to that, for although I have read and heard so much about the Queen liners have never seen them in reality. Following a quick trip to New Brighton we eventually arrived at the Bears Paw Restaurant for the "festival dinner."

Six hundred of us sat down to a seven course dinner, I need only say it was excellent and the entertainment which followed was superb. There was a Welsh contingent of singers and they were well worthy of their country. After the show was over we caught a train which was going to Halifax only that meant we had to stay at the Temperance Hotel until early morning. A beautiful day, a beautiful dinner, an education but clouds just round the corner.

We had been led to believe that miners were the only people who came on strike but when the dispute between the wool combers and employers cumulated in a six months strike I for one changed my mind. All the mills were silent and these being the only source of employment in Bradford things were very, very, very glum indeed. My wife wrote to her mother at Hemsworth and enquired if there were still any houses left vacant, the reply was "yes" but Hemsworth colliery was still on strike. I was eventually reinstated at Hemsworth with a house also.

I had only been back a few weeks when I ran into Tom Garbett the late bandmaster for Kinsley band, we were very glad to renew acquaintances and we decided to go and see the colliery manager Mr. Beach and after a successful interview he agreed to lend us ten pounds to liberate our instruments from the Kinsley Hotel landlord Mr. Elstone.

He also asked us how many bandsmen we could get at once and when we replied eight he immediately gave orders that any bandsmen wanting a job at Hemsworth was to be signed on right away. Furthermore he ordered a new bandstand to be made and the top floor of the washer was cleaned out and fitted with electric light, to be used for practice purposes. That was the beginning of a very successful band for not quite two years later we won the junior cup at Crystal Palace in 1911. Unfortunately in 1910 I had a serious accident coursed by twisting a tub on a wet flat sheet this caught a prop and down came the roof, my two brothers managed to escape the fall but I was completely buried. They all worked very hard to liberate me but I could feel every stone that was lifted off me, after a terrible journey to the pit bottom, home, thirteen weeks of it. May I add that one of the old Faithfull's in first aid treatment in those days was Friars Balsam.

More strikes, I was fed up to the teeth so off I went to another pit, to be precise Frickley Colliery. This turned out to be the best pit I had ever worked in and as now their band took some licking.

War broke out in 1914 and I remember plainly queuing up for meat and margarine. Those who were there early were fortunate those who were late were not so lucky. Rationing facilities were poor and the food situation in World War 2 was heaven compared with 1914 1918. One night a Zeppelin was over South Elmsall and it was apparent he was following a train from Doncaster, the train driver however was crafty, and he pulled his engine under a bridge. After circling around for some while the Zeppelin made off and dropped a bomb in Pontefract Park.

It was in 1916 I was told of a little business, a small grocers shop at Ferrybridge near Pontifract. With a family, now four boys, we went to look over the place and decided to take it, this meant getting another change of colliery, this time at the Prince of Wales Colliery, Pontifract which was only two miles from Ferrybridge. Whilst I worked my wife looked after the business. Everything looked rosy for us especially as they were laying the foundations for the huge power station, but it was not to be, The river Aire was soon in flood and that curtailed the power station job, (and I hope you don't get bored, another miners strike,) this strike in 1921 lasted sixteen weeks. This busted us good and proper, we let out so much credit to starving families that we were absolutely flat. None of the money was ever retrieved as those years were very lean indeed, but we had to foot the bills to various warehouses and we were paying back on court orders or many, many years to follow, that is what came of being good and kind to ones fellow men. The last two or three years had completely ruined my wife's health, and now with six sons and a daughter we were really up to our neck in it. Back to the pit again this time Askern Main with the pleasant thought that there are plenty more pits in Yorkshire if I fail here, I never threw up the sponge although god knows I sometimes felt like it. We moved to Askern in 1923 my interest still being in music and two years after joining Askern band I was appointed secretary and helped to build up a contest band.

Whilst at Askern I had one of the greatest tests in my mining career. It happened on the Pollington district, my mate was Jack Jones and we were packing and drawing off, whilst at the top of the face was William Evans, Hugh Jones and Owen Williams. They were driving a road through a huge fall of roof and were using what we call a puncher, a machine with a steel rod six feet in length that holed under the coal, this in turn was blown down then cast up onto the pans which conveyed it to the gate end, to say that the noise was terrific was putting it mildly. One hundred yards was the length of the face and the waste had never broke down, it resembled a great forest, I attached a chain to a very stout prop and released it, immediately the roof seemed to lower and rapidly too, we had to leave all our tools. The roof didn't break up it just wanted to come down in one piece and that is exactly what it did. Jack Jones went off to warn the Deputy whilst I ran terrified up the face to warn the others. They knew what I was getting at and ran for their lives whilst with noise like thunder, props breaking and huge lumps of coal busting from the face we prayed to God to keep safe for just a minute or so. Luck was with us we just got through in time then the whole lot fell in, a full eighty yards was completely blocked burying pans and material which to my knowledge may still be there.

A few years later on one of my sons Lawrence was in an engine house on the Barnsley district when a run of tubs broke away hit the engine house and completely buried him but not one piece of stone touched his body. It was a stroke of luck that pieces of timber had fallen about him providing him with a temporary tent of safety, those who rescued him will have something to remember all their life's and I would like to extend my thanks to those gallant chaps.

Injuries and illnesses and were beginning to tell their tale on me and I lost numerous weeks and was off work when war broke out in 1939 but this didn't stop me from joining the Askern A.R.P. station. My son Douglas joined the army with the Royal Engineers and went over the top on D-Day finely finishing up in Germany in 1947. Clarence was on a mine sweeper in an electrical capacity. Maurice was in the R.A.O.C. until 1946 and my only daughter passed with honours at Doncaster Technical Collage as a shorthand typist. In conclusion I might say that I have lived through the finest age ever known and have seen everything that moves, turns or flies come in my time. All this however would have been impossible without a loving and caring wife who passed away at 56 years of age hers was a struggle from start to finish but we do not know what is to come our way and probably it is a good thing too, so I wish all my six sons, one daughter, twenty-six grandchildren and nine great grandchildren all the best of luck and health in huge proportions.

James Canning
Born 1879 - Died 1973

This is the story of Douglas Canning

Son of James Canning, Brother of my Father

Douglas Canning

Born 19th March 1919 - Died 28th July 1988

What follows is a copy of an article

Written by Douglas's son Dennis

274

Operation Overlord

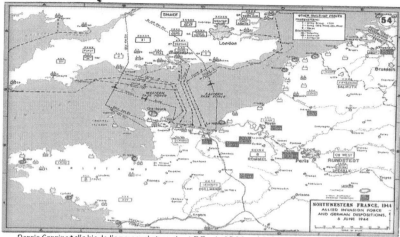

Dennis Canning tells his dad's personal story about D Day in 1944 and dedicated this article to his
mam and dad:

Operation Overlord was the codename for the Allied invasion of North West Europe which began with D
Day on 6th June 1944 with the assault on five Normandy beaches. The landings at Utah, Omaha, Gold,
Juno and Sword were the culmination of three years of joint strategic planning by Great Britain and
the United States. It was the largest seaborne invasion force ever assembled in military history.

An invasion force of 6,500 vessels landed over 150,000 allied troops on D Day. Around 12,000
aircraft bombed German defences and gave cover and support. The airborne landings saw some 2000
aircraft and 850 gliders of the RAF and US airforce used.

By the end of the month, some 850,000 men, 148,000 vehicles and 570,000 tones of supplies had
been landed on the Normandy shores. This began the reconquest of Europe from the Germans.

Dawn on D Day at Hermanville-La-Breche, Sword Beach
As dawn broke all along the Normandy coast, there was a heavy sea mist. The German army were in
their bunkers and trenches unaware what was about to be unleashed upon them. To their
astonishment, out of the mist there appeared the biggest armada of ships ever assembled in the
history of warfare, firing large guns inland. 6,500 ships of all kinds and landing craft with 150,000
British, Canadian, American, French and Polish troops.

Among the troops approaching the shore was Douglas Canning of Adwick-le-Street, a miner at Askern
Pit. He was nervous and seasick and, like all his mates, wondering,
'Will I make it through this day?'

275

Four Years Earlier – November 1940

It was while he was working at Askern Pit that my dad received his call-up papers. My parents lived at Adwick at this time and dad travelled to work at the pit by bus. The war was not going too well and after the disaster of Dunkirk everyone knew that there would have to be what was called 'The Second Front'.

Douglas was enlisted into the Royal Engineers on 12 December 1940. He had been married just less than a year and was just 21 years of age. He became 2135621 Sapper Douglas Canning RE.

After his initial training he was to spend many months training in chemical warfare. When this was completed he was posted to the Royal Engineers Field Squadron at Boxhill near Dorking in Surrey. Here he began training to build bailey bridges. As 1944 approached, the training took on a new challenge in learning how to destroy beach obstacles which the engineers would encounter on the D-Day beaches. This was done on practice beaches in the south of England using plastic high explosives.

On May 4th 1944 Douglas and his squadron took part in a very important practice landing called 'Exercise Fabius' and later that month the squadron was inspected by the king, George VI who dad always remembered had a bad stutter and was so pale he looked like chalk.

On May 28th the squadron was moved to a marshalling area where they were to waterproof all lorries and other army vehicles and prepare all the plastic explosives needed for the demolition of beach obstacles.

Such was the secrecy of Operation Overlord that no-one was allowed to leave the area or to contact anyone outside by 'phone or by letter. They were totally penned inside wire fences with guards patrolling carrying guns. The agony was made worse for the men when the whole allied invasion was postponed for 24 hours because of terrible weather in the English Channel. This, together with the fear that the Germans might find out what was happening increased the tension and nerves amongst the men who, by now, just wanted to get on with what they were doing. Even by this time, Douglas and the rest of the soldiers in Britain had no idea where they would be landing.

Landing in Normandy on D Day, 6th June 1944 – the start of Operation Overlord

At 7.25 in the morning Douglas landed with the British 3rd Division on the Normandy coast at La-Breche, part of 1 Troop 629 Field Squadron Royal Engineers on Queen White Sector on Sword Beach. As the squadron approached the beach in their landing crafts (think of the opening scenes in Saving Private Ryan), they were met with a withering hail of machine gun fire and mortar bombs. To make matters worse, they found the beach obstacles in 5 feet of water, almost submerged, each one attached to mines which would have exploded had the landing craft touched them. It was quickly decided that the men would have to jump overboard into the rough sea and remove the mines by hand. Some of the men did not even make land and were drowned as the sea swept them away!

Douglas risked a moment to look behind him and was amazed at the sight: the sea was covered in ships of all kinds all firing missiles inland. The noise, he remembered, was deafening. Hundreds of soldiers were wading through the water trying to reach the beach. Many, of course, did not make land – some drowned, some were shot and some blown up. Eventually men from Douglas' squadron made it onto the beach and were able to clear areas for tanks and vehicles to get through safely which was absolutely essential for the invasion to succeed. Whilst this was going on, the men were being fired at by a sniper from one of the beachside houses. A message was sent to one of the battleships off the coast which fired a shell at the house blowing it to pieces. The sniping stopped!

Douglas and an army pal had a lucky escape when they both trod on a mine. It was the sort of mine that was designed to blow up tanks and was only triggered by the weight of a tank going over it. They were lucky – many others weren't. Another scene Douglas remembered from D Day was that of a journalist, a war correspondent, sitting in the sand dunes tapping away on an old-fashioned, heavy typewriter to get his story back for the newspapers in England!

By around midday, the beach was captured along with hundreds of German soldiers who were put on ships and sent back to England as prisoners of war. It was around this time that Douglas and his pals noticed a French civilian wearing a fireman's helmet running along the beach, stopping and kissing British soldiers on both cheeks. He had a bottle of wine in his hand which he was sharing with his liberators! It turned out that the man was the Mayor of the local town, Colville-Sur-Mer, who was completely drunk but wanted to show his appreciation to the soldiers for the liberation of his town from the Germans.

629 Field Squadron Royal Engineers lost 23 men killed, 43 wounded and 4 missing, believed killed, on D Day. Douglas survived the rest of the war unscathed but did lose many of his friends. He saw action throughout Normandy, through the rest of northern France, into Belgium and Holland, and then finally Germany itself. When the war ended Douglas applied for his old job back at Askern Pit. He was released to Army Reserve on 6th January 1946 and was still an army reservist until 1959!

Sometime in the 1970s, I learned from my uncle Sam that my dad had witnessed the horror which the Germans had left behind in Belsen Concentration Camp. Dad had never mentioned this to us all through the rest of his life but he did continue to have nightmares well into the 1960s and I remember my mother having to wake him from such bad dreams on many occasions. Today, he might be diagnosed with Post Traumatic Stress Disorder.

This is the story of Gordon Robinson

Brother of my mother and a prolific writer

He wrote several novels. He unfortunately did not know how to get them published, although one was published as a serial in a newspaper. There are no copies or records of this available within the family papers.

This is an abbreviated but mainly word-for-word account of his life and times as written in 1982.

"A Brief Visit in the passage of time"

The "war to end all wars" was reaching its climax. Fate decreed that I should enter this mad, mad world a few minutes before midnight on the third of November, 1918.

My entry was destined to be in a small terraced cottage, two up and two down, built from local stone and unwisely on a steep slope. The local quarry had created a land slip, so the whole terrace was shored up at the lower end with huge baulks of timber.

It was pinpointed on the local survey map, as 181, Stonedale Terrace, Snydale Road, Normanton, Yorkshire. England.

The house itself was freezing cold and the bedroom lit only by a couple of small candle stubs.

[Gordon's story describes his and his family's upbringing in sheer poverty, moving from village to village, living on meagre rations, and his continuous suffering from poor health and deafness, which kept him in bed most of the time and unable to go to school.]

I was almost thirteen years old now and something happened that was to change my whole life. It happened when I was eating my breakfast. My mother had settled down for a breather after getting the rest off to school. For some unknown reason I sneezed quite hard and something cracked inside my head. Then I was aware of a loud clucking noise, together with many other noises that seemed to come from everywhere. I remember clapping my hands over my ears to try to drown them out. My mother spoke and her voice was deafening. I could hear the wheezing in her throat. I sort of whispered to her what had happened and she laughed.

"Sounds like your hearing has come back. You know you were not born deaf. It only happened when you caught meningitis.

Now I could hear the kettle bubbling on the hob and the grating of the rocker as she moved back and forth. Evidently she was very happy for me, but I couldn't bear it, so I shot out of the house and fled for a patch of waste ground at the rear of the village. For a couple of hours I lay in the grass until my ears settled down. Even then I swear I could hear the grass growing.

For the next couple of weeks I steered well clear of the house and the now noisy village. I now entered a new world of sound and was able to integrate and began to understand the world we lived in. I must confess it was not as good as the world I knew, but nevertheless it had to be faced.

I found a friend of my own age, though a little different, for his Father worked on the railways. My friend knew he would follow in his footsteps and felt obliged to predict my future. It was simple and very much to the point.

"Seeing that you have never had any schooling, there is nothing else for you to do. Down the coal hole you must go and when you come up I will not be able to recognise you, for you will be as black as a nigger, like all the miners when they come up the pit lane."

It was a sobering thought but boys of thirteen do not dwell to long on serious subjects. We were soon distracted looking for bird's nests. Nevertheless, in May of that year I was shocked at being told that I was to start school. I never knew what prompted my parents to have this odd idea, maybe it was official pressure, but in due course I started. Of course I was well out of my depth, stumbling from one class room to another, unable to master any of the subjects. I made a little progress in the woodwork section, and my favourite subject was geography and learning about other countries, but that seemed to be the sum total of my achievements.

The day I left, after six months, I felt sure the teachers never even noticed. Saturday was my fourteenth birthday and Father took me down the pit to see if I could be set on. It was probably a hopeless exercise, but we must go through the motions. Then we were stood in front of the under manager and I was petrified. The stories I had heard about him had made my blood curdle. He had earned the title of "Black Jack" and it was no compliment. I could easily visualise him with a pirate's hat on and a black eye patch. He looked at me wearing a terrible scowl, as if we were a bad smell that had blown in. After an eternity he grunted and said, "See the clerk over there. He will sign you on and you will start Monday." I wanted to ask questions but my Father shook his head and we left in silence.

We were half way back up the pit lane before he found his tongue and then he couldn't stop. He was amazed that I had been set on. Then, he went on to the savage rules that must be obeyed without question. Never talk back to an official, obey with speed whatever they ask you to do, never fight down the pit and never let anyone see you resting. Any deviation meant the sack with no redress. It began to sink into my mind that I wasn't going to enjoy this life very much.

There was a rush to provide me with suitable pit clothes. Hand me downs soon solved that, though precious pennies had to be spent on a water bottle and snap tin. My school boots would have to serve a dual purpose.

The weekend flew by and all too soon I was seated at the table, eating bacon sandwiches at half past four on Monday morning. At five o clock, I was crushed with thirty other men and boys on the top deck of the cage. I clutched tightly the dirty jacket that reached into my face that only reached waist high to the huge man. He must have felt it for he moved and gripped my shoulder, "You'll be right tich gets everybody the first time." Tich was rather appropriate, for it seems as if I was the smallest lad in the pit. On the first drop into the bowels of the earth, the stomach rises into the mouth, then as the cages passed each other, one gets a feeling that the cage is rising again. In reality it was not so and a few seconds later we bumped gently on the bottom. Then I found out what a wet shaft meant. The water fell like a thunderstorm. It never ever stopped.

Father took me to the pit bottom deputy, and then hurried away to his own work. He was a huge man with a big walrus moustache. He scowled at me and set off with another lad to work on the empty side of the shaft. The work was heavy and none – stop, for the cage threw out its load of empty tubs at the rate of one load a minute. At the end of the shift I was shattered and was hardly aware of coming up the shaft. It was almost a shock to come into the peace of the surface after the violent noise of underground. From that day on, I learned what hard work really meant, for each new job got progressively harder. There was no easy work down the mines. In nineteen thirty two. At the end of the second shift, I hurried home to tell them all the news of how I had been working inby and crawled along the coal face. "About a mile and a half it is." I crowed, and then Father walked in with very sombre news. He and five other older miners had been given the sack. The fact that six lads had just been "set on" told its own sordid story.

In the event of this event, I had to take over the rent, the rent arrears (for everyone had them) and the coal leading. My wages were only a few coppers a week, often as little as a penny. Once again the family had to tighten their belt.

[Several years passed by very quickly for Gordon, the family moving from pit to pit following work and wages. He became obsessed with reading about other countries although he didn't think he would ever visit them. He and his friends had fun with their girlfriends and as he got older, life became sweeter, but soon to turn into misery for many.]

The clouds of war were building up and it seems we were to pay for our brief period of happiness. I received my call up papers in May. It appeared that I was in the first militia to report to Aldershot. June the first. I was told by everyone, the manager included, that mining was a reserved occupation, but I just laughed. My dream of foreign soil was about to come true. Time to say "goodbye" to the hard grafting coal mines, to see for myself the countries I had only read about. With the ignorance of youth at twenty one, strong and bursting with vitality, I was ready to take on single handed the Germans to realise my dreams.

My dreams were rosy as I boarded the train for Aldershot.

The next few months tore holes in my dreams and ego. It was to be expected that the Army would need to install discipline into the new conscript Army, but I was constantly amazed at its stupidity. To train a man into the arts of drill, to teach him to be fully conversant with a few weapons we were offered was one thing, but to completely annihilate his thinking ability was something quite different. We were subjected to every possible indignity to achieve their desired aim, a mindless robot. It was drummed into us so many times. A good soldier was someone who never had any ideas, never thought for himself, they would do all that for you. Obey every order, no matter how ridiculous, even to scrubbing stone steps with your own tooth brush on a Sunday afternoon. Can one imagine one hundred and twenty men, lined up with their tooth brushes to scrub flights of stone steps? There were many many other mindless exercises, for the only wished to produce mindless gun fodder. Their thinking hasn't improved from the last war or even the Thin Red line of years ago. The men hated the NCOs. The NCOs feared the officers, who in turn crawled to each other, or vented their spleen on any lower rank. Folk often referred to Hitler as a dictator, but the Army made thousands.

From the day they were given their first stripe or pip, it was as if all signs of humanity disappeared, for they all became obsessed in demanding unthinkable obedience. Lots of men found themselves in the "glass house" army prison on field punishment for the most trivial misdemeanours. Sad but true. As for pride in units or battalion, well I firmly believe it only existed in the minds of NCOs and officers. Everyone I knew had only one ambition and that was to get out, but the system had us trapped, for we were in a state of war and as such came under Martial law.

It seemed I had made the greatest mistake of my life, but what can't be cured must be endured, though I was at odds with the army to the day I left. I learned to obey every order, no matter how insane, yet even at that, I was once charged with dumb insolence, for the look on my face and that earned me ten days fatigues. At least this idiotic army rule is no longer in existence!

At the end of basic training, I was posted to a driving school. The fact that I could drive and passed a simple driving test promoted me to Instructor. A sort of job that can give a man grey hair long before his time. It took three months to lose that job and I did it by volunteering for the B.E.F. I was given seven days leave before leaving for France. All I could think about was a foreign country, for only three months ago I had never been more than twenty miles from home.

After a lot of muddled travelling, we arrived at Sus St. Ledger a small village near Arras and quite close to the Belgium border. Our company was Lord Gorts G.H.Q. I only saw him once and that was on a bombed out pier at Dunkirk. That was the day he was supposed to make his historical speech. "I surveyed the beach and saw no one." There were thirty thousand men on that beach!! Could be he had his eyes were closed, or that he was surrounded by so many Staff Officers that he really could not see.

The weather was perfect and we only had routine stores, petrol, ammunition and rations to move about. We got on well with the "Froggies" and I began to enjoy life. Suddenly the war broke out. The bombers came and flattened a village only two kilometres up the road. There were many troops there and we buried a lot of men the next day. A new urgency swept through the group and we moved tons of stuff in the next few days. Then we moved into Belgium and within a week we were trying, desperately, to get out. The Germans were far too clever for us. We were still thinking in the old trench warfare of 14/18, insomuch, I once found myself with hundreds of others, in a shallow ditch and told to be ready for a bayonet charge. It was quite a shock when hordes of tanks rolled over the hill and we were scattered far and wide. We only had our rifles and eighteen inch of steel bayonet wasn't a great deal of use against these monsters. Unashamed, we fled and by some miracle, I found my own vehicle in a ditch. I sweated blood getting it out of that ditch and before I had settled on the road, it was loaded to capacity with bodies, hanging on everywhere and screaming at me to get a move on. A few miles down the road we came to a halt at a small cross road. An M.P. stopped us and directed us to Dunkirk. For a minute I thought we were to be slung into another makeshift trench, but the powers to be had decided that discretion, not valour, was the order of the day. I prayed it would hold out.

After about fifty miles we ran into a solid mass of transport and troops. All troops were ordered off and I was told to take my truck over the hill and destroy it. To my amazement, there were a lot of our own lads there and we pulled out our own personal gear. We were then treated to the best lunch for days. We had a regular Corporal with us, a real Earl Haig type complete with waxed moustache. "Stand back" he barked, "I'll show you how this is done." He knelt on one knee, less than three yards away from a Bedford truck, brought his rifle up to aim and fired directly at the engine block. The resulting in ricochet as it flew back past his ears scared the daylights out of him. The verbal beating he took from all around him, in their choicest language completely deflated his ego. A tiny cockney in a quiet voice explained. "All you need to do Corporal is to dig your bayonet into the petrol tank and throw a match in to it and bobs your uncle." I have many reasons to bless the cockney unit I was with, least of all, the cheery none-stop banter when even in the tightest of corners.

It was their wit and humour that kept us sane during these mad, mad days. We trailed along with the rest on the ten-kilometre ramble to Dunkirk, but never arrived at least on foot.

Our C.S.M. met us and we were given new orders. We were to go back and grab any vehicle and start to ferry troops to Dunkirk. It helped to cut down the congestion on the roads. I can't remember how long we did this for but it seemed forever. As fast as one truck died on us, through lack of petrol, we scrounged another. Then the Germans closed in on us and we were forced to fall back into town. "Make for the beach and try to keep together," was the last real order. I spent four days in the town under a nonstop barrage and one night on the beach. Then it was my turn to race down the battered pier. I even had to jump for the small destroyer as it moved away from the side. We ran into a vicious attack as we cleared the smoke cloud then it was plain sailing on a sea like a millpond. We were given tea laced with rum and I am afraid I slept most of the trip home. Then I was prodded awake to see the White Cliffs of Dover.

TAKEN 1941

We were rushed to Blackmoor and I felt very guilty at the reception we received from everyone. It was thought that we were heroes and I for one, never felt like that.

My first taste of battle was over and to be candid I wasn't overjoyed with it. Someone somewhere, had slipped up badly and I reflected that I really should have been born with that silver spoon, I shouldn't be at the beck and call of these idiots who had started this caper. The local civilian population tried to make heroes out of us but I could never agree with them. We had been ingloriously booted out of France and that to me was no victory. I loathed the B.E.F. flashes we were ordered to wear, for it made us clear targets for these poor souls. We were given a weekend pass and the family at home tried to do the same thing. Mother was worried and my appearance did nothing to reassure her. My hair was almost white and my deafness had returned, it wore off after a few weeks.

[Gordon spent the rest of his war days travelling half way round the globe on Troop-ships, and fought with the Eighth Army in North Africa and Italy. At least he fulfilled a major part of his dream to see the world. After the war he and his family travelled to Australia to live. They returned to England, where he spent the rest of his days following various occupations and writing about his adventurous life. He never returned to the pit.]

Gordon Robinson
Born 1918 - Died 1987

Printed in Great Britain
by Amazon